GLOBAL FILIPINOS

GLOBAL FILIPINOS

Migrants' Lives in the Virtual Village

DEIRDRE McKAY

Indiana University Press
Bloomington and Indianapolis

This book is a publication of

Indiana University Press
601 North Morton Street
Bloomington, Indiana 47404-3797 USA

iupress.indiana.edu

Telephone orders   800-842-6796
Fax orders   812-855-7931

Library of Congress Cataloging-in-Publication Data

McKay, Deirdre, [date]
    Global Filipinos : migrants' lives in the virtual village / Deirdre McKay.
        p. cm. — (Tracking globalization)
    Includes bibliographical references and index.
    ISBN 978-0-253-00212-9 (cloth : alk. paper) — ISBN 978-0-253-00205-1 (pbk. : alk. paper) — ISBN 978-0-253-00222-8 (electronic book) 1. Filipinos—Employment—Foreign countries. 2. Foreign workers, Philippine—Foreign countries. 3. Migrant labor—Philippines—Haliap. 4. Globalization—Social aspects—Philippines—Haliap. 5. Haliap (Philippines)—Social conditions. 6. Haliap (Philippines)—Economic conditions. I. Title.
    HD5856.P6M45   2012
    331.6'2599—dc23
                                                                              2012000165

1   2   3   4   5   17   16   15   14   13   12

James George Brett (1929–1998)
in memoriam

CONTENTS

ACKNOWLEDGMENTS

My deepest debts are to my friends in my field site of Haliap who have gener-ously shared their triumphs and frustrations with me over many years. Keeping their real names confidential and blurring some of their identifying details is the least I can do to protect their privacy; this precludes a roll call of all my key respondents here. I offer my friends who have chosen to be known as Angelina and Luis, and their extended families, special thanks for agreeing to let me retell what I have learned of their stories to a wider public.

While doing fieldwork in the Philippines, I have had the good fortune to be sustained by my own much wider network of friends and family too. They have shown me the myriad ways one can be and become Filipino. In Baguio City, Professor June Prill-Brett advised me on my project and showed me the flex-ibility of Filipino kinship firsthand, adopting me into her family. I owe much to her hospitality and that of her husband, the late James Brett, and to Heather, Sigrid, James Jr., Wrenolph Panganiban, and their families. My colleague and collaborator Padmapani Perez continues to be a source of sustenance, both intellectual and culinary. Padma's comments on "villagizing" in American colo-nial history helped me identify key themes in this book. In Sagada, Mountain Province, I enjoyed the hospitality and friendship of Teresita Malecdan Baldo, Mayor Thomas Killip, and the Cangbay family, and in Kiangan, Ifugao, the Sakai family gave me a base from which to travel.

My research has also been shaped by an overlapping and equally impor-tant set of academic connections. Anthropologists Villia Jefremovas, Joachim Voss, and Susan Russell introduced me to Philippine fieldwork, while Harold Conklin and the late William Henry Scott helped me comprehend the com-plexities of history in my field sites. Visiting Research Associate positions at the University of the Philippines Baguio supported my research and introduced me to Carol Brady, Ben Tapang, Del Tolentino, and Lorelei Mendoza. In Manila, Jun Aguilar made me welcome at Ateneo de Manila University, and Maruja Asis and the Scalabrini Migration Centre encouraged my work. In Canada, Fay Cohen, Tania Li, Jennifer Leith, and Arthur Hansen supervised my initial fieldwork as part of a larger project at Dalhousie University. At the University of British Columbia (UBC), Terry McGee, Gerry Pratt, Derek Gregory, Tineke Hellwig, and Maureen Reed advised me when I returned to the Philippines to undertake my PhD. I benefited enormously from the lively intellectual atmosphere in UBC's Department of Geography with Nadine Schuurmann, Lynn Stewart, Bruce Braun, David Demerrit, Philip Kelly, Jennifer Hyndman, and Gisèle Yasmeen all influencing my reading and thinking on theories of development, both self and state. Colleagues at the Australian National University— Katherine Gibson, Kathryn Robinson, Andrew McWilliam, and Monique Skidmore—then helped to hone my writing and thinking about Southeast Asia by reading what became chapter drafts. My theoretical approach owes much to Ian Buchanan's unparalleled ability to make Gilles Deleuze's abstruse theory clear for the non-philosopher. Finally, Pnina Werbner at Keele University and Danny Miller at University College, London, have encouraged me to become a better migration scholar. They, along with Mirca Madianou, Theba Islam, and Martin McIvor; my partner, Ben Smith; and Rebecca Tolen at Indiana University Press deserve thanks for their generous comments on the manuscript. At Keele Beverly Skyes and Lisa Lau copyedited, while Keith Mason and Andy Lawrence redrew maps and polished my figures. All photos are my own except Figures 2 and 5 which were supplied by "Luis."

Funding from the International Development Research Centre and the Canadian International Development Agency enabled me to begin the fieldwork that informed this project (1992), followed by support from the Social Science and Humanities Research Council of Canada, through an Eco-Research Fellowship (1993–1997), a Doctoral Award (1998), and a Postdoctoral Fellowship (2000–2001). The Australian National University then funded follow-up visits as well as my work in Hong Kong (2005–2007). In the United Kingdom, Keele University sponsored my travel to Canada (2009). My writing has been supported by a research fellowship within the Arts and Humanities Research Council's Diaspora, Migration and Identities Programme (2009), and a Visiting Research Associate position at University College London, Department of Anthropology (2009–2011).

Sections of chapters 4 and 5 have been developed from articles previously published in the *Asia Pacific Journal of Anthropology* and *Mobilities*.

ON TRANSLITERATION

People in the Philippines speak nearly seven hundred languages. One of these many languages is a distinctively Filipino variant of English. Most of my respondents in this project speak four or five Filipino languages as well as English, switching codes as the context demands. In transliterating the terms they use, I have, for the most part, followed the accepted conventions but respected their preferences for pronunciation and spelling. Filipino English terms with specific local meanings appear in italics at their first use. Words from other Filipino languages are also italicized and defined at first use. For words from local indigenous languages I indicate the language of origin. The exception for this is Tagalog-language terms that my respondents recognized as being used nationwide: being Filipino language. All translations are my own, or report my respondents' translations made for me, except where otherwise specified. Finally, some place and ethnic names have been modified—Ayangan to Adyangan, for example—to more accurately reflect indigenous pronunciations.

GLOBAL FILIPINOS

INTRODUCTION ◆ The Parade

A LONG LINE OF people marched up a winding road toward the summit of the hill. In the lead were gray-haired older women. Bare-chested and wearing bark-cloth skirts, they carried baskets of sweet potatoes on their heads. The women walked behind a placard reading "The Stone Age." Their bare feet felt their way gracefully around the potholes in the road. Men wearing red loincloths followed closely behind, brandishing spears and shields. Limbs glistening, they stamped the ground, raising small puffs of dust, and the breeze carried the distinctive odor of their Johnson's Baby Oil toward me. The men carried a sign labeling them "The Spanish Era." Next came ranks of women and men marching together under the banner "Modern Times." These people carried smaller signs proclaiming them to be farmers, teachers, health workers, a mothers' group, churches, youth groups, and, finally, senior citizens. Their roles were also evident from their accessories—clipboards, books, rosaries, stethoscopes, hoes—and all wore rubber flip-flops or boots on their feet. Among them, the farmers' contingent sported battered straw hats that contrasted with sparkling-clean white T-shirts labeled "Bay-Gro" (a brand of fertilizer) and "Pigrolac" (a hog feed). Finally, behind the farmers a phalanx of men in dark suit jackets marched into view. They carried imitation-leather satchels with paper labels reading "OCW" affixed to the sides. These letters, standing for "overseas contract worker," designated the men as international labor migrants. As they moved off, the heels of their well-polished dress shoes flashed in the sun. The next group then appeared, with slightly different costumes and accessories, again elaborating on a story that transformed them from a primitive prehistory through anticolonial warfare, agricultural development, and, finally, overseas migration. In this parade a number of different villages were competing with one another, vying to see whose performers could best tell this story of progress.

It was April 1996, and I was staying in Haliap, a village in rural Ifugao Province, in the Cordillera mountains of the northern Philippines. I had come out to support my parading neighbors in their efforts to win the competition. Haliap exemplified the kind of marginal place that was being drawn into the global labor market as a migrant-sending area in the mid-1990s Philippines. Located on a resource-rich frontier and itself the product of a long history of still-contested colonial displacements, the village remains a prime target for efforts to develop while conserving the forest; to renegotiate claims to land; to make local customary arrangements amenable to government control; and to bring its often recalcitrant people into various programs to tax, administer, and educate them. After a popular uprising overthrew the Ferdinand Marcos dictatorship in 1986, one of the changes its people hoped for was a new balance between better government services, on the one hand, and political autonomy, on the other. However, attempts to reinvigorate democracy in the Philippines have not delivered anything like the Anglo-Saxon governance people thought they desired. Voters have often elected demagogues who engage in vote buying and patronage. In this system, sparsely populated upland provinces like Ifugao remain both irrelevant and vulnerable. A largely rural province populated by indigenous people—descendants of the original inhabitants of the Philippines who have retained their customs and traditions, resisting Spanish and then American colonial power—Ifugao has been assessed as one of the country's poorest areas.[1] Successive national governments have been so beholden to special interests that they have been unable to do much more than lurch from one crisis to the next and have neglected rural development there. Ifugao's minerals, timber, and water nonetheless remain possible sources of government revenue, offering lucrative concessions for government cronies and potential sites for mega-project development to jump-start progress. Struggling against the resulting land and resource grabs and seeking further political autonomy on the basis of their indigenous cultures tends to exclude such villages from the benefits of wider national belonging. As a result, places like Haliap are confused by the state.

To me, from the crowd, this parade seemed to be, above all, an exercise in obtaining civic compliance. I estimated that nearly four hundred people were marching in front of an audience of fifty. This audience was made up of a few tourists, some government workers, local media, and a group of dignitaries traveling with Ifugao's congressman, who was judging the competition. As the parade ended, the congressman expressed his approval and announced the winners, praising the municipality for its efforts to promote tourism. He then chided the performers for replacing the grass roofs of their native houses with galvanized iron sheets. Tourists, the congressman advised them, would not want to see inauthentic houses. Around me, I heard people sigh, barely concealing their frustration. Grass roofing might be scenic, but it requires days of labor and annual maintenance; most villagers considered low-maintenance galvanized iron roofing to signal prosperity. The congressman then announced that he would build a new road, linking Ifugao Province to the major market center in the mountains of northern Luzon—Baguio City. This road had been planned since the early 1900s. People cheered the news about the road. When I visited the village again, a decade later, tourism had failed to take off, the houses still had galvanized iron roofing, and the road had yet to be constructed. The parade, however, remained an annual event.

In the parade's story, labor migrants epitomized progress. It was clear to me, however, that women's absence from the parade's ranks of overseas workers disguised a public truth: even here, in a remote mountain village, the majority of Filipino migrant workers were female. The 2000 census would report that 2.5 percent of Filipino women between the ages of fifteen and forty-nine were overseas workers. Women then comprised 78.1 percent of all the nation's workers abroad, with female migrants having a median age of thirty years and approximately 30 percent of them having either some college education or a degree.[2] Unlike the male office workers portrayed as marching up the hill with briefcases, these female migrants were taking on domestic or caregiving work in Hong Kong, Singapore, Israel, Italy, the United Kingdom, and Canada. Such migrants risked fraud, abuse, and exploitation while enduring long periods away from their families. Among the crowd watching the parade, a woman holding a video camera represented these women. As she panned her camera across the scene, several of my female friends watched her with envy. She was "one of the lucky ones," they told me. The gossip was that she had gone to Canada to work as a live-in caregiver but had married a Canadian and become what people called a *permanent* (meaning a permanent resident, landed immigrant, or citizen). Stories of her success quickly segued into requests that I facilitate my friends' own migration.

I begin here because the parade maps the changes that were at work in the village at the time. The tale the parade told came to matter in the ways villagers felt and thought about themselves in the world. To reveal how and why this happened, this book unpacks the parade through its vignettes. Most importantly, by mapping Filipino labor migration onto local history, the parade endorsed the importance of an imagined global realm while simultaneously bringing that realm into being.[3] The parade condensed and expressed globalism: the desire for the global. But the global desired by the parade's performers was an imaginary—something they had not quite defined or understood. What gave substance and meaning to their desires was globalization, meaning a set of late-twentieth-century development programs and government projects attempting to expand foreign investment and transnational trade, to increase the consumption of international brands, and to create a worldwide market for labor and thus bring into being the global.

Like many Filipinos, villagers here found themselves on the margins of globalization's flows of value and information. In 1996 villagers' global imaginaries were based largely on vicarious experience, delimited by their ties to already-migrant friends and kin. The global realm they desired was a space of free movement where they might achieve economic security and be respected and recognized for their merits and talents. Global connections, material security, easy movement around the world, respect, and success—my friends in the crowd wanted what they imagined the woman with the video camera enjoyed. The parade tied their vicarious desire for the global into the public rituals of Filipino culture and village life in a way that transformed the village.

On my return a decade later, I would find that the biggest change in the village was in my friends in the crowd. Many had themselves become migrants. As I have followed their lives over the intervening years, I have asked, "How do these people cope with globalism? What has happened when their real-world lives do not match up with their global imaginaries?" The answer is that my friends have used their migration to bring together their sense of place, their sense of being and feeling as selves in the world, and their engagements with the government into a new form, what I call the virtual village. But before I sketch what that means, we need to understand a bit more about globalism.

Performing Globalism

The parade told a story that took its shape from mid-1990s national development initiatives that focused Filipinos on the global. Government offices had then promoted globalization as a cultural form, with President Fidel Ramos exhorting people to "imbibe and expand" the "culture of globalization."[4] Newspaper advertisements had challenged people to become "the global Filipino"—a young man in a shirt and tie, sitting in front of a computer monitor. The government, however, was unable to generate enough well-paid professional jobs either at home or abroad to bring into being the dreams it inspired among a fast-growing, well-educated, underemployed population. While government campaigns encouraged citizens to desire global futures, the jobs on offer through the Philippine Overseas Employment Administration (POEA) were rarely permanent professional jobs for male breadwinners. Instead, the POEA's greatest successes were in placing a predominantly female workforce in unskilled and semiskilled short-term overseas contracts, building on an already established market position; the Philippines had been exporting contract workers to earn foreign exchange since 1974.

During the 1990s globalization had typically shifted economic power from governments to global markets. In the Philippines, globalization featured the now familiar export-processing zones and foreign investment that characterized this shift, but it was most strongly expressed through the deployment of migrant workers to meet demand in an expanding worldwide market for temporary labor.[5] Opening recruiting to privately owned labor-placement agencies, the government also instituted its own training and accreditation programs to support would-be labor migrants in the 1980s and 1990s. The Philippine elite, including the families of senior elected officials, then invested in labor recruiting and training, enriching themselves as labor migration expanded. While migration generated wealth for a few at home, most of the jobs available abroad remained low-skilled and low-status. Ordinary Filipinos perceived that they were being forced to seek menial work outside the country rather than being offered equitable development at home. People were deeply upset that government institutions regulating migration were geared to meet the demand for female workers to take on unskilled domestic or sex-related work abroad.[6] With the expansion of migration, a growing number of overseas Filipino workers were murdered, abused, or arrested as they worked abroad while, in the worst cases, the families that the migrants left at home suffered neglect and abandonment. In the mid-1990s the country's national media focused on cases from this shadow side of migration. Filipinos were both saddened and angered by the huge sacrifices that the now established migration regime was extracting from individual migrants and their families.

Between the 1970s and early 1990s, overseas migration had become a definitive part of what it meant to be a Filipino—a member of a "Global Nation," as the migration-related section of the national newspaper, the *Philippine Daily Inquirer,* proudly announced. The POEA began marketing Filipino workers as a self-consciously global workforce. By the end of the 1990s, the Philippines had the world's largest per capita temporary migrant labor force deployed outside of its national borders. In 2005 their numbers made Filipinos the world's third-largest group of migrant workers, outnumbered only by migrants working beyond the borders of India and China.[7] The new millennium marked the high point for women's deployment for land-based contract work, and then male migrants began to catch up, having previously been largely seafarers. Between 2004 and 2009, the numbers of male workers deployed for land-based overseas jobs more than doubled. In 2007 and 2008, for the first time slightly more men than women left the country for land-based work, largely in construction, information technology, services, and manual labor.[8] Since 2006, Filipinos have recognized that overseas migrants make up approximately a tenth of the Philippines' 93 million people, remitting money to support about half the country's households.[9] Though the amounts sent home by migrants remained comparatively small when considered individually, ordinary people know that when the amounts are added together, these flows are their resource for development. Remittances in 2005 outstripped overseas development assistance and foreign direct investment combined.[10] In villages and neighborhoods across the country, Filipinos expect that the money remitted by their migrants abroad will enable them to progress. Yet much of the country has failed to develop, despite the promises of progress that are implicit in the government sponsorship of labor migration.

Government policies to deliver development and create a global nation through migration have touched local villages like Haliap through a wide range of activities. Among these are recurring civic rituals, like the parade, that are intended to mold dreams and identities. While the parade I saw was supposed to be a collective, harmonious display of progress, uniting people and government in shared civic aspiration, it seemed to me to be working largely by promising a monetary reward. Advertised as "ethnic parades," such events feature prominently in annual festivals across northern Philippine municipalities inhabited by indigenous peoples. These ethnic parades are part tourist attraction, part popular education exercise—celebrating participants' indigenous customs and traditions—and comparatively lucrative competitions. Village councils are usually desperately in need of the prize money to supplement the small amount of central funding they receive to support their local development projects: road repair, water systems, and the like. Staging the parade as a contest between groups of performers from different villages disguises two key facts: first, the Filipino category of indigenous people does not map onto the concept of village very easily, and, second, these villages are not, and have never been, discrete and bounded, nor ever simply local.

The government's aims of instilling pride in citizens belonging to indigenous ethnic minorities, sustaining local culture and customs, and attracting visitors to the mountain region seem praiseworthy. But, unofficially, these parades work in almost the opposite way, not so subtly demonstrating to their performers that they are located on the periphery of both their nation and the global economy. Only by performing the story correctly, the parade suggests, can the performers free themselves from the history of underdevelopment in which they are mired. Thus the competition is judged on the quality and sincerity of the performers' efforts. These criteria include the order of the marching ranks, the coordination of marchers' movements, the seriousness of purpose they express, the perceived completeness of their narrative—including the number and detail of signs they carry—and the authenticity of performers' dress and deportment. To mark this particular parade as an ethnic occasion in 1996, the municipal mayor had directed the female marchers and spectators to wear the "native uniform": a white blouse and *tapis* (woven skirt). Casual business clothes distinguished the male judges, other elected male officials, those men representing OCWs, and a few men in the audience. Thus the parade's story of progress from primitive tribal people to cosmopolitan professionals was made common sense by combining bodily actions, performances of social identities, and material reward in a highly gendered way.

I watched the parade beside my friend Sylvie, who worked as an administrator for the municipality. She deeply resented the mayor's edict that she wear native uniform rather than her preferred business dress to introduce the congressman's speech. In response, she had threatened to dress me in local finery as well. I should parade as my own exhibit—my placard would be "Researcher"— she joked. Her office mates dissolved in fits of giggles as Sylvie explained her plan. Sylvie had a management degree from a Manila university. Her brother was an academic, studying agriculture in Japan. Her former husband had migrated to the United States. Sylvie herself wanted to pursue further study overseas. She considered herself a global kind of person and my peer. Joking about dressing me up too, Sylvie made the point that she was no more a merely local kind of girl than I was. As Sylvie and her office mates watched the parade, they pointed out flaws in people's costumes and performances, most of which brought on more laughter, shared between themselves and the marchers. Yet it did not seem to me that this jollity necessarily undermined the more serious purposes behind the exercise.

Over the ensuing decade, I saw that people in Haliap really did try to transform the parade's ideal of global progress into something sensible and solid in their everyday lives. People took on the challenge of the parade, however, not by taking on identities inscribed by the placards and costumes but by transforming their own global imaginaries, transposing the elements of globalism as they came to know it and reworking their own ideals for village life.

Writing the Global

Taking the parade as a starting point to explore globalism, my approach both differs from and complements more familiar multisited or institution-based studies of globalization. I study globalism by expanding on a more traditional village. I have adopted this strategy for two reasons. The first reason to take a village study global is that while research may have moved on to study new social networks and cultural phenomena, villages remain salient forms of social organization for many people, perhaps even the global majority. Villages continue to be made and remade, and although they are sometimes superseded in importance by the other social networks in which people participate, they are certainly not passé or irrelevant. Villages are likely becoming more important, rather than less so, with the global upswing in temporary labor migration and expansion of new communications technologies. While we do not know exactly how many rural people have become international contract migrants, development experts see that their sheer numbers are dampening growth in rural agriculture production because the money they remit competes against innovation in the agricultural sector.[11] Migrant workers and their families now account for about 90 percent of the current total of 214 million international migrants, and the Philippines—the country most affected by global labor migration— had an estimated 3.6 million of these people overseas as temporary migrants in 2007.[12] Data on the regions of origin for Filipino temporary migrants suggests that 82 percent of them come from areas outside the capital, Manila.[13] For these people, their sending villages, their home villages, are the sites of the familial, political, and economic ties that keep them connected to home as they sojourn abroad. Village life thus shapes their migration experiences.

Abroad, such migrants can rarely remit, invest, return, settle, or move on without activating some form of village relation. Thus, in order to connect global migration to development, to political change, and to cultural shifts, we need to consider village ties. And we can see such ties being made increasingly visible through cell phone contact lists, in website chat rooms, and on "friends" lists on social networking sites—if we know what and who to look for. This electronic mediation does not necessarily mean these connections are somehow less constituted through place, kinship, and ritual than face-to-face relationships in the village. Indeed, what this pattern suggests is that a study of village migrants can tell us interesting things about the way place and intimacy are being changed by the global world.

Studies of globalization make it clear that place has never had any absolute power to broker relationships across some firm boundary between its inside and the outside world. Thus, despite their familiar caricatures, looking more closely we see that villages have almost never been the "tightly territorialized, spatially bounded, historically unselfconscious and culturally homogeneous" objects of anthropologists' study.[14] In fact, the classical anthropological approach that described villages as closed and homogeneous has long been challenged within the discipline, having been a problematic methodological presupposition rather than an empirical fact. In the 1960s heyday of village studies, only a very few projects actually treated the village as entirely isolated from broader society or as entirely self-sufficient. Some anthropologists studying villages did, of course, seek to retrieve something purely local and filter their data to offer an account of a more bounded culture, but this was rarely seen by their peers as more than a strategic choice to emphasize continuity of culture. And while there is certainly a large body of mid-twentieth-century anthropological work that has been criticized for representing other cultures in ways that suggest they have always been isolated communities, that story of the isolated, timeless village often emerged more from the ways governments and development planners took up village studies material than from the anthropological research itself.[15]

The classical ethnographic approach to the village would have us focus on the ways kinship, symbolism, ritual, and cosmology constituted its sense of place—which they do—while relegating migrants, media, movements, and other global influences to the margins of the study. But global agents and flows have likely always been central to villagers' senses of self and place as well, and vice versa. Thus, even in a Facebook age, kinship, symbolism, ritual, and cosmology should still be able to tell us about the priorities, practices, and desires of migrants abroad. We would expect that people abroad remain pivotal within their home villages, but be only one among multiple agents of change.

A strong strand of work on globalization suggests that people on the move actually become untied from village relations. This, the approach advocated by the new mobilities paradigm, would encourage us to focus largely on movement and change rather than localizing the subjects of research as villagers.[16] I think this approach would overreach the mark. Moving beyond ideas of society as fixed to territory would encourage us to obscure the importance that territoriality still retains for most people's sense of being and feeling about themselves in the world—their subjectivity. While globalization does not transcend place, the opposite idea—that globalization could solidify rather than dissolve some places—is one I think is worth exploring in considering village migrants. My premise here is that globalization is actually making some rather particular places solid and more substantive. This starting point allows me to describe how the sense of place behind the new, virtual form of village is emerging.

The second argument for a village approach to the global lies in the shortcomings of multisited approaches to studying globalization. Where a multisited approach has succeeded, the results are dazzling, revealing novel connections and histories. But unless these ties are also real, and very important, for the ethnographic subjects whom researchers study, readers rarely come away with transferable concepts and methodologies other than multisited-ness itself. This book builds on the strengths of multisited approaches but does so by understanding the village as itself its multisite. By taking a more traditional village study global, it offers a diachronic view of who villagers are and how they understand and feel about themselves in the world, demonstrating how village relations and identities both constitute and are shaped by globalism. In order to think about the ties between places and persons in a more nuanced way, we need to distinguish between the qualities of social relations that ground people's sense of "placeness" and the physical forms of their settlements themselves. The persistence of placeness tells us about subjectivity in a global world, showing us how with globalization the problem of sustaining place becomes the problem of locating the self-aware, and self-shaping, subject. Thus, in order to understand how the global transforms ties between place and subjectivity, I follow the same persons across an extended site rather than drawing together encounters with different people in distinct places.

THE VILLAGE IN CONTEXT

Though the village I explore here is in some ways unique, it nonetheless exemplifies wider trends. In the northern Philippines, global chains of meaning and global institutions reach out to touch every facet of local lives, much as Anna Tsing and Tania Li have shown for the remote corners of Indonesia or Ara Wilson has argued for the urban communities of Bangkok.[17] While other ethnographies of globalization in Asia examine chains of meaning that articulate different groups or trace histories of global institutions governing people's lives, I follow a village that has extended into the world in a variety of ways. By mapping personal networks and new forms of meaning generated by Ifugao villagers on the move, I use individual biographies to show how, even as migration thrusts them away from their village, temporary migrants remain embedded within and intensify village social relations and affective ties. These ties mean that villagers carry with them a durable and even expanding sense of placeness on their sojourns overseas.

My approach to the village here extends a long tradition of double-ended studies of migration. This tradition was perhaps inaugurated by William Watson's study of Mambwe migrants to the Copperbelt in the 1950s, in those days the limit of the global world for Zambian tribal villagers.[18] Later, Katy Gardner's study of a Sylheti village in Bangladesh and the migration of many of its residents to Britain highlighted the emotional dimensions of villagers' local-global movement, while studies such as James Watson's work on Chinese lineages in Hong Kong and London and Michelle Ruth Gamburd's research on Sri Lankan migrants in the Middle East have explained migrants lives abroad through their ties to home.[19] More recently, Peggy Levitt analyzed the movement of villagers from the Dominican Republic to Boston, describing them as "transnational villagers."[20] At the same time, new research on hometown associations has highlighted the way local places mediate ties between members of national diasporas.[21] Few studies of Filipino migration, however, have taken on this double-ended approach.

Research on Filipino migrants has focused on lives lived overseas and the structural factors shaping migrants' engagements with host societies—for example, Nicole Constable, for Hong Kong, Pei-Chia Lan, for Taiwan, and Rhacel Parreñas for Italy and the United States.[22] Other scholars such as James Tyner, Anna Guevarra, and Robyn Rodriguez have produced detailed studies of institutions regulating migration and migrants' experience within them.[23] Scholars working in the Philippines have tended to concentrate on the impact of migration on people left at home, such as the work of Rhacel Parreñas and Alicia Pingol on left-behind husbands and children.[24] My Filipino colleagues Filomeno Aguilar and Raul Pertierra have argued for the need to contextualize migrants within their village networks to understand Filipino migration.[25] Following their example—describing how both those at home and those abroad belong to a single field of sociality—this book explores what global migration means for personhood and placeness, not at home and abroad but across a single field of sociality.

TAKING A VILLAGE STUDY GLOBAL

My approach here builds from my village fieldwork, where I observed that people's desires are what create change in their world through their lived lives. To make my argument, I rely on individual life histories set in a wider village context. By tracking my respondents' moves, I show how the contemporary form of the village has actually been shaped by long-standing local practices of mobility. Village mobility thus prefigures my friends' international migration at the same time that it suggests we should query the naturalized categories of nation and identity on which that migration depends. Much of my analysis is inspired by Lila Abu-Lughod's strategy of "writing against culture": taking apart national and other collective cultural norms to show how people's individual understandings and practices both challenge and constitute such norms.[26] First, of course, I need to set out the culture against which I write. I do this through what is a more conventional—rather retro—village checklist that covers the classic themes of social anthropology: politics, economy, kinship, and religion. Setting individual biographies within this context then allows me to challenge and expand our understanding of Filipino migration.

My approach differs from that of much scholarship on Filipino migrants. Most research has focused on workers' circumstances abroad, the government's labor export program, and the institutions, like POEA, that manage it.[27] Researchers have documented the exploitative employment relations that migrants encounter overseas and revealed how host governments rarely regulate migrants' conditions of employment effectively. This work has demonstrated that the conditions of migrants' work overseas are shaped by discourses of gender and nation that are attached to migrant Filipino women by migration's governing institutions.[28] Yet, when described in such accounts of regulating migration, Filipinas can almost take on the role of a human kind of export commodity. As migrants, they should come to know themselves through the discourses attached to them—by institutions like the POEA or by their overseas labor agencies and employers—as being naturally oriented to caring work. I use my village study here to broaden this literature and reassess some of the fundamental assumptions about personhood, place, and the power of governing institutions that underpin more institutional approaches. I decided to explore migration from this village viewpoint because I found that my respondents' own accounts of their lives were quite different from what the institutional studies of migration might predict.

To my surprise, I found that my village respondents did not consider their encounters with the seminars and paper-processing requirements of labor export to be the most profoundly transformatory part of their migration experience. And they were able to cope with their overseas employers, even if their coping strategies were restricted by the regulatory regimes through which their host nations managed migration. My respondents expected government restrictions and attempted to circumvent the rules governing their mobility by building strong interpersonal ties. Rather than defining themselves by their Filipino nationality, my friends located their identities, motives, and dreams for the future within their village relationships. Thus not only their migration trajectories but also their self-knowledge and resilience continued to depend on village ties, even a decade or more after their initial departure.

When the institutions governing their migration classify them as migrants or Filipinos and categorize them by nationality or skill, these people work with such identities out of a practical and strategic necessity. In their daily lives they are much more engaged with the local identities and interpersonal or familial ties that make their village. They do not try to take on a Filipino identity so much as they attempt to open up and redefine the category of Filipino itself. By assimilating their village-ness to being Filipino, they demonstrate how the nation can be continually remade by the new members it recruits. They are subjecting themselves to intrusive international regulatory regimes of work and visa requirements, and they are forging new social relations, so the ways they think and feel about themselves in the world necessarily change. However, some of their most profound changes often happen in response to new village demands. Migrants continue to sustain and even intensify their valued village ties, objectifying them through economic exchanges imbued with affect. These exchanges, both monetary and emotional, anchor their sense of self in a local place or neighborhood and define their way of being in the world. That village ties and identities are strengthened rather than attenuated by contract labor migration helps to explain why Filipino migrants are reputed to be hardworking, self-effacing, and compassionate. At the same time, village ties account for how many migrants remain skeptical and strategic about the national and gendered discourses attached to migration.

FEELING CONNECTED

My analysis here builds from data on feelings and exchanges as they shape villagers' ideals for themselves and the world. Observing the parade, we can see how affective connections both make and unmake effective performances. However glorious it may have been in the collective imagination, the ethnic parade I observed was a rather unruly event. Among the ranks there was some distracted nose-rubbing. Several gossiping marchers were wearing outfits that did not match those of their companions—"in the wrong uniform," people observed. The marching ranks were largely uneven. One farmer pointed to his battered straw hat and rolled his eyes. His clowning made a small cluster of spectators to my left laugh. Then we noticed that the migrant workers' briefcases were all-too-evidently children's schoolbags. At this, Sylvie and her friends erupted into another round of giggling. And, finally, the one identifiable OCW present was female, not male. The performers knew all of this; some laughed along. So did the judges and other observers. Some performers certainly did not seem to take their roles at all seriously, making faces, catching the eyes of friends in the crowd. The parade's bodies and signs thus jostled against one another rather than making a unitary account. However, as a concept in the minds of the observing officials and marching participants, the parade seemed to be working as a seamless whole, mapping out an ideal for local progress. This ideal was expressed through the enthusiasm and excitement of the performers, the competitive and historical distinctions being made among them, the congressman's judging, and the monetary reward. Their uniforms and placards, by labeling participants as certain kinds of subjects and locating them within the parade's time line of progress, should have motivated the performers to improve both themselves and their village. Though the parade was intended to discipline performers' desires, this outcome of improvement was undermined by the affective connections among the marchers and crowd. Shared laughter more than once threatened to send the whole exercise up as a self-indulgent piece of state-sponsored puffery.

Here, by "villagers' ideals" I mean the set of shared standards through which people judge things against the future they imagine and ideals they expect. Bringing the everyday world more closely into alignment with these ideals requires villagers to engage this disparate set of institutions. These institutions, with their messy, overlapping, and contradictory projects and discourses bring into being and then administer the village/parade as a set of bodies, signs, and techniques for desiring the global. Such institutions comprise what Stephen Collier and Aihwa Ong—after Gilles Deleuze and Félix Guattari—call the "global assemblage."[29] Assemblages govern the tangible world through projects, processes, and programs, making social groups and attaching identities to individuals. Assemblages act as a channel for affect—the energy that motivates people to connect and transform—coupling together networks and making flows of matter, energy, and information move. It is affect that enables assemblages to govern people by modifying their relations to others. A global assemblage brings into being and governs an assemblage of the global—the global realm—by shaping desires about self and other into imaginaries of globalism. Like any assemblage, this global governs the everyday world by channeling affect through projects, processes, and programs that order persons, their relations, and conduct. But the outcomes of this governing are contradictory. Thus the global assemblage must manage contradictions by balancing things that seem to justify each other, like the village and the nation. All of this means the assemblage is much more than simply what we might recognize as the formal institutions of the government, and it brings the global into being by juxtaposing and then blending together these opposites.

In thinking about how villagers experience the workings of connecting and flow, it is affect that best describes the way people's sense of self comes largely from ties to others. Affect springs from gut feelings rather than originating in self-conscious reflections. These feelings are not always at the forefront of people's minds but are revealed to them in moments of crisis, of self-discovery, through surprise and sudden internal shifts. Affect is not simply expressed through words chosen in speech. What makes it visible—performs it as shared—are things like the energy in a potent silence or a shift of the shoulders, the falling away of a voice. Rendering affect into text by reporting conversational exchanges is very difficult without the observer's explanatory voice intruding. One way to do it is to show video clips where sound track, camera angle, and lighting can all help to convey mood and then write about affect in the clips shown. This methodology works because facial expression, bodily *hexis,* vocal tone, and spatial placement are all involved in the quotidian dynamics of affect. These things can only be brought into a book like this through the observing, descriptive authorial eye. But this brings with it a number of problems. Too much authorial self-positioning can turn the text away from respondents' lives and toward an intimate account of the author's experiences and the possibilities of fieldwork. Yet the reader must come to trust the author's ability not just to learn language but also to recognize and connect affect to emotion across cultural difference, to learn the emotional grammar of her hosts. Here, I try to balance the two, offering verbatim quotes blended with my own recounting. Many of these verbatim quotes are in Filipino English. English is both a lingua franca in my field site and the language in which my respondents work in Hong Kong and Canada. Many of their English phrases appear as short snippets of conversation that illustrate my key themes. I offer definitions or contextual examples where doing so seems helpful. I alternate with my own observations to suggest how my relationships with my respondents ebbed and flowed as our interests changed over time. And I also want to allow my respondents' moments of profound feeling and affective outbursts to stand out against the rest of the text, much as they did against the backdrop of daily life. If fieldwork has taught me anything, it is that affect is not always predictable.

Affect itself is ambivalent—positive and negative, constructive and destructive. People have flashes of love and hate and then recognize them as feelings of admiration and resentment. They may repress feelings at one moment and then throw them about in public the next. Thus the same exchanges and relationships we might imagine would sustain the story of the parade and the authority of the local government can very rapidly reconfigure in ways that threaten to undo the assemblage.

We can see glimpses of affect being channeled by this governing assemblage in the elements of the parade. Villagers are governed and their desires are shaped not only by elected officials and the institutions of government—departments, extension programs, schools, taxes, and land and birth registries—but also by a whole series of other institutions that govern their conduct and identities. These institutions include nongovernmental organizations, citizen groups, churches, multinational companies, international agencies, development projects, popular movements, and media, some of which are allied with the state-making activities of government while others work alongside or against them. The congressman represented the national government. The Bay-Gro logo on the farmers' T-shirts marked the global—in this case, the transnational agrochemical arm of the multinational Bayer pharmaceutical company. Other signs distinguished the marchers as members of global churches and beneficiaries of series of international development agencies and donors. Some accessories, like the shiny dress shoes, positioned people as global consumers. Gathering these signs, symbols, and performances together, the parade exemplifies how assemblages work. Like the other everyday rituals that bring the state into being, the parade produces embodied, sensuous social patterns that translate—albeit imperfectly—intangible ideals into programs and practices of ordered conduct.[30] This parade/assemblage produces a map of winners and losers: those who achieve, enact, and embody progress, and those who fail its challenges. People have feelings, good and bad, about their places on this map.

To understand villagers' globalism, we thus need to supplement the already strong institutional analyses of migration with accounts that explain how these feelings arose. By focusing on the stories that villagers told about themselves and their village, I show how their ideals are held in constant tension with the village form promoted by the national government. Exploring how relationships and institutions govern these conflicts, we will see how these village contradictions shape people's attachments to place and the ways they come to think and feel about themselves in the world. It is through ties to others and through the feelings these ties generate that villagers experience and understand their global dreams and disappointments and develop personal strategies to cope with risky moves, changing themselves and the village in the process.

Becoming a Virtual Village

Because village ties persist and remain the ground of feeling in which migrants find themselves, I describe how their village becomes virtual in three senses of the term. First, and most obviously, village ties are now supported by new communications technologies that enable people to stay in touch with home when they migrate. Second, village ties inhere in a shared imaginary of the village that migrants leave behind as a site of underdevelopment and lack. Finally, the village then emerges in the ways migrants reimagine it as having a radical potential to become a new—and better—kind of place. This idea of village perfectibility then becomes an article of the faith that enables migrants to cope with the demands of sojourns abroad. My virtual village friends thus still conceive of themselves as locals—but locals who have always thought of themselves as belonging to a more porous and labile kind of place. This sense of placeness is consolidated, rather than dissolved, by migration. Laying out how this new virtual constellation for the village emerges from local history then returns us to more fundamental questions about place, personhood, and government.

That village ties persist and even expand makes the global nation of the Philippines something of a paradox. People do not leave the nation when they migrate for temporary work overseas; they join it instead. In Haliap, villagers learn how they are not truly Filipinos through village-level experiences of governance and development like the parade. As indigenous peoples and rural Filipinos, they live at some remove from, and are confused about, the purposes and workings of the national bureaucracy. Because the nation-state in the Philippines emerged from non-state societies that were unified by and then liberated from different colonial powers, the nation has always had an uneven geography. What the state is, what one can expect it to do, and where it ends all remain a puzzle for villagers.

Far removed from the locus of political power in Manila, villagers in Ifugao tend to be ambivalent about their Filipino identity. Yet they often attribute poor local governance to the flaws of the (so-called) Filipino character. They share a popular discourse that blames "poor Filipino values" for political strife and underdevelopment. Both critical of the government and self-recriminating, in

Ifugao this discourse identifies failings coming from elsewhere while recognizing that local people, too, share in a kind of being-Filipino founded on complaints about government inefficiency or nepotism. These complaints persist even as the complainants seek personal benefits from their own government ties. Where people explain deciding to migrate as their response to the outcomes of poor governance, their migration itself becomes part of this political critique. For my Ifugao friends in the mid-1990s, it was global migration, rather than government-led development, that they envisaged would create an equitable society of mutual respect. They shared this ideal of creating progress through migration with many of their working-class and peasant Filipino countrymen.

FOLLOWING LIFE HISTORIES

This book follows the lives of Luis and Angelina, two of my village friends who became overseas contract workers. Their individual stories and those of some of their neighbors frame my study of Haliap, tracking the way that village lives both follow and diverge from the parade. Setting out the context and circumstances that see Angelina and Luis depart for work overseas, I follow both of them through their sojourns overseas and returns home. My data come from interviews with them, their kin, and neighbors and long-term participant observation, as well as surveys, media reports, oral histories, archival data, photographs, video grabs, voice calls, text messages, supplementary interviews, and participant observations collected in Haliap, across settlements in the Philippines, in Hong Kong, and in Canada. To explain how accounts of their struggles, disappointments, and successes in coping with a global world exemplify more general circumstances, I draw on theories of state, subjectivity, and cosmopolitanism. These theories help me to suggest what my friends' lives can tell us about the global world more generally. The virtual village that comes into being through their experiences describes a new constellation of personhood, place, and state emerging from temporary migration from the rural third world.

If all migrants were themselves a nation, they would now be the fifth-largest nation in the world.[31] In the decade between 2000 and 2010, the total number of international migrants increased by just under half, and migrant workers came to make up 3 percent of the global workforce. This expansion in migration has brought the global into villages and enabled village dwellers to grasp at new kinds of global futures. The global brought into being by their migration is shifting not only local and national economies but also the ways we all can come to understand ourselves in the world.

CHAPTER 1 ◆ Finding the Village

TO FIND A VILLAGE like Haliap, we could locate a dot on a map or a cluster of buildings and fields on Google Earth. We could even use Google to map Haliap's presence in the news or consult platforms such as Facebook or Friendster to chart the social networks of its inhabitants. Yet it would be a mistake to interpret any of these ways of representing the village as evidence that Haliap's migrants depart from some stable, bounded place. Haliap's name labels nodes, networks, and dynamic ties that both represent and elaborate on a complex history of local mobility. We can trace migration back to the founding of the village, itself an act of migrants. Yet this rich history is constantly obscured by the stories people are required to tell themselves about progress: the story they act out through the ethnic parade. Disjunctures between local history and its ritualized performance reveal to villagers that their claims to land, identity, and livelihood are fundamentally insecure. Villagers cope with this insecurity by innovating within a dynamic indigenous tradition and by departing for elsewhere.

Haliap is a particular example of a more general situation in which insecurity produces migration. Insecurity in Haliap is attached to people's indigenous identity, but similar kinds of insecurity affect ordinary people living in rural and urban areas across the Philippines. Even middle-class citizens discover that the law deems them to be living as squatters on the properties of absentee landlords or corporations, find their previously secure titles to land disputed in the courts, or learn that records held in the local land registry have somehow been altered. People in these circumstances are pushed to migrate. They may try to out-argue and out-evidence those who would dispossess them, but they need money to do so. Moving on—either to explore the agrarian frontier, to seek work in the city, or to take up contract work abroad—allows them not only to earn money but also to reinvent themselves. This kind of insecurity is familiar across much of the migrant-sending developing world, but its specifics are always particular to the history of a local place.

Haliap: A Personal History

Haliap on a December day in 2005: I see seventeen wooden houses with galvanized iron rooftops. Garlanded by clothes drying under the eaves, the houses cluster around a T-junction. Most people are inside, avoiding the drizzle. The country's 2000 census tells me that Haliap is home to 914 people in 177 households; the hamlet at the T-junction is a small part of a wider whole.[1] Its houses, several small shop fronts, and a water tank are dwarfed by a wrought-iron gateway reading "Barangay Haliap" that arches across the road. Behind the houses, the damp greenness of forests and fields stretches up to the mountainous horizon on all sides.

Luis and Angelina Dulnuan own one of these houses. They work in Hong Kong, and I am now an old friend, visiting their family home. Luis is his Christian name; friends and family call him Chanag, his native name. Dulnuan, his grandfather's native name, is now the family surname. Luis marched as one of the parade's progressive farmers. He spent some of his childhood in Manila, the national capital, where his father worked as a laborer. During their years in Manila, his family converted from Catholicism to the Philippine Protestant church, the Iglesia ni Cristo (Tagalog: Church of Christ). Despite new church-based networks in Manila, his father could not find a stable livelihood. Luis returned to Haliap with his parents and nine siblings in the middle years of his elementary schooling. The family brought their Iglesia faith back to the village. They continued to follow indigenous Ifugao practices for marriage and inheritance. As the fifth child, Luis did not inherit any land.

Luis's village of Haliap occupies the eastern slopes of the Antipolo valley in the municipality of Asipulo, Ifugao Province. At the 2000 census, the Asipulo municipality had a total population of 13,336 persons in 2,404 households and occupied an area of 11,980 hectares, while the province of Ifugao had 180,815 persons in 36,232 households, with an average household size of 5 persons and a population over age eighteen that was 51.5 percent male.[2] Asipulo lies in the foothills of the Cordillera Central, the mountain chain running parallel to the east coast of Luzon, the largest island of the Philippine archipelago. Its village of Haliap is approximately fourteen hours' travel from Manila. Haliap proper or *centro* (central) is accessible by jeep via a gravel road. The village's more remote hamlets lack road access and require a hike of an hour or more over rough trails. Settlements are nonnucleated in Ifugao, thus the village is spread out over the landscape. Hamlets are called *sitios* and are tucked into patches of forest on the slopes, separated by stacks of bench-terraced rice paddies. Haliap is a recent settlement by local standards. While some areas of the Cordillera have been cultivated since 500 AD, terraces in this part of Ifugao date only to the late 1800s, built by people from the lowland plains fleeing Spanish colonial rule.[3] A former place of refuge, Haliap remains remote. It has no telephone landlines. Cell phone service and electricity are recent arrivals. Haliap is the kind of place metropolitan Filipinos call a "far-flung *barangay*." By dint of its very location, it lacks progress and its inhabitants are thus considered backward yokels.

The green vista beyond the gateway reminds me that Haliap's relationship with the government is a paradox. There really has never been much government here at all. Yet, other than a few government jobs in schools and local offices, there is still not much more formal economic activity other than that I first observed on my initial stay in the village in 1992. Beyond a few small stores and some—mostly visiting—traders in agricultural commodities, there is little evidence of a market. Villagers travel to buy food, goods, and services. They farm for their own subsistence and grow a few cash crops to sell at the weekly regional market—a forty-minute trip by public *jeepney* (passenger truck) to Ifugao's provincial capital, Lagawe. On a day-to-day basis, people sustain themselves through exchanges with their neighbors.

Passing a familiar shop front, I recall how in 1996 I was sitting with Luis, listening to the radio, when we heard a snippet of opinion floating, without context, between music and news: "The ethnic—tobacco, G-strings, betel nut. Now we have Hope, Levi's, Juicy Fruit—the modern *Pinoy* [Filipino]. The ethnic is now in the far barrios, never seen here in the center. Fading away . . . That is the fate of the ethnic."[4] Luis, sitting beside me on the shop's bench, palpably recoiled. Many of his uncles and cousins were still such ethnic men. They smoked loose tobacco in pipes. They wore traditional loincloths, or "G-strings," to plow their fields. Most men over about age thirty chewed the nut of the betel palm as a stimulant. These habits distinguished villagers as ethnics from the far *barrios* (villages) rather than Pinoy from the progressive center. When I first met him in 1992, Luis himself wore Levi's jeans, chewed Wrigley's Juicy Fruit gum, and smoked Hope cigarettes. Like his young, single contemporaries, Luis consumed things that helped him fit into a broader Filipino culture defined by the Tagalog-speaking, metropolitan lowlands. The radio DJ's observations expressed a widespread understanding that ethnics were not part of the nation until they, too, joined in these projects of shared consumption. But Luis wanted to retain his cultural traditions while exploring the global world opening up to him.

In the mid-1990s I observed how villagers attempting to recreate Haliap as the parade's site of progressive agriculture had engaged in a wide range of institutions and programs. Much as people wanted to have a united, progressive village, they found that history, economy, and religion were pulling them apart. Most Haliap people thus described their village to me as *kurang* (lacking or insufficient). The village was insufficient for their needs and ideals for security and prosperity and lay outside the imagined community of the nation. Villagers found themselves struggling to perform the kind of ethnic identity that would give them secure access to land while seeking economic and personal progress. Their fundamental problem seemed to be one of their ethnicity and its history. In this period Haliap was attempting to distinguish itself from its neighbors as being the territory of a distinct cultural group with a particular history and set of norms—customary laws—for self-government.

I was living in Haliap while studying land tenure as part of a Canadian-funded development project. Local leaders and elders found me a willing student for their auto-ethnographic version of a village study. Villagers were retrieving and rehearsing their history in order to support their claims to land. Their strategy was to make use of my research activities on land tenure to present themselves as a culturally distinct ethnic group, possessing their own well-defined customs and traditions. While the overview of village culture I have reconstructed from my interviews and reading, below, reflects their classic ethnographic checklist, what I learned about their village through this exercise explains the social networks and life histories of my migrant respondents.

Being Indigenous

In the Philippines progress has long been understood as people evolving from one social stage to the next. The idea dates from the American colonial era (1898–1946) when administrators used an evolutionary ladder to distinguish between the ethnic groups they had inherited from the previous colonizers, the Spanish. Americans classified some groups as primitive and assessed others as comparatively more evolved and thus better prepared for self-government. People from Ifugao exemplified this "Upper Primitive" category.[5] The colonial idea of an evolutionary hierarchy of ethnicity continues to inform popular Filipino understandings of the ties between people and place. Metropolitan Filipinos tend to imagine villages like Haliap as untouched by progress and globalization. Some commentators argue that such communities should resist the demands of the external world and be left alone to conserve their supposedly authentic culture. Others claim that this cultural authenticity is already lost, irretrievably transformed by colonialism, development, and, now, globalization. Either way, villages like Haliap, ranked at the bottom of the hierarchy of development and located far from metropolitan Manila, are usually considered to lie beyond the political boundaries of the imagined nation.

Haliap is what Filipinos call a barangay. The smallest Philippine political unit, a barangay is equivalent to an urban neighborhood or ward. The word comes from the Filipino term for boat. Before the Spanish arrived, each barangay was distinct from other communities, its people joined together by personal allegiances based on kinship. Thirty to one hundred households led by a *datu* (a hereditary chief) comprised the typical barangay.[6] In most precolonial Filipino societies, people owed allegiance to this datu rather than to any wider community that could be described as a tribe or a nation. The Spanish found that this highly localized form of governance facilitated colonial rule. The barangay became a useful unit through which to collect taxes and organize labor. The Spanish made the barangay a formal political unit by appointing leaders, *presidente,* to replace the datu, sometimes appointing the former datu himself. In places like Ifugao, where people were organized into acephalous societies rather than hereditary chiefdoms, the appointment of a presidente consolidated local elites. The Spanish then applied the political term *barangay* to what they had called a *barrio* or, in rural areas of sparse settlement like Ifugao, what they had called a *rancheria* (a small native village). Later, under American rule, appointed presidente were replaced with democratically elected barangay captains, a system that has persisted. Because so many relationships in a village are based on kinship and affinity, barangay politics are emotionally intense, multiplex, and intricate. This is the view from the village, where one's belonging is contingent on engaging in this politics through its exchanges and rituals.

Belonging in the Philippine nation is defined through ties of mutual obligation that are rather like those forming the village. Scaling up village relations explains much of how Filipinos experience nation and national government. Collectively, Filipinos form the *bayan* (Tagalog: people, town, or countryside). Bayan signifies nation in the sense of being a people, a collective public, or a mother/fatherland—a kind of metaphorical national body. The president is *pangulo* (Tagalog: at the head) and is leader of the national body. As president of the republic, he or she also leads *bansa* (country or nation). People expect the president and other senior elected officials to govern wisely by redistributing care and progress to those who have elected them. Every election thus sees numerous projects and programs launched or relabeled to suggest they are gifts to the voters from the president or other senior politicians. The term *bayan,* in the sense of people or town, or the countryside more generally, is often used in much more local ways. *Kababayan* (meaning co-ethnic or fellow national) describes someone who shares commonalities with others, being from the same village, town, or ethnic group. Filipinos are kababayans for one another abroad, but at home the term applies to people from the same language group or region, if not village. Bansa is about membership that can encompass difference, while bayan is about commonality and belonging, describing the nation as a more homogeneous space in terms of culture and social ties—a timeless, collective body of the people. Thus it is possible for indigenous people, with their distinctive cultures and languages, to be governed within the political and administrative networks of bansa but not considered to fully belong within the collective Filipino bayan. In the Philippines I found it rare for a Haliap person to refer to lowland Filipinos as kababayans and vice versa. The term usually refers to someone located in interlocking networks of meaning and exchange at a much more local level.

DRAWING BOUNDARIES

Daily life in Haliap is less defined by any imagined national culture than by the complexities of local ethnic groups and networks. People in Asipulo speak several indigenous languages of the Ifugao subgroups across the municipality: Tuwali (found in south and central Ifugao, also known as Kiangan Ifugao), Hanglulo (also known as Kallahan or Kalanguya, in western Ifugao), and Ayangan (eastern Ifugao). In Haliap, people are Ayangan speakers, a term they pronounce and spell with an extra *d,* as Adyangan (and sometimes spell Adyjangan).[7] Adyangans also speak the Tuwali Ifugao dialect as a common language across the province. The Tuwali word *Ayangan* has become the name of Haliap's dominant ethnic group in Filipino English.[8] Haliap villagers learn both Filipino (Tagalog) and English in school, and they access radio, newspapers, books, and videos in both. They often use Ilokano, the language spoken in neighboring lowland provinces, for regional travel and marketing. When Haliap people talk about kababayans, they usually mean village-mates, other Adyangans, or fellow Ifugaos. Haliap and its neighbor, Panubtuban, are the only Adyangan-speaking barangays in the municipality of Asipulo. To the north, villagers identify people as Tuwali speakers; to the east, Hanglulo (or Kalanguya); and to the south, Keley-i (a distinct dialect of Kalanguya). The boundaries between these ethno-linguistic groups have become blurred at the edges by intermarriage and land transfers, particularly along the main road.

The ways Haliap Adyangans hold land and act politically have never fit with the national government's administrative frameworks. Many Haliap residents cultivate rice fields that lie in Barangay Panubtuban, to the west. Together, Haliap and Panubtuban form one contiguous area, and people living in both barangays long considered themselves a single community.[9] But not all of the people who claim rights to cultivate land inhabit houses within the village's administrative boundaries. One cluster of Haliap houses lies within the boundaries of Keley-i-speaking Barangay Antipolo to the south. Several more hamlets lie on the north side of the Hagalap River, in Tuwali-speaking Barangay Duit, part of the Kiangan municipality. Following Asipulo's inception as a separate municipality in 1992, the setting of its administrative boundaries, four years later, adjudicated between conflicting land claims by drawing a boundary along the Hagalap River. Thus some of Luis's family's rice fields and his father's house lot are now in Kiangan. When it comes to deciding where to reside, accessing public services, and choosing which party's list of candidates to support in local and national elections, Luis juggles conflicting advice and claims on his loyalty.

KINSHIP AND EXCHANGE

Adyangan kinship, like English kinship, is bilateral or cognatic. People typically acknowledge relatedness to both maternal and paternal kin to descendants of common great-great-grandparents. Village social relations are shaped by customary exchanges between relatives and links to other villages through intermarriages. Haliap people can draw on their relatives for support but must in turn support them. Adyangans accord people status to recognize their generosity and willingness to redistribute their wealth, so redistributing money, food, or connections brings prestige. Close relatives are expected to assist each other with regular exchanges of goods and labor. More distant relatives can make claims on one another on special occasions, such as religious festivals. Villagers also tend to be tied to their neighbors by cash debts and food exchanges associated with life-cycle events and religious festivals, just like urban-dwelling Filipinos. But their indigenous customs also stipulate exchanges of a wide variety of gifts, days of labor, and cash donations, which occur across the agricultural calendar, mark public rituals, and discharge obligations to kin.

Haliap's sense of place is founded on shared labor: "We work together so that we will eat." Exchanges of labor between households locate people in the village social network, whether people cultivate for sale or for home consumption, repair shared irrigation systems, or help each other erect or renovate houses. Working together enables villagers to move or raise a house in a day, maintain kilometers of irrigation canals, and plant or harvest rice fields in quick, coordinated succession. Shared work takes two main forms: *changa'*—a daylong working bee, open to all, where workers are given a big meal and lots of rice wine—and *ubfu,* a smaller work group that rotates days of work among members' fields, providing lunch and refreshments. Households keep records of their ubfu obligations in notebooks, writing down the days owed to them and the days of work they owe. Changa' is a broader community obligation. Villagers note who attends their working bee so as to repay them with future cooperation and political support.

Reciprocity in Haliap is about mutual accountability. People can shame their kin and neighbors publicly if they fail to reciprocate as they should. This obligatory reciprocity underpins governance in what was, before colonization, a non-state society. Political power and personal influence remain intertwined, both depending on social relations that must be continually validated through exchange. Relatedness, or being *close,* can never be taken for granted. All village relationships need ongoing renewal in order to be recognized and thus sustained. Haliap's locality, its sense of placeness, is thus constituted by the embodied actions of working and eating, worship and ritual that also produce its agricultural cycle. Work is an extension of the body and one's ties to others. Property—created by an originary mixing of labor with land—extends kinship into community, with rice terraces held in trust for owners from within the kin group and for future generations, though the work is done by a mixture of household and ubfu, or exchange, labor. Intimate ties shaped by these exchanges give villagers a sense of satisfaction in numbers. "*Ado kami* (our company is many)" is something my friends regularly exclaimed with pleasure when involved in inter-village weddings or representing their barangay in the annual municipal fiesta. Being alone remains among the worst things that could happen to a person. Even living outside Haliap, people locate their sense of self by connecting to others, finding they feel satisfied and recognized when they give and receive.

Transfers of value between persons and households enact the practical love and care that are necessary to—as expressed in English—*show* and *share* what people call *feeling*. Villagers cannot easily refuse to cooperate in work, to lend material goods, or to redistribute unexpected windfalls. To do so would be *hardheaded* or *hard-hearted*, to *insist on your own* (property or course of action), or to be *closed-minded* or *stingy*. These are among the worst things that can be said of another person. Instead, people cultivate the virtues of *taking pity on, accommodating* or *entertaining,* and *sharing to* (redistributing excess). Exchanges of work, food, and goods are tied to affect, shaping personhood by increasing or decreasing the esteem in which people are held by fellow villagers.

Adyangans expect more or less generalized reciprocity among household members who are close relatives. Norms of private property are not strongly attached to smaller items such as cooking utensils, decorations, clothes, pens, books, and DVDs. In order to avoid the humiliation of being refused a request from a close relative, many relatives do not ask before borrowing. More balanced reciprocity characterizes relationships between households of more distant kin. As well as keeping records of exchange labor obligations, villagers record larger loans of cash and agricultural equipment, mortgages on fields, and sharecropping arrangements, often with witnesses. They exchange days of work on a like-for-like basis between households, with members substituting for each other in case of a double booking. Restitutions never seem to even out to a point where both sides believe their obligations have been equalized. Exchanges either persist for a lifetime or collapse acrimoniously, one (or both) side(s) claiming that the other refuses to recognize the value of labor donated or goods received.

Villagers regularly seek to receive redistributive gifts from patrons outside the village.[10] As clients, villagers offer their patrons an opportunity to redistribute that demonstrates patrons' humanity and generosity and thus raise their status. Patrons include a variety of politicians, religious organizations, development projects, and government offices. Villagers expect these patrons to receive political support and labor in return for cash, goods, recognition, and the possibilities of political alliance. However, villagers rarely consider themselves satisfied with the donations of patrons when compared to the work they have offered in return. Patrons are often criticized, though rarely face-to-face, for being stingy, unappreciative, and demanding—not showing proper humanity—in their relationships with villagers.

Despite these gripes, Haliap people consider themselves to be good at building relationships. They tend to see the wider world as a series of collectives of persons to whom they can relate rather than a network of abstract institutions operating through knowable rules and regulations. Their approach to the world is thus characterized by personalism.[11] Villagers understand that they share a set of moral norms with their consociates—other collectives or individuals with whom they exchange labor, goods, or symbols of affiliation or political loyalty. Without public institutions that merit their trust, they assimilate strangers into their world by converting them into consociates through exchange. Giving, of things and of selves, is the way Adyangans establish and maintain kinship and kinlike ties. Thus villagers who donate counterpart labor to a development project or ask a patron to stand as a sponsor at a wedding or baptism are trying to create kinlike relations to extend their personal networks. Adyangan kinship is flexible; it is quite common to develop close affective ties based on reciprocal exchange with non-kin, and many households include members who have been adopted, fostered, or absorbed into the family as fictive kin. Reciprocity between households and with patrons often arises with co-residence, which is then solidified into kinship through marriage, adopting, fostering, or godparent-child relationships. Personalism helps Adyangans build security in an uncertain world, leading them to cultivate diplomacy and patience and to become disposed to display care for others, an ethos they maintain in migration.

FAITH

Haliap people tend to see religion as a separate sphere of social action, but their faith expresses their beliefs and norms of community cohesiveness, moral purpose, and ways to create an enduring set of ties outside the household. These norms are very much the same principles on which local politics are founded.

Approximately half the village follows what they consider traditional Christianity, combining Catholicism with what they call Adyangan paganism in a syncretic system of beliefs. Haliap Catholics maintain exchanges with a Christian God through weekly church services and daily prayers. Most also maintain another vital set of exchanges with a variety of supernatural beings through the offices of Adyangan *munfahi,* or native priests, who preside over rituals sustaining the agricultural cycle and marking life-course events. These rituals require the sacrifice of pigs and chickens to the spirit world. Blood sacrifices alleviate people's feelings of heaviness in the body, anxiety, and discomfort, producing calm, optimism, and light-bodied feelings that suggest capability and a positive future. The distinctive feature of this ritual practice is the contractual nature of the ties between humans and the spirit realm, with each side obliged to reciprocate. Sacrificing animals assures people of good health, wealth, fertility; protects people from disease and disaster; and gives them success in their endeavors.[12] People tend to understand Catholic teachings through the same rubric of exchange, with worship and prayer being donations to God to ensure desired outcomes. While the Christian God may sit above all the other spirits that people recognize, local spirits, particularly those of departed ancestors, seem to exert the strongest influence over village lives.

The non-Catholic half of the village is divided into Pentecostals and followers of the Iglesia ni Cristo. As Protestants, both groups reject Catholics' so-called pagan practices, considering them to be the work of the devil. Members of each church claim that their own religious observances and networks are actually more civilized and *in line with* projects of Philippine development than Catholicism. Though Protestants, both churches nonetheless maintain a similar exchange-based understanding of worship, offering prayers and tithes intended to ensure that eventual material security and prosperity will be provided to their members by God.

MOBILITY

Village sociality extends Haliap's locality well beyond the administrative boundaries of the barangay. Both Haliap emigrants and circular migrants remain in regular text message and phone contact with areas of outmigration: rural settlements in the nearby provinces of Nueva Viscaya, Quirino, and Isabela; Lagawe, the capital of Ifugao; Appari, in Cagayan; the towns of Solano and Bayombong in Nueva Viscaya; the Cordillera region's metropolitan center, Baguio City; Manila, the national capital; frontier areas on the southern island of Mindanao; and Singapore, Hong Kong, Dubai, and Canada. If they are able, migrants in these areas return for the major shared labor events of their household's year: planting and harvest. Migrants' arrivals and departures and visits to their home villages mark the everyday life of the community.

Some villagers travel by bus to and from the homes of relatives in Isabela or to new farms they have cleared in logging areas near Maddela, Quirino Province. Others go south, riding three or more long-haul jeepneys through

Nueva Viscaya to arrive in their citrus orchards near Kasibu. When workers in Manila visit, they bring supplies and gifts from metropolitan department stores. Travelers carry agricultural products, goods, and stories back and forth across the region, and cash, letters, and more boxes of goods arrive periodically from contract workers overseas. When people cannot come in person, they send goods and money as their way of participating in shared work. Combine all of this interchange with links to churches, religious orders, NGOs (nongovernmental organizations), and overseas visitors, and the result is a village anchored to a site in Ifugao but with an extensive, expansive, and inclusive valence to it.

Luis's own biography reflects this pattern of mobility. During his last years of high school, he moved to Kasibu, Nueva Viscaya, where his maternal aunt and uncle, a childless couple, sponsored his studies and offered to adopt him. He declined their offer and, after graduating, worked in a small-scale mining camp belonging to Ifugao migrants, where he describes his job as *helper*. He then moved on to Manila, where he worked as a wood-carver in a factory and as a helper in a garage. At that point he ceased to be an active member of the Iglesia church. Then, after unsuccessfully applying to the U.S. Navy, he returned to Haliap in his early twenties to live with his widowed father.

Luis identifies by his ethnicity, calling himself Adyangan, or by his place of origin, *Ihaliap,* to distinguish himself from other Ifugao people. During the 1990s, Haliap people increasingly began to describe themselves as *IP*s, meaning indigenous peoples, differentiating themselves from the nonindigenous, mainstream Filipinos who inhabit the lowlands. Villagers' multiple ways of identifying themselves reflected their interests in place rather than their mobile livelihood strategies. Conflicts between their mobile livelihoods and their indigeneity became a pressing concern from the mid-1990s.

Resource Politics

The idea of something called *the government,* as a set of nationwide institutions Haliap people need in order to organize their lives, is a relatively recent and sometimes troubling imposition. The series of government plans and programs that engage the village offer a compelling set of future possibilities, a series of largely irrelevant and intrusive activities, and fundamentally destabilizing challenges to security, often simultaneously.

The major problem for governance arises from the village's history of migration, placing Haliap in conflict with its neighbors. Tuwali people consider Adyangans to be *kaingineros* (shifting cultivators) rather than expert rice terrace builders. Haliap villagers do cultivate significant areas of terraced pond fields dating back at least seven generations. Adyangans are reputed to be shifting cultivators not because of their activities in Haliap—where their swidden are integrated into the rice terrace system—so much as from their migratory history. In lowland provinces bordering Ifugao, Haliap migrants use slash-and-burn cultivation (swidden or *kaingin*) to informally claim and improve land. They plant these plots with cash crops such as squash and citrus trees and sell the crops to other migrants. Where Tuwali and Adyangan claims to land conflict, Adyangans tend to be vilified as destructive shifting cultivators who could be resettled elsewhere.

Nationally, late-twentieth-century concerns over deforestation led the government to introduce measures to conserve the remaining forest. Under the Revised Forestry Code (1975), land over eighteen degrees in slope became forest reserve, part of the public domain.[13] In southeastern Ifugao only 7 percent of the entire (former) municipality of Kiangan had been certified as below eighteen degrees in slope and thus "alienable and disposable," meaning available for titling. Haliap's steep slopes meant that only some of the occupied land area would be available for individual applications for land title. On the map, much of Haliap/Panubtuban fell within the limits of the Santo Domingo Forest Reserve, an area reserved for conservation or future government-initiated development. Haliap people had always cut logs in their forests and often earned money by selling lumber. In 1992 the government introduced a ban on logging in all the Philippines' primary growth forests. Villagers suddenly found themselves described as squatters on public land, pursuing illegal livelihood activities.

Control over Haliap's forest resources was the preeminent political concern in the late 1980s and early 1990s. Tuwali people claimed rights to the forest on the north slopes of the Hagalap River and began logging there in the mid-1980s. Haliap's barangay council appealed to the (Tuwali-dominated) provincial government to stop thefts of timber, with no success. Villagers then approached the communist insurgents, the New People's Army (NPA), for help. For some months guerillas lived in a small encampment in the forest near Luis's family home. In 1990 the Philippine army shelled the Antipolo valley to drive them out. The army has since stationed troops in the valley to keep the peace. In the mid-1990s the military themselves became the biggest contributor to the demand for cut lumber.

Villagers intensified their logging activities to supply the soldiers. In 1992, when soldiers of the 56th Infantry Battalion departed, they took with them a load of cut lumber for which they had not paid. The army claimed the lumber had been seized from illegal loggers in support of the Department of Environment and Natural Resources' new total log ban and that they had simply been enforcing the law. Villagers claimed the soldiers had broken a verbal contract of sale. They contacted DZNV radio (a Nueva Viscaya–based station popular in Ifugao) to broadcast an appeal for payment, but to no avail. As agents of the government, soldiers seemed to enjoy immunity from justice. Whatever Haliap people thought they might do in response to such thefts, they could foresee that the government could use their response as a pretext to dispossess them.

Haliap was not alone in this situation. To redress the problems faced by indigenous communities, the national government created a new category of land tenure intended to exempt lands from the Forestry Code: ancestral domain. From the mid-1990s, Haliap took part in the ancestral domain claims process. Ancestral domain delimits particular kinds of indigenous identity and links these identities to equally specific forms of place, relying on a circular argument that assumes land and people are inseparable.[14] Its enabling legislation, the Indigenous Peoples' Rights Act (IPRA) of 1997, recognizes "ancestral domains . . . delimited by indigenous cultural communities who are defined by their ancestry; or, indigenous cultural communities . . . contained by ancestral domains which are defined by their prior settlement by indigenous or autochthonous populations."[15] To meet the requirements for recognizing ancestral domain, applicants must demonstrate to the National Commission on Indigenous Peoples (NCIP, established in 1997) both the evidence of their ancestry and their control of a defined and bounded domain. The NCIP requires people to document at least six generations of continuous inhabitation in order to recognize a community's indigenous status. While ancestral domain appeared to offer Haliap people a way to have their claims to their land formally recognized by the government, they first had to demonstrate historical control over domain and define village membership through ancestry. Quite clearly, ancestral domain anticipates an indigenous village with the kind of history told by the vignettes of the ethnic parade rather than Haliap's convoluted past.

Colonial History

Haliap emerged from Spanish rearrangements of people along the nineteenth-century colonial frontier. The village has no written records, and the colonial archive itself is fragmented, so people must rely on oral histories to learn about their past. This is problematic, not least because village elders described displacement and resettlement in a series of places that are no longer on official maps, using names that few contemporary people remember. Most of the old native place-names along the colonial frontier were replaced with the names of twentieth-century Filipino politicians.

Spanish rule in the Philippines began in 1521 when Magellan claimed the islands for Spain. Almost a century later, Spanish forces entered the area called Ituy, along the Magat River, in the contemporary province of Nueva Viscaya.

In Adyangan, *hituy* means "here." Initial attempts to convert the population of the Ituy area began in 1591.[16] When Spanish missionaries failed to convert the local people, they then tried to subdue the scattered hamlets with military force. People fled. Spanish forces withdrew and returned several times over the next three centuries, starting missions in the foothill areas and river valleys. Many of these missions were populated with people brought down from the mountains into *reducciones* (lowland resettlements).

The original inhabitants of Ituy practiced shifting cultivation, with some wet-rice agriculture along the river valleys. They also participated in long-distance trade in goods (pots, baskets, textiles), dried meat, deerskins, salt, gold, and slaves. Trade underpinned political and cultural exchanges that linked their upland communities to those on the foothills and plains and, finally, across the South China Sea to Chinese metropolitan markets. People in Ituy inhabited temporary houses that were located near swidden tended by women. Men devoted much of their time to game hunting, trading journeys, and warfare. Much of Ituy was malarial, so while people lived on the heights, hunters moved across extensive hunting grounds, *panganopan,* on either side of the Magat River. Language groups, including Ilongots, Gaddangs, and Ibanag people, eventually shared these same hunting grounds, encountering one another in the forest.[17] The various groups formed trade alliances through parental marriages that crosscut their linguistic differences. Since there was much land available, no one group claimed anything more than a few house lots and fields for their exclusive use. Spanish attempts to settle these groups in mission towns along river valleys disrupted trade and agriculture and exposed them to disease.

Life in a Spanish mission was demanding. Filipino converts paid the *cedula* (head tax), and all men from sixteen to sixty had to provide forty days' labor each year, building churches and roads. In return, the Spanish offered people new technologies and crops alongside religious salvation. The Spanish introduced the plow and the water buffalo (*Bubalus carabanensis—carabao* or *kalabaw*), which enabled wet-rice cultivators to enjoy a significant increase in productivity.[18] But Spanish religious discipline demanded constant presence in places where natives were accessible to their governance: in town and in church. Even initially willing converts found it impossible to tend swidden, hunt, and trade and remain good Christians. Malaria was endemic in many of the missions. People fled the reducciones and returned to the uplands as *remontados* (runaways), bringing with them new tools for farming.

Spanish records identified religious confessions, not language groups: Christian converts were *nativos;* non-Christians were *infieles*. Administrators were rarely able to recognize linguistic or cultural differences among infieles living beyond the missions. In Luzon they called these infiele groups *Ygorrotes*.

This term came from *igolud* (*i* meaning "from" and *golud,* Tagalog for "mountain") and entered English as "Igorot" (a term that would later be transmuted to "gook" during the Philippine War of Independence, 1899–1902). Spanish records of the groups in Ituy are particularly confused. During the 1700s, Ygorrote raids, death from disease, and converts deserting to flee to the mountains saw the missions in Ituy continually fail.[19] Spanish attempts to punish raiders and deserters resulted in whole settlements being abandoned, pushing outlaws farther into the hills. In this period Ituy was inundated by several waves of migrants fleeing the Spanish elsewhere. People began moving upstream into the headwaters of the Cagayan River, away from the Spanish presence along the river's lower reaches. At the same time, more people crossed the Baler Pass from Pangasinan, fleeing Spanish haciendas and towns along the Ilocos coast.

Most arable areas in the mountains were long occupied. Those fleeing the missions had to fight or trade for land. Many appropriated land through *ngayaw,* head-taking warfare. The frontier became increasingly violent, characterized by what, to the Spanish, seemed to be random head-taking raids, disappearances, and thefts. Groups seeking access to land through trade sent raiding parties back to the missions to procure water buffalo and sometimes slaves. In response, the Spanish made further punitive raids across the frontier, attempting to discourage more Ygorrote incursions. People from the upper and middle Magat River seem to have fled Spanish control during the 1700s. In 1748 the Spanish made the first of many punitive expeditions into a Ygorrote area called Paniquy, attempting to put an end to raids on the new missions at Bagabag and Bayombong, in present-day Nueva Viscaya. The abandoned Paniquy settlements on the Ganano and Magat River flatlands are potentially the origins of the group who fled to Adyang and then eventually settled Panubtuban.[20]

PLACE OF CURSING

In Haliap, Luis's uncles told me stories of Spaniards burning their ancestral villages, followed by flight and head-taking in the struggle to find a new place to dwell. These ancestors settled in the Antipolo valley after an arduous journey from the eastern side of the province. Known as I-Adyang or Adyangan, they had traveled from the headwaters of the Alimit River, a tributary of the Magat, in the 1870s. They had retreated to the Adyang area from lands along the Magat several generations earlier. Arriving in Adyang, they made *habal* (swidden or kaingin) and grew *camote* (sweet potato) because of a shortage of land suitable for rice fields. There was insufficient land at Adyang to feed the growing population, and in the early 1870s there was a famine. A group of people left Adyang to return to their old lands along the Magat River. They arrived at their former settlement of Ibong (now Villaverde, Nueva Viscaya) after several weeks of hiking but found their fields occupied by Ilokano-speaking Filipinos from the mission. The Ilocanos were infected with malaria. Before departing Ibong, the Adyangans took some Ilocano heads as payment for the land that had been lost. Led by a young woman, Bugan, the group then traveled from the western bank of the Lamut River to what was the most westerly Adyangan settlement at Bolog—"sailing across the land like a boat on the water" is the phrase used in Haliap ritual chants. Members of the group had kin among the Bolog Adyangans, and they agreed that the Adyang people should move into the Antipolo valley to the west.

Like other Ifugao groups, Adyangans worshipped spirits of nature, deities attached to particular places, and their own ancestors.[21] Male priests (munfahi) sacrificed animals to contact spirit patrons, determining the cause of and cure for misfortune or sickness or ensuring the fertility of people, crops, and animals. The well-being of ancestors in the next world depended on the sacrifices offered up by their descendants before and after their death and burial. Ancestors could mediate with gods. Gods, in turn, needed to be appeased with sacrifices, because men and women were indebted to them for the good fortune they enjoyed and the misfortunes they avoided. Meat from sacrifices to the ancestors and gods was eaten by relatives of those sponsoring the ritual, with shares distributed in order of kin precedence. During these rituals, munfahi chanted long myths and family genealogies, marking funerals, weddings, and harvest rites. Prestige feasts, too, required munfahi to chant genealogies and boast of ancestral exploits as the host redistributed food to the community. Daily activities that involved risk or doubt also required people to consult a munfahi, who would propitiate their ancestors to ensure a good outcome. Illness and death were believed to be caused by jealous ancestors calling people to the next world, so each household sponsored an annual round of rituals, plus special sacrifices as needed, to maintain their good fortune.

The new arrivals found the land along the Hagalap River "almost empty." The upper valley had a Spanish-built cement kiln, some abandoned rice terraces, and a few rice fields cultivated by Hanglulo people. The Adyangans *pioneered* the lower valley by building an extensive system of rice terraces. They first built houses from trees they felled on the slopes by the river. In the cleared area they made rice terraces, watered by a creek from a spring up the slope. Along the banks of the creek and above their house lots, they cleared land for habal. Having established their presence and secured their livelihoods, the people held a ritual. Led by munfahi, they slaughtered pigs and chickens in order to *mun-tubtub* (curse) the Ilocanos at Ibong so that they would not become ill themselves. They called their new settlement "place-of-cursing," or *panubtuban*. Learning of its success, more people came from Adyang, expanding the community. In 1997 the oldest lineage of inhabitants could trace their residence back eight generations.

Oral historians offered conflicting accounts of the origin of the rice terraces. Some claimed that their forebears built all the terraces. Others reported that their ancestors had taken over empty fields, previous Hanglulo cultivators having gone down to lowland missions. A few claimed that their great-grandfathers had frightened away the Hanglulo inhabitants with magic and ngayaw or had acquired land by arranging marriages between Hanglulo and Adyangan children. Their Hanglulo neighbors recall that Adyangans purchased rice fields from them with kalabaw. (This history was unfamiliar to many younger Haliap people who listened in on my interviews and claimed "we've always had carabao" because "we're not that primitive.") Draft animals enabled Hanglulo people, who were, like the Adyangans at the time, still tilling their rice terraces with wooden spades, to increase the land area under cultivation.

The name *Panubtuban* commented on colonial rearrangements of the Adyangan people. Panubtuban may have been their place of refuge, but it was part of a much wider colonial world in which they understood themselves to be resisting Spanish control.

HURRY UP

When Luis's elderly relatives took shortcuts, the slippages in their stories revealed resistance to colonialism. Luis's uncle, Lakai Ngabit, once told me the name Haliap came from the commands given by a Spanish overseer shouting at a worker to "hurry-up, hurry-up." I suggested that perhaps he meant an American because he spoke in English. Lakai Ngabit shrugged his shoulders and replied, laughing: "It doesn't matter. They're the same thing. . . . A letter needed to be carried to Kiangan, and they called to the man they chose to 'hurry up' to make him go fast. So here we said it was the place of *holyap*." In his cheerful rejoinder, Lakai Ngabit saw governments as interchangeable, continually sending agents to push villagers around and give their places new identities.

In 1898 the Americans replaced the Spanish as the colonial governors of the Philippines, an outcome of the Treaty of Paris that ended the Spanish-American War. American administrators quickly established a consolidated presence on the Cordillera. Arriving in the Antipolo valley, they found a zone of conflict.

The place-name Panubtuban first appears in a 1904 report from First Lieutenant C. J. Bates to Captain W. E. Thompson, senior inspector of Nueva Viscaya. According to Bates's report, three men and two women from "Panitubang" were traveling to Ibong when they were attacked by "Igorots" hiding along the trail. One woman, Imuc, was killed with spears and her head was taken. Her companions returned the body to her kin. News of the murder came to Bates from Dominga Alandada, a female presidente of a nearby rancheria. She had met with the first American expedition to Ifugao in March 1903, first at the American headquarters in Kiangan and later in her home community of Dullayan (Barangay Cawayan, Asipulo). Bates planned to visit Panubtuban to investigate: "If I succeed in getting the guide I will leave here on the 31st. I cannot inform you how long I shall be on the trip, not knowing where the place is, but will stay out until I find it and will try to capture the outfit . . . that committed the murder."[22] Bates, on Alandada's advice, was seeking people from "Banhitan," likely the present-day sitio of Banetinon in Panubtuban.

The Americans soon replaced the old Panubtuban with the new name Haliap, consigning its history of carabao rustling and head-taking to the past. They built a road through the valley that saw new hamlets spring up along it and trade expand, effectively quelling conflicts over farmland and pacifying the warring tribes. By the 1940s, Haliap Adyangans had given up hope of reclaiming lands at Ibong. Instead, after the Second World War and Philippine independence, they began to return to what they consider to be their old hunting grounds in the upper Cagayan Valley. Collective memories of late Spanish-era displacements underpin even more recent migration back into the lowlands, particularly to the string of settlements between Kasibu, Nueva Viscaya, and Maddela, Quirino.

Becoming Tribe

Tribe was the key word organizing the American administration of peoples living on the Philippine Cordillera Central. American colonizers brought the concept of tribe along with them from the American Great Plains. Tribe framed the identities of peoples and places, simplifying complex histories and relationships for easier governing: those who inhabited the former Spanish-governed towns and cities had become civilized Filipinos, and those who dwelt along and beyond the old Spanish frontier remained primitive tribes. American approaches to classifying Philippine tribes elaborated on details provided by soldiers, academics, missionaries, and travelers for the lives and customs of groups of people previously living outside effective state control. Behind these practices of classifying lay an assumption that place and people's physical appearance could easily be linked. So, rather than their historical location outside the boundaries of state governance, tribal categories in the Philippines typically revolved around descriptions of physical appearance as they do in the rest of Southeast Asia. This idea of indigenes as physically different from mainstream populations is the origin of the short, dark-skinned, curly-haired characteristics that Tuwali speakers attribute to Adyangans and that metropolitan Filipinos (equally mistakenly) ascribe to Igorots. Anthropologist Tania Li calls this sociopolitical space occupied by indigenes "the tribal slot," observing that the physical stereotypes attached to indigenes make them into outsiders against which a mainstream national population can consolidate its identity as unified, contemporary, and progressive.[23]

The ways tribal classifications are connected to physical appearance suggest there should be some essential differences between indigenes and mainstream groups. This is not the case. Across Southeast Asia, groups now categorized as national or ethnic minorities have only somewhat recently become distinct from the mainstream population, and this is true, too, in the Philippines. While in Indonesia or Vietnam ethnic minorities are seen as backward, they are nonetheless considered merely less-civilized versions of metropolitan nationals. The Philippines is an exception to this pattern.

In the Philippines, American colonialism drew explicit parallels between indigenous Filipinos and North American indigenes, or Indians. "Tribe" was imported as a category applied to Great Plains Indian groups to distinguish legitimate natives from bands of outlaws.[24] Authentic tribes were people who could demonstrate their settlement in a particular place, and name a specific individual as their leader. In the United States, tribes had made a dynamic ethnic landscape legible as the former American colonies expanded westward. But in the Philippines, tribe carried with it the idea that the state, with its project of progress, was being similarly imposed on primitive people by an ethnically and culturally much different—more advanced and sophisticated—settler society. Today mainstream Filipinos tend to think of indigenous peoples as tribes that represent distinct groups of primitive first inhabitants, the Filipino version of American Indians. They imagine these first inhabitants were displaced by later arrivals: their own ancestors, who were Malay-speaking migrants from mainland Southeast Asia and who introduced civilization to the archipelago, much like European settlers civilized the American West. This idea of increasingly civilized waves of migrants, famously put forward as anthropologist Otley Beyer's wave migration theory, is not supported by contemporary linguistic and archaeological evidence, but it remains prominent in the popular imagination.[25] Few metropolitan Filipinos recognize that the social and cultural differences distinguishing indigenous peoples from the metropolitan mainstream date only to the later Spanish period. Fewer still realize that they deal with Filipinos almost every day who could identify themselves as these IPs in metropolitan Manila, in regional urban centers, and in the diaspora.

American officials used regional names and place-based and religious descriptors inherited from the Spanish as well as their own surveys to establish these tribal identities. After it won independence from America in 1946, the new Philippine government retained these now solidified categories. The result was an ethnic landscape with a particular geography. Tribal names proliferated and were fine-grained, acknowledging complex ethnic histories and self-appellations for localities that were tied more closely to missions, colonial administrators, and prominent scholars. For the rest, more general terms applied, such as the pan-Cordillera descriptor of Igorot (the Spanish *Ygorrote* and Tagalog *igolud*). Classified as non-Christian tribes, it was Igorots' animism that supposedly distinguished them from lowland, Christian Filipinos. While the Spanish colonizers had seen religious confession as the distinctive mark of a civilized person, the Americans established education and professional qualifications as the key features that separated primitives from progressive peoples. Bringing these ideas together, Filipinos came to understand that the progressive, developing part of the newly independent Philippines—amenable to scientific reason and state planning—was that composed of Catholics. Paganism marked backward regions. National development thus necessitated religious conversion, because only those people who had abandoned what they considered pagan beliefs would be amenable to governance.

When indigenous villages on the Cordillera were less than enthusiastic about post-independence government programs and projects, it was easy to blame their less-than-perfect understandings of Christian religious precepts. Elite Ifugao villagers responded strategically, emphasizing their own Christian faith and seeking professional qualifications rather than pursuing agriculture. The elite soon gained the qualifications needed to take over administrative positions in local government themselves.

In Haliap the concept of tribe did not really begin to intrude into daily village life until the mid-1990s. Until then, the term *Adyangan side* (meaning the Adyangan section of the province, largely in the south and east) described a swath of interrelated Adyangan communities extending across Ifugao Province from Madyjodyjao (Mayoyao) to Asipulo. Villagers described themselves as part of this side or as Adyangan Ifugaos, a subgroup of Ifugao people. However, a 1990 Socioeconomic Profile of Ifugao produced by the National Statistics Office listed more than forty (mostly) Barangay-based tribes belonging to four Ifugao linguistic groups.[26] Haliap people were perturbed. Ihaliap was listed as a Tuwali-speaking tribe. People complained that many of the names on the list were simply the place-names of barangays, reflecting administrative rather than cultural divisions, and that the names did not reflect the dialects people spoke. Yet these ethnic names were vital; place-based tribes would shape local visibility in the national political sphere and thus access to government revenue.

The ancestral domain process required the village to perform a kind of tribal identity that could be recognized by the government's National Commission on

Indigenous Peoples. Haliap people tried to build the patronage relations necessary to promote village claims to territory by exchanging their performances of ethnicity for flows of resources from the new NCIP bureaucrats, as well as provincial and national politicians. Attracting the government's notice to their history of transience and the ways their village might not be quite the bounded or local group that the category "tribe" anticipates carried risks. Villagers needed government to perceive Haliap as the right kind of tribe: one with the requisite ethnic traditions but, fundamentally, Christian and progressive, interested in and compliant with government projects and programs.

Yet villagers did not entirely trust the ancestral domain process, largely because of the personalism in Philippine politics. Elsewhere, previously accepted tribal identities were challenged and rendered illegible by political contests, identities being easily reframed by those who had the best access to the bureaucracy. Links between tribal names and territory remained unstable, with new names appearing and previously accepted identities being rejected on the NCIP register. In 2002 the NCIP listing for Ifugao Province described the Asipulo valley as the territory of the Hanglulo tribe, with no mention of Tuwali or the Adyangan presence. In 2005 the NCIP listed a total indigenous population for the Philippines of 11,718,190 persons, 1,252,962 of these people living in the Cordillera Autonomous Region. The total national ethnic population included 17,049 Tuwali people and 22,039 Ikalahan, 5 Hanglulo, and 110,819 people who identified as Ifugao, offering a problematic admixture of overlapping categories that worked across several scales.[27] Haliap people wondered if omitting the category of "Adyangan" was an oversight or if it indicated that their neighbors were preparing to contest their claim to the land occupied by the village. And what were the 110,819 people doing who had ignored ethnic subgroups in favor of an Ifugao identity? Everyone in Haliap wanted to resist the idea that *Ifugao* really meant "Tuwali speakers."

Luis, who identified himself foremost as a progressive farmer when I first met him in 1992, was initially skeptical of the idea of an Ihaliap tribe. He soon began to appreciate the necessity of ensuring that the government's category "tribe" coincided with the administrative divisions of the barangays. He was not alone. Haliap's claim to domain went forward as part of the larger Asipulo municipal ancestral domain claim in 2004. In 2005 a process of delineating boundaries began, with the NCIP assessing conflicting claims on specific land areas against each other. To minimize conflict and ensure speedy recognition, each barangay in Asipulo agreed to act as a tribe and respect all current administrative divisions. Thus tribe had effectively been mapped back onto barangay divisions. Unfortunately, a boundary dispute—both the provinces of Ifugao and Nueva Viscaya claim Asipulo's Barangay Camandag—stalled the process.

SEDUCTIONS OF IDENTITY

The category of "tribe" worked to change the ways villagers thought and felt about themselves in the world. Tribe promised them a chance to become part of the nation—if they modified their histories, identities, and desires appropriately. Mapping tribe onto the village involved answering in advance several important questions about settlement, belonging, and livelihood for Haliap people. Though a tribe was supposed to be a legitimately settled group, Ihaliap people remained both rooted and mobile, engaging in both legal, settled agriculture in Ifugao and illegal logging and shifting cultivation in the lowlands. Lands in Ifugao claimed as the domain of an Ihaliap tribe might be legitimately farmed, according to village custom, by returning migrants from Nueva Viscaya. These people could reactivate their hereditary land rights in Ifugao if they so chose, but were unlikely to be recognized as Ihaliap tribe members under the NCIP's new rules. Though these multilocal livelihood strategies were important, villagers considered security of tenure in Barangay Haliap to be more so. Thus villagers were persuaded to think of themselves in new terms.

In 1992 Luis described himself to me as part of an Adyangan side, proudly explaining that his uncles could tell me about the historic migration from Ibong. Just a few years later he was speaking of himself as an IP whose ancestors had inhabited Barangay Haliap since "time immemorial." By 2004 he was actively seeking a certificate of indigenous identity from the NCIP, listing the birth villages of his mother and father in boxes labeled "Tribe." He was glad he belonged to a Protestant church because, he explained, Catholics were known to be "superstitious." While he wanted to maintain his indigenous culture, his vision of a virtuous village, deserving of progress, no longer had a place for "pagan beliefs." Though Luis may have been a landless IP, he had been able to depend on his landed relatives to farm. Yet his relatives, comparatively well-off villagers, could easily have lost their lands and livelihood, too, if the government had decided to relocate the village to conserve the forest. With the outcome uncertain, Luis and his family were hedging their bets, intensifying efforts to open new land on the rural frontier, in areas not covered by ancestral domain. Here, they were—like everyone else—migrant peasants. Migration was, for them, a strategy to transcend the limits of this reinvigorated tribalism.

Insecurity and Migration

Village history reveals how insecurity in Haliap is not simply about poverty, but also about political power and the ability it has to shift previously accepted categories toward new and unpredictable meanings. Haliap thus exemplifies a more general link between insecurity and migration. To attain security, people must transform the ways they think and feel about themselves. Thus, quite abruptly, but equally sincerely, people become something different in their own understanding. Rather than losing a bounded village per se, here people lost one way of thinking and feeling about themselves in the world and gained another. This shift in self-understanding is what Deleuze describes as territoriality and reterritorialization. These concepts map how losing one's sense of self-in-the-world only to gain another can happen even when one remains in place. Villagers hedged their bets, some moving on and others staying and complying. In doing so, they sought to make an opening—a space for a vital, contemporary culture that could incorporate their mobility and allow them to retain much of their familiar way of being in the world. Thus, even as they marched in the ranks of the parade, they knew that their village was not the ideal the parade enacted. They responded to this disjuncture between history and how it was represented in the parade by coming to define themselves, not through their present circumstances, but through their dreams of something more and different. This something lay in the imagined global realm, and to find it they sought work abroad.

CHAPTER 2 ◆ Becoming a Global Kind of Woman

AROUND THE WORLD, WHAT women do and don't do—and how they look while doing it—is evidence of civilization and development and a matter of national pride. To understand the Philippines, with its land-based migrant labor force predominantly composed of women, we need to understand why and how village women, who are the majority of the country's peasant and working-class female migrants, approach both being women and becoming overseas migrants. Thus we need to explore how women's work and social roles have changed over time and learn how women come to understand themselves with and against different models of femininity. In 1990s Haliap, women found themselves unable to enact proper Filipina, or *housewife,* identities when at home and dreamed that working abroad would make them over into their own global kind of woman. These dreams no doubt expressed feelings of frustration and inadequacy they shared with women elsewhere in the Philippines and across the developing world—women considered too poor, too backward, or too uneducated to really matter in the public life of their nation.

During my stay in Haliap, I learned that gender gave a particular shape to progress. Though women were not the figures of anticolonial resistance or global migration portrayed in the parade, my early 1990s interviews with local elders retrieved oral histories that were populated by female actors, and my household surveys indicated that women comprised the majority of the village's overseas migrants. But local ideas of global femininity were both powerful and proscriptive. In 1996, Peter, a former Haliap barangay captain, completed an interview about local history, and his comments sparked my curiosity. To the question "What improvements have Haliap people experienced since before the Spanish time?" he had replied, "Bras and panties for women." Was he serious? Was he teasing, resisting what he may have found to be an intrusive question? When I asked Peter to explain, he said that wearing underwear was what people had learned about progress from the Americans. He then cautioned me against drying my own bras and panties on the clothesline under the trees outside my rented house, in case "someone would steal them." So should I have understood this as a profound insight, progress being best encapsulated by undergarments that nobody should actually see but that shaped the female body into a more acceptable and attractive form? At the nearest market I examined the bras on sale. All had formed cups that promised the wearer a shapely bustline; a woman's own natural shape was apparently inadequate. Peter's comments suggested that femininity—how women performed themselves as gendered—acted as a powerful and widely accepted metaphor for progress.

Angelina

Seeking women's thoughts on the shape of bras and progress, I found single women in their mid-twenties scarce. The census told me that many of them were away completing education, working in the lowland urban centers, or seeking work abroad.[1] Married women were busy with their businesses or their farming and rarely had much time for a regular woman-to-woman chat with me, then single and childless. I went to the shops—called *sari-sari* stores—on the main road, where people hung around. The female shopkeepers could chat while they worked. My friend Otag Manghi, known as Angelina, owned one of these sari-sari stores.

Angelina had grown up in Haliap but left in her mid-teens as what Filipinos call a *working student*. She did domestic work for the household of distant cousins in the lowlands while completing her high school education. She then enrolled in college for two years of midwifery training; however, her parents could not afford to fund her third year of college. She had learned that it was very difficult for qualified midwives to find work. Haliap had several unemployed midwifery graduates, and there were already too many applicants for the jobs available in Asipulo, so Angelina decided against returning to college. Her parents gave her part of her inheritance early, before her marriage, so that she could support herself. This inheritance was a plot of land along the main road and a small amount of money with which to build and stock a sari-sari store. Angelina's parents also engaged a traditional matchmaker to find her a husband. She became engaged to Mark, the youngest son of one of Haliap's comparatively better-off families. After the *fonong*—a ritual payment of bride wealth in pigs, consumed at a village feast—Mark withdrew from the contract. Angelina was pregnant and the baby was not his. Thus, in 1992, when I first met her, Angelina was a single mother living with her parents and running a failing store. Her customers could not pay their outstanding accounts, so she could not replace her stock. She spent her days listening to the radio. People stopped to chat with her on their way up and down the road. Before returning to Haliap, Angelina had already explored some of the opportunities opened up by becoming a shapely, urban woman herself. She was happy to introduce me to her relatives and female friends to chat about their dreams and plans for work abroad.

To describe the changing agricultural economy and emerging migration opportunities, I juxtapose two stories, or cases, that we discussed at Angelina's store during 1995–1997. Both are stories of women who may have committed murder. In telling and retelling these tales—asking "Could she or couldn't she?"—people revealed how their ideas of the global led them to reimagine who a woman could be. Working between local histories and the news broadcasts Angelina followed on her radio, I show how speculative stories of women's actions underpinned village debates on women's roles and self-concepts, and I then suggest how these debates came to shape labor migration.

A Murderess?

On August 14, 1868, José Lorenzo, a twenty-nine-year-old Dominican priest from the Spanish mission at Lagawe, Ifugao, was found murdered. Records held in the archives of the Dominican missions in the Philippines report that Father Lorenzo was killed while attempting to collect a debt of several pesos from Bumidang, a man living in Tuplac, along the Kiangan-Lagawe trail. Fellow priests investigated Lorenzo's death. Their correspondence reports "que el Padre Lorenzo había sido muerto por los igorrotes de Tuplac" (that Father Lorenzo was killed by the Igorots [masculine, plural] of Tuplac).[2] One investigating priest, Father Corujedo, questioned the two teenage Christian converts who had accompanied Father Lorenzo from Kiangan to Tuplac. According to their accounts, Father Lorenzo died at the hands of five or six Ifugao men with spears. The investigators were at pains to assure the Church and the government that the motives for killing Father Lorenzo were explicitly not religious.

Years later, historian Josefina Lim Pe collected a number of oral histories to create an alternative, Ifugao, account of the events. Domonyag, the wife of Bumidang (the debtor), had been weaving at a back-strap loom under her granary when she saw a man enter her rice stores. The man began removing seed rice that had been stored for the next planting, and she attempted to stop him. That failing, she hit him across the neck with the "sword" (heddle) from her loom. The blow killed him. Lim Pe was not disposed to accept this version. The Spanish records did not report the circumstance of the woman and the seed rice. Lim Pe concluded that "the natives . . . imputed the murder to Bumidang's wife, and they thought their story would be more credible if they explained why her anger was aroused which is exactly what they did by inserting the circumstance of the seeds."[3] Lim Pe thought the story of Domonyag had been invented to disguise the shameful facts of the murder. Her interpretation rests on the improbability of a woman killing a grown man.

I encountered the Ifugao version of this story several times during my research in Haliap. It circulated as part of wider debates over anticolonial resistance and was offered to me as an example of someone killing a Spaniard in response to colonial abuses. In the mid-1990s, local leaders were retrieving such stories of resistance to support community claims to ongoing settlement in the valley and "domain" for the ancestral domain claims process. Villagers were fascinated by the details of the conflict between the local and Spanish versions of the story. When they retold the tale for me, they added their own interpretive gloss, which I have synthesized here as follows:

> Domonyag, the wife of Bumidang, killed the priest for taking seed rice from her granary. Domonyag was young and strong at the time. She had just married and come to Tuplac with her husband's family to farm there. She was a *kadangyan* (a member of the elite), because she and her husband were very hardworking farmers with much inherited land. Many poorer people had approached her for help during the famine of that year. They offered their labor in exchange for rice, either at that time or as a debt in the future. She had much rice in her granary and was known to be industrious.
>
> When the priest arrived, Domonyag, not a Christian herself, despite her husband's conversion, saw his request for rice as she would any other. But he did not offer her labor, goods, or money. Instead, he claimed—through the translation of two small boys who accompanied him—that Domonyag was obliged to pay the debt of her husband, Bumidang. This idea, that the wife would be responsible for the debt of the husband, was not recognized under Ifugao customary law. Debts incurred separately by spouses were not enforceable against conjugal property. The seed rice was Domonyag's own inherited property. It represented her industry and knowledge in farming and her choices about what seed grew best, year after year. When Father Lorenzo took the seed rice, he committed theft. Since he had effectively removed the next year's entire harvest, Domonyag took the heddle from her loom and struck him dead.

When he told me his version of this story, another Haliap elder, Lakai Joaquin, explained that the story expressed Ifugao anger at Spanish abuses of Filipinos. The Spanish had abused the Filipinos by imposing a new set of property relations on them without regard for local gender norms: Ifugao rice fields were held by individuals unless they were acquired jointly, in which case they were shared. Lakai Joaquin's retelling described a broader Ifugao culture, which he then extended into the present:

Sometimes the Spaniards really stole some rice from the *allong* [rice granary]. Such a case is the one of the woman at Tuplac who killed a Spanish priest when he was removing her seed rice from the granary. She hit him in the neck with the bar from her loom. He thought to take the seed rice because it looked the best of all the bundles. Her husband was indebted to this priest. . . . Her seed rice was not part of her husband's debt. A creditor of the husband could not collect against the wife's inheritance unless she too had agreed to the loan. But the Spanish refused to recognize this practice. Even today, to borrow money or land, both husband and wife should agree and both should be there when you give the money.

Lakai Joaquin asserted the continuity of Ifugao custom against Spanish patriarchal norms found in the lowlands. Outside Ifugao, a Filipino man, as head of a household, could indeed borrow money or mortgage land without his wife's consent, but not vice versa. In Ifugao, Lakai Joaquin claimed that the old customs of gender equality were being maintained.

GENDER ROLES AND STATUS

In Haliap, people expected both men and women to work to support households. Women's work, they said, was lighter but longer; men worked harder but in shorter bursts. Neither kind of work could be more important, because both were necessary to sustain households. Despite church teachings that described men as breadwinners and women as housewives, most villagers understood the conjugal contract to be an equitable one. Both women's and men's productive roles were deeply enmeshed with reproductive work and caring labor. This local gendering differed from the lowland mainstream. Radio soap operas described dependent and restricted women, but Angelina and her friends considered these programs to be just dramas, entertaining accounts of how people lived elsewhere rather than scripts for their village lives.

The Spanish introduced the patriarchal nuclear family to the Philippines.[4] Though male-headed nuclear family households have been the objects of government regulation ever since, such legal fictions had rarely impinged much on everyday lives in the village. Haliap households are dynamic nodes within broader, extended family networks. Within these networks women are encouraged not so much to be natural carers as they are to be industrious, self-sustaining, and knowledgeable in ways that will make them *big* persons in a local redistributive politics. Just like Domonyag in the story of the rice, women's knowledge and capacities remain an important part of their household's—and extended kin's—strategy for security and success. A kadangyan household was respected not because the family was wealthy per se, but because its members treated those less well-off with respect and charity, redistributing their wealth. Traditionally, kadangyans performed prestige feasts, sacrificing more animals and entertaining more guests at life-cycle and agricultural-cycle rituals than ordinary villagers did. In contemporary Haliap a woman's ability to contribute to and manage redistributive provisioning; juggle hired labor; donate food; and feed large crowds at weddings, baptisms, and wakes goes some way to defining her as elite. Her status can be maintained only by reciprocating properly with the spiritual world, kin, and neighbors.

Haliap accounts of Father Lorenzo's murder thus described a woman's identity shaped by local institutions rather than by universal or national norms. My interviewees notably did not speculate on Domonyag's self-awareness as a woman. They did not describe her as a housewife defending her family or a Filipino engaged in anticolonial struggle, though they were familiar with both ways of talking about women. And they did not imagine her emotional state. When I asked, "So could a woman kill?" Roger, a customer at Angelina's store, offered, "I think she could have done it. Ifugao women are . . . strong, not afraid to work, to do what they think." Even more people refused to come to any conclusion at all about the gender of the murderer. Felipe explained, "Anybody could kill anybody, if she had a reason. . . . You'd really have to see the body, the weapon . . . to think . . . if it is a woman or man, but maybe it cannot be told." Angelina and her friends Edna and Lourdes agreed, "If a woman needs to, she can do that." Rather than suggesting it was beyond the capacity of a woman to kill, villagers deferred to the specifics of the case. Instead of describing a time-less, generic woman, they situated Domonyag within particular obligations and entitlements as a self-sufficient woman on whom others depended. Nobody spoke about a woman being naturally oriented to care and thus unable to murder. No one speculated on her internal struggle to overcome some natural reluctance to kill. Villagers did not draw on dominant Filipino ideals for women as physically delicate and wives as submissive helpmeets.

Years earlier, American colonial administrators had been puzzled by the version of female virtue that prevailed in early-twentieth-century Ifugao. Rather than valuing a woman for beauty, a pleasing nature, or childbearing and rear-ing, Ifugao people considered industry in tending to rice fields and hillside shifting cultivation gardens (swidden) to be the definitive attributes of a good woman.[5] When the Americans arrived, men repaired the rice terraces and then hunted and traveled beyond the boundaries of the community for trade and warfare while women tended the rice fields and swidden. Villagers still con-sidered women's work in cultivating the crops and maintaining the fields and house lots, which they called *cleaning,* to inscribe evidence of human habitation on the landscape. A woman who *could see what to do* worked hard, built social relations, and exercised good judgment to achieve kadangyan status for herself and her husband, engaging reliably in reciprocal labor exchange and redistributing wealth, as well as making her work visible in the community. By the 1990s, however, the scope of women's action had long extended beyond agriculture into business and the professions. Nonetheless, people still described a good woman as a person who *knows what to do*. This knowledge meant strategically combining subsistence and cash-oriented agricultural activities with nonfarm earnings, particularly from migration. Rice and rice fields—owning them and growing the rice crop—continued to be the fundamental measure, if not of wealth, then of security. Rice cultivation, however, had begun to change when the "green revolution" and its new high-yielding varieties and agrochemicals finally spread to Haliap in the early 1980s, and these changes brought with them new gender roles.

Rice and Knowledge

Owning real property, as Domonyag's story suggests, is the key to social status and livelihood security. Terraced rice fields have always been the most secure form of real property in Ifugao. Individuals hold rice fields in trust for family lineages. To sell, rent, mortgage, or sharecrop rice land required consent from the wider kin group. To transfer ownership, a buyer had to compensate the owner and his or her extended family—up to third cousins, if they might reasonably have expected to inherit a particular field. However, changes in rice farming started to produce tensions in this customary system after hybrid rice varieties began to be planted in the village.

Only ten women were planting traditional, or native, rice varieties in the 163 Haliap households I surveyed in 1992. These female farmers retained locally important knowledge of the kind Domonyag would have had, including which seeds were likely to be most productive in the micro-conditions of particular fields. Farmers conveyed this information to one another in exchange labor groups, participating in ritual chants and planting songs. Women working in these ubfu groups transplanted native rice seedlings in February and harvested in August. They weeded by hand throughout the summer and harvested with handheld knives. Their fields produced only a single crop. Native rice growers applied sunflower leaves and stalks to their fields, turning the rice straw back into the soil to maintain its fertility. At the harvest, they set the heaviest rice panicles aside. Women who were expert in judging productivity selected those panicles to be used for the next year's crop. These were stored separately, to be germinated in a purpose-built transplanting bed. Men and women together bundled the harvest, and men carried it to the granary for drying and storage. Households processed native rice as they needed it, taking bundles from storage, pounding it to remove the husk and bran, and winnowing it before cooking. Pounding and winnowing were usually, but not always, women's jobs. Each day, the soft thud-thud of pounding filled the valley in the late afternoon, signaling that people had started to prepare their evening meal.

By the mid-1990s, hybrid rice varieties dominated Haliap's agricultural landscape. Hybrid rice is cultivated from seed bought from a supplier in the market and requires what the Filipinos call *medicines,* meaning chemical fertilizers and pesticides, in order to thrive. In 1992 I watched people plant two crops, in January and July. Men joined the transplanting groups, working alongside women. In the harvest, mixed working groups of men and women cut the crop using scythes. They then threshed the rice from the stalks on a frame erected in the rice field. Threshing being *heavy work,* this labor group was predominantly male. Men placed the threshed rice in *cavan* bags (fifty kilograms each) and carried it to the road for transport to a rice mill. The field owner burned the straw on the field to return some of its nutrients to the soil. When the milled rice came back to the owners' house, some was stored for short-term family consumption, and the rest was sold to a dealer who would, in turn, sell it into the national market. Because this rice was sold for cash, field owners hired day laborers rather than using ubfu. Men, though less skilled in planting and harvesting, were paid more than women. Because men were needed to do the heavy work of threshing but would receive higher day-labor rates for other kinds of work, such as hauling, carpentry, and logging, rice farmers had to compete for their labor. Women found fewer opportunities in the village for paid work.

People growing hybrid rice were becoming entangled in complex debt relations. The advantages of hybrid rice were a purported doubling in yield per field and the potential for a cash return on a proportion of the harvest. Two crops per year suggested that people with smaller fields could grow enough to feed their families, offering food security denied them by the *timawan* (yearly) native varieties. But growing rice for sale and then buying rice for household consumption from the market had its drawbacks. People purchased seed, medicines, and labor power for each crop, spending again to transport and mill their harvest. When they did not have money to buy these items outright, they arranged credit, borrowing with interest against the sale of their harvest. Rice, however, sold at the prevailing farm gate price. This price fluctuated in response to yields elsewhere in the Philippines and to imports (sometimes illegal) of much cheaper rice from other countries. People initially imagined that the cash proceeds of rice sales could be invested in other crops, housing, travel, and education. Instead, they found that hybrid rice was a cash-hungry crop. Their costs rose with the increasing price of petroleum.

Hybrid rice thus bred resentments. Not all villagers switched to the new crop willingly. Some felt compelled to *follow* their neighbors to avert conflicts arising from different sets of demands on water and from pests moving between fields. People also found that exchange labor relations were transformed by growing rice as a cash crop. Farmers competed to access a secure labor force in the short planting and harvesting seasons. Farmers who had previously provided lunch and work in return for an ubfu team found that almost all available workers—even kin and neighbors—wanted to shop around for the best pay-and-lunch deal. Hybrid rice farmers began to cut lumber or grow vegetables for sale to earn more cash to pay day-labor rates. Their households also sought to secure regular wage labor or salaried jobs off the farm. Some households did well; others struggled.

Becoming "Housewife"

Villagers initially approached the gendering of new crops and new kinds of work in a pragmatic way. Work was about knowing what to do and the opportunities available. Men were challenged to join women in planting and harvesting hybrid rice by the large harvests they saw on the farms of lowland relatives. In the lowlands, the introduction of mechanized tractors, hand tillers, and mills and the distribution of new rice varieties had freed female labor from agriculture two decades or so earlier. Significant numbers among the first generations of lowland women exempted from farming had gone on to secondary and tertiary education. The most successful among them secured salaried professional work, married into more prosperous families, and often migrated to live in urban centers. Haliap women wanted to follow this same path. Angelina's cohort pursued college and university studies at rates much higher than their male counterparts.[6] But there were simply not enough salaried jobs for women in rural Ifugao. The government services that would employ graduates of the professions had only so many openings for teachers, clerks, midwives, and nurses. These professions became the new *thing to know* that determined a woman's value as a daughter or spouse.

Young female graduates like Angelina and her friends explained to me that they felt "obliged" to find salaried work. They had enjoyed financial support from their families for their studies to become professionals, so they wanted to practice their profession to repay their debts. Their families expected that monies they earned before they married would be fed back into familial exchange networks. After starting their own households, they would continue to make gifts and help out in emergencies. Like Angelina, Edna, and Lourdes, few of the village women had the resources and personal ties necessary to secure well-paying work in urban centers. To find jobs elsewhere in the Philippines—in export-processing factories, for instance—they would need to move their households, commute, or relocate. But these low-skilled jobs paid salaries that were barely sufficient to sustain a single person. Young female graduates sought government jobs in the towns nearest Haliap. These jobs, unlike factory work or salesclerk roles in the cities, offered salaries that, compared to the local cost of living, enabled women to avoid farming and live their lives as what villagers called, in their Filipino English, housewives. Indeed, becoming a housewife was the future Angelina and her friends most often identified to me as their ideal. By this, however, they meant something rather different from what I understood by the term.

Across the village, people consistently described women who no longer worked in the fields to me as *maybahay lang* (Tagalog: a simple or plain home-maker)—or, in English, a housewife. Since many Haliap houses had room for sleeping and some storage only, with cooking and laundry done outside, using the term *housewife* this way seemed to depend on a rather ambiguous extension of this house to include the house lot and landscape beyond, where most domestic tasks and child care took place. Yet being a housewife as they described it seemed to have very little to do with staying in and around the house. I questioned Angelina about what I initially thought must have been my misunderstanding of local English, but I had grasped what was being said well enough. In response to my skeptical approach to accepting a new and apparently contradictory way of defining a familiar English word, Angelina and her friends compiled an exhaustive list of housewives I had met for me to reflect on. This list included the female midwives; teachers; government and NGO workers; shopkeepers; dealers of rice, vegetables, and crop inputs (fertilizers, pesticides, and seeds); and moneylenders. Angelina explained that the key distinction was that a housewife did not do manual labor, particularly farming. Instead, she worked outside of the home to earn income to support her family. If a housewife went to the fields, it was only to "help out," but not as her full-time job. Even if she was not actually practicing her profession, a "true housewife" was expected to be someone people called a *professional,* meaning college-educated and running her own business. These Ifugao-style housewives rarely stayed at home with the children all day. Instead, they delegated child care and other domestic tasks to older children, younger relatives, working students, and husbands as required.

Angelina explained that local women were really following the lead of the nation's first female president, Corazon Aquino. Aquino had famously described herself as a "simple housewife" when she took over leadership of both a political party and the allied popular political movement for social change after her husband's assassination. Explaining why they were aspiring to business or professional practice, village women said they, too, could "be like Cory." To help their family and nation, they were not so much cloaking their ambitions in a domestic rhetoric as redefining the domestic sphere for themselves. Angelina's cohort, leaving college in the early 1990s, identified as professionals as opposed to farmers. Their dreams were of careers that would recognize their innate intellectual abilities, interpersonal skills, and creative capacities, garnering respect from their kin and community, and giving them the good life they saw in the lowlands and the media. Angelina, her friends, and their male peers all dreamed of owning large houses with "complete [electrical] appliances," eating meat at three meals a day rather than once or twice a week, owning a family car, traveling for pleasure, and educating their children to work in the professions too. This was the kind of development women could provide for the Philippines.

For Angelina, Edna, and Lourdes, the best example of someone pursuing this housewife lifestyle in Haliap was Nora, Edna's sister-in-law, who had been working in Hong Kong since early 1991 and had returned for occasional visits. Even though she did not live with her family year-round, her household had the material trappings and consumption practices that featured in the others' dreams. Nora, they were sure, would return home eventually, but "not to plant rice." Angelina's friends were making, as best they could, real-world, everyday plans to enact their own dreams of having a similar lifestyle. In doing so, they began to compare their households and families not just to Nora's but also to the family model used by lowland Filipinos, the educational system, and the programs on the radio.[7]

This local account of the housewife role offered Angelina and her friends who hung around at her store particular ways to talk about what motivated women to migrate and how they should feel about themselves in their most significant romantic and kin relationships. And the norms and dreams attached to this concept of housewife enabled other women in the village, such as the midwives and teachers, to publicly criticize the family practices and work of less economically secure households in village meetings. While women's work outside the home remained about knowing what to do, people in Haliap soon began to discuss women's life choices by referring to their roles as wife and mother. Launching a new public health campaign in 1996, Susan, a midwife, explained that a housewife was naturally oriented to domestic concerns and thus recognized her duty to *sacrifice,* to put aside her own self-interests in order to care for her family. Susan's approach to being a housewife sounded more familiar to me, but it was constantly being debated and transformed into something rather different by women like Angelina and her friends.

For example, Angelina's cousin Rachel, back from college in the city and waiting to see if she would have a teaching job in Asipulo, told me her dream was to become a housewife. She was among a group of young women who were engaging in cash-crop cultivation but who saw farming as what they referred to as a *remedy,* a temporary solution, rather than a lifelong vocation. Sitting at Angelina's store one afternoon, Rachel explained to me that her plan was to marry and become a "true housewife." But her desire to become a housewife did not preclude her teaching career; teaching would support her domestic plans. She explained that if she could not find a teaching job locally, she would set up a vegetable trading business or look for work abroad, "like Nora," an older neighbor known to be a successful migrant in Hong Kong. She would, she told me, be sure to select a husband who could manage to take care of their children with the help of her mother and sister so that she would eventually be able to go abroad. Thus, rather than consolidating a woman's attachment to the everyday affective and sensual engagements of a house-based domestic realm and the kind of daily self-denial celebrated as women's sacrifice in Susan's comments, Rachel's dreams of becoming a housewife had the opposite effect. To become a housewife, Rachel planned to seek work beyond the village and away from her home and family.

BECOMING MIGRANT PROFESSIONALS

Overseas, the jobs available to Filipina migrants are closely related to a more familiar, even global, ideal of a housewife as someone whose knowledge, skills, and desires are delimited by caring for the home. Filipina migrants—particularly women from peasant and working-class backgrounds and provincial origins—are hired to work predominantly as maids, caregivers, nannies, and factory laborers. Given the exchange rates, the salaries for these jobs are much better than what Filipino college graduates would earn from many highly skilled professional jobs in their own country. But most of these overseas jobs are considered unskilled or semiskilled work. To fill them, employers and recruiting agents seek women who are generally disposed to be the ideal housewife: women who are tolerant, family-focused, shy, reticent, maternal, biddable, have limited horizons and ambition, and are willing to sacrifice for the economic well-being of the families they leave behind.[8] Employers and recruiters do not anticipate that the women applying for domestic work and caregiving roles will consider themselves, like Rachel, professionals for whom the move overseas is part of a personal career strategy.

Ifugao women who take such jobs abroad consider themselves professionals who are, albeit somewhat indirectly, practicing the skills they have learned through their training in the caring professions—teaching, nursing, and midwifery. It is their professionalism that enables them to make do and *cope up,* as they say, with work abroad. They focus more on the status their earnings garner them at home rather than on the nature of their actual work.[9] They do not consider themselves part of an unskilled female workforce somehow naturally inclined to undertake menial or caring work. Working overseas is, instead, part of their personal plan to become an Ifugao-style housewife at home. They migrate to earn capital that will enable them to invest in land (to be registered in their own name), start their own businesses, build houses for themselves and their families, and educate their children in the professions. Understanding themselves as providers and entrepreneurs, they believe their approach to both work and family life fits within and properly expands, rather than contradicts, their Ifugao version of the housewife role.

Villagers think women are generally better able than men to cope with the mismatch between their own education and aspirations and the work and working conditions they encounter abroad. By the mid-1990s only a very few men from Haliap had migrated for work as seamen and as construction laborers. Men did not apply for domestic or caring work abroad, not because they were less caring, but because they had not traditionally pursued the educational routes that produced professional caring skills. Villagers suggested that men generally made less successful migrants for unskilled work because their *higher pride* was more easily offended by being treated as *low, small,* or *ignorant* in overseas or even urban Philippine worksites.[10]

I found it interesting that *sacrifice* was not a term many villagers often used to explain their life choices in the early 1990s. Instead, people focused on how well they were able to cope up based on their innate ability to *see how it would come out* and to know what to do. As migration from Ifugao accelerated throughout the 1990s, villagers like Susan began to borrow the rhetoric of maternal and migrant sacrifice. My respondents then began to describe men as being unable to "sacrifice their pride" as migrants. Women, they thought, were less proud and better able to budget and could more easily endure the "hardships" of forgoing material things and life-cycle events to provide for those at home. While the village's migrant women saw themselves as aspiring professionals in extended family networks, other villagers began to talk about them as self-sacrificing mothers supporting nuclear family households. Initially this was comparatively rare. Villagers were, at least in 1995–1997, more interested in the ways migrants' earnings could repay debts, both monetary and symbolic, fulfilling their roles as dutiful daughters and generous sisters as well as provisioning mothers.

A shift in the way villagers viewed women's migration evidently took place over the decade. By 2005 virtually all of my Haliap respondents described women's migration to other countries as a sacrifice befitting an idealized Filipina's disposition. This combined their earlier secular use of *sacrifice* to mean self-denial with an account inflected with both nationalism and religion. Migrant women were now imagined to be placing the material needs of their children and spouse above their own emotional attachments and thus offering their lives to their family and the nation. In Tagalog, a *martir* is a person who himself becomes an offering, or *hain,* for a national cause, and the term is central to a discourse of sacrifice that extends and reworks one of the fundamental themes of postcolonial Philippine society—that of faith, martyrdom, and transformation.[11] From the mid-1990s this discourse was specifically applied to domestic workers in the national media.[12] Haliap villagers picked up on this narrative of female sacrifice in ways that subsumed their older Ifugao knowing-what-to-do femininity within a national story of migration and martyrdom. Thus, virtually at the same time they were discussing Domonyag's story, my Haliap friends were also following the coverage of women, particularly migrants overseas, in the national news. Between 1995 and 1997 their two quite different accounts of woman became blended together in a watershed moment where a specific migrant's sacrifice brought the relations between government and bayan (people, nation) to a crisis.

A Martyred Housewife

A Filipino OCW named Flor Contemplacion was hanged for double murder in Singapore on Friday, March 17, 1995. Contemplacion had been convicted of murdering her friend, fellow Filipina domestic worker Delia Maga, and Maga's four-year-old ward, Nicholas Huang.[13] Haliap villagers were both horrified and fascinated by the unfolding events, following the story on the radio and in the newspapers. In doing so, they participated in a nation-building exercise infused with a moral discourse on family and a universal account of woman.

According to the police who arrested Contemplacion in Singapore, Maga had been strangled and Huang drowned. The victims were discovered in the Huang family flat. The police identified Contemplacion through an entry in Maga's diary. She had visited Maga on the morning of the murders, dropping off a box of gifts for Maga to take back to the Philippines. A police search of Contemplacion's room revealed some of Maga's possessions. On questioning Contemplacion, the police claim she confessed. She then apparently made four statements to police admitting her crime, following which she was silent until her high court trial. At trial Contemplacion entered evidence of a diminished mental state: "I was not myself during that time."[14] Between being convicted and being executed, Contemplacion made no public statements. Press reports in Singaporean publications emphasized details that portrayed her as deviant, criminal, and mentally unstable—for example, "She was put in the punishment cell four times: twice for fighting with fellow inmates, once for tattooing herself and once for attempting suicide."[15] In the Philippines, human rights activists and labor leaders suggested Contemplacion had been drugged and coerced into confessing and then (falsely) assured that pleading insanity would lead to clemency. They claimed that Singaporean authorities had overlooked evidence that instead suggested Maga had been killed by her employer. Several Filipino newspapers published unsubstantiated claims that Contemplacion had been stripped and tortured into confessing when the police had interrogated her. Other reports suggested she had been sexually assaulted. Authorities in Singapore maintained that her trial had been fair and transparent and that Contemplacion had not been mistreated.

After Contemplacion was executed, her body was repatriated. The First Lady met her coffin at the airport. President Ramos spoke of her as "a national heroine."[16] She was given a public funeral, with thousands of people lining the route of her cortege. The Filipino response to how Contemplacion had been treated after death shocked Singaporeans. Singapore considered her a criminal; how could Filipinos receive her as a martyr? Filipinos took to the streets and burned Singaporean flags. Overseas Filipino workers staged protests in front of Singaporean embassies in other countries, attempting to create a global form of censure. The Singapore media reported on the protests, and diplomatic relations between the two nations hit a historical nadir. These protests worked through what Vicente Rafael called a "necropolitics," a politics in which the martyr's body itself and the attendant discourse of sacrifice circulating around her death enabled the Filipino public to make political demands.[17] On Contemplacion's execution, the public demanded their government change the way it treated migrants. People wanted to see absent migrants fully included in the daily life of their nation, accorded belonging, respect, and protection at all times. To meet this demand, the Philippine nation-state had to extend beyond its territorial borders into migrants' overseas sites of sojourn and dwelling.

As this global nation mourned Contemplacion, it became more global through the collective processes of mourning. Contemplacion's death cathected outrage, anger, and despair over the treatment of migrants abroad. Activists organized mass demonstrations not only on the streets of Manila but also among Filipino contract workers in cities overseas. This global Filipino public apportioned blame to employer nations and Philippine politicians and bureaucrats alike. The public outpouring of emotion expressed the long-suppressed guilt of the middle classes and elites over the fate of migrants. At the same time, the public response attached familiar middle-class ideals for family and femininity to the previously largely working-class phenomenon of Filipino women's migration: "When husbands and wives are separated by vast oceans, the children suffer, as do the bonds of marriage. As does society. We feel guilty that this is happening. . . . We feel even guiltier when we realize that for our economy to keep afloat, our women have to lead bestial lives abroad. This kind of pressure cooker was building up for years."[18]

In media reports, Contemplacion personified the nation in an individual, female body. She was variously described as a "national saint" and the "flower of national rage," and as "the martyr that is the Philippines" while her funeral was covered as "requiem for a people."[19] Significant numbers of Filipinos believed as a matter of national pride that Contemplacion must be innocent. When journalists and members of the public asserted her innocence, it revolved around her roles as a wife and mother. "Many Filipinos just cannot believe Contemplacion could have done this. They say, she is a mother, she left home to provide for her children, she and the other maid are friends. How can she kill?"[20] Opinions from neighbors, psychologists, and NGOs described Contemplacion's disposition: "If she ever cooks anything like a chicken, she has to ask her neighbor to kill the chicken. So how could she even kill a person? She is not a violent person. It is not in her nature."[21]

Speculating on her feelings, people asked how an evidently hardworking, God-fearing, family-oriented person—a typical housewife—could commit such a crime. A minority opined that if Contemplacion, a former washerwoman, were guilty, she had "run amok" because of the stress of her husband's infidelity or the long time she had spent away from her children. Press coverage described her as a tragic figure: "a mother who, in her last hours, could not hug her own children to say goodbye; a wife who came home in a box all dressed in white, and then was photographed being kissed like a sleeping bride by a philandering husband who had last seen her six years ago."[22] For Filipinos, transforming Contemplacion into the idealized housewife-turned-migrant both consolidated the emotional truth of the case and concealed the class politics of female migration.

Public guilt quickly turned to anger. The execution of a Philippine national by a foreign jurisdiction, despite the diplomatic overtures of the country's president, Fidel V. Ramos, undermined the ruling party during the run-up to the 1997 election. Maga had been strangled, Contemplacion hanged, and President Ramos was quoted as saying: "It's my neck that's on the line!"[23] Activist groups and journalists demanded the government investigate the evidence in the case to prove Contemplacion's innocence. Journalists speculated that she had been framed in Singapore because of her "utter vulnerability" as a Filipina: "because she carries a passport originating from a country whose women have become synonymous with the lowly maid or the cheap and easy whore."[24] Editorials accused the government of "abandoning its nationals to maltreatment, prejudice and abuse" overseas.[25] Activists claimed that the legal counsel Contemplacion had received from Filipino diplomats had been grossly inadequate, thus making the government complicit in her execution. Her case revealed how President Aquino's new heroes were really being treated as disposable human beings. In response, the government temporarily banned the deployment of domestic workers to Singapore, and the president forced the foreign secretary and labor secretary to resign, suspended the ambassador, and ordered an inquiry into the criminal culpability of officials who had handled Contemplacion's file. Advocacy groups argued for the ban to be extended to other receiving nations reputed to abuse migrants and demanded more support services for workers abroad.

Two films retelling Contemplacion's story were quickly produced. Both films depicted Flor being framed for a murder she did not commit and then abandoned by a ruthless and uncaring Filipino bureaucracy. Publicity for both films suggested they offered an authentic account of Flor's life because they were realistic or politically transgressive. *The Flor Contemplacion Story* (1995), directed by Joel Lamangan, starred the country's then most popular actress, Nora Aunor, supported by Contemplacion's real-life twin sons playing themselves. Director Tikoy Aguiluz filmed *Bagong Bayani: OCW* (1995; translated as New Hero: Overseas Contract Worker but known in the United States as *Unsung Heroine*) at the actual sites of events in Singapore, ignoring the usual permits and government channels of approval. Aguiluz consulted Amnesty International reports that confirmed victims of torture exhibited behaviors similar to those reported for Flor provided by sympathetic witnesses from Changi Prison. Aguiluz's film brought the class politics of representing migration to the forefront by choosing a mestiza actress to play Flor.[26] Helen Gamboa— married to a prominent Philippine senator and spokes-model for a line of home appliances marketed to "the Filipina housewife"—seemed to many an unlikely choice to play a migrant worker. One critic offered the following description: "she of the porcelain complexion playing a flat-nosed, brown-skinned salt-of-the-earth."[27] Debate on Gamboa's casting revealed the class tensions underpinning the Filipina identity, suggesting that the qualities that made a woman valuable as a citizen in the eyes of the Filipino media—and, perhaps, broader public—were being contested through debates on migration. The two films did not come to Haliap, where there was then no video screening, but people followed publicity for them in the newspapers and on the radio.

The Philippine government eventually constituted a seven-member commission to investigate Contemplacion's conviction. In an exercise reported as a kind of public theater, the Gancayo Commission reopened the forensic investigation of the remains of the Filipina victim, Delia Maga. Testifying before this commission, experts from the Philippine National Bureau of Investigation maintained that Maga had been severely beaten before she was strangled. According to these experts, her injuries could only have been inflicted by a man.[28] Singapore contested these findings. Singaporean reports portrayed Filipino investigators as incompetent and the commission process as driven by nationalist political interests: "When certain statements were made, they were applauded by the gallery, others were booed and shouted down. It was a kind of show."[29] Neutral American pathologists were called in to settle the dispute, only to find that Maga's remains could not be made to reveal the gender of her killer.

Though Contemplacion was never formally exonerated, many Filipinos believed she had been framed, and it was her gender that, for them, made the case against her implausible. The furor around Contemplacion's execution consolidated what was already a dominant nationalist ideal of the Filipina-as-housewife. Through the public outpouring of feeling around Contemplacion, the nation accused the government and its bureaucrats of being indifferent—willfully blind, even—to migrants' sacrifices. According Contemplacion a martyr's burial publicly revalorized migrants, symbolically restoring them to full citizenship, but this was only accomplished by consolidating the shared belief that she had been an innocent housewife—self-sacrificing, focused on her children and household. The Contemplacion case thus tied a nationalist vision of idealized femininity to very specific ways that female migrants were supposed to think and feel about themselves in the world.

MIGRANT LIFE AS BARE LIFE

The Contemplacion case did a very important kind of political work in the everyday lives of the Filipino people. Hanging out at Angelina's store, I followed the case on the radio and in the papers, discussing the latest news with Angelina and her friends. Just after Contemplacion's funeral was broadcast, a young man approached me and asked where I was from. I replied, "Canada," and he looked down at the ground, then back to my face, saying, "What I know is . . . in your place, a Filipino is just *scratch*," meaning scrap paper—a low-quality, disposable material with low value, little better than garbage. *Scratch* seemed an apt way to describe the collective "utter vulnerability" of migrants abroad that Contemplacion's execution revealed for many Filipinos. The word also described how villagers understand their experiences of being treated as small by the government and by their neighbors—as disposable people whose lives, and the livelihoods that sustained them, did not count. This use of the word *scratch* resonated with me, and I held on to it as an important comment. It seemed to condense and express widely shared feelings of insecurity and being excluded from the national body politic among rural, poor, and working-class Filipinos.

In Haliap, Contemplacion—this single word is how villagers referred to the events of this period—marked a shift in the public understanding of migration, confirming that the government had not been properly caring for migrants. The case offered Haliap people a new language with which to speak about migration. Talking to me about migrants' sacrifices, Luis quickly took up an argument contending that by working overseas migrants were actually struggling to become and remain citizens at home: "They suffer abroad, our women, so that they can have respect at home. Because the government will not give them their needs, they must provide for themselves." In this argument, by sacrificing themselves for their families and communities, migrants were, by extension, developing their country—doing the work the government had failed to do because they could see what to do and the government could not.

Scratch, as a popular Filipino English concept, coincides with the theoretical terms in which the political philosopher Giorgio Agamben describes "bare life."[30] Bare life is that of a disposable human being, someone who can be killed without that killing being a sacrifice, without any mediation from the law and without any guilt attached to the killer. Rather like scrap paper, such a being is intended for disposal, never able to become the real citizen whose life carries value. Bare life inhabits what Agamben calls a space of exception. In such spaces the law gathers individual persons together to form populations on which new kinds of regulation can be imposed, like making tribes or regulating IPs. In these spaces the law is decided and administered in a discretionary way, and governing institutions refuse to recognize peoples' rights. Spaces of exception lie neither entirely within the legal order of the state, nor are they completely excluded. Instead, these spaces remain in an active relationship with the state through its agents of government, even though this relationship may be one of studied ignorance, refusal of claims, and neglect. Spaces of exception allow populations to be effectively abandoned by a society that refuses to recognize them fully under the law. Haliap villagers already knew they occupied such a space when it came to land tenure. As Luis explained, "We must think to leave here now because . . . what can we do? The government does not like to listen. They say they own the land, while we are the ones caring for it." But leaving one such space does not necessarily guarantee migrants can escape it, nor necessarily avoid entering into another.

Global migration has itself seen such exceptional categories proliferate. There are the obvious exceptional acts and spaces—a variety of special "stateless" zones where would-be asylum seekers are detained and excluded from receiving societies, for example. Global migration has also diversified and expanded the categories of noncitizen residents. Governments have created these categories by imposing citizenship tests, adding new qualifications and waiting periods for citizenship applications, and introducing new temporary labor migration programs. But focusing only on the practices and policies of regulation that underpin these categories can obscure the key lesson from Contemplacion: how exceptions also arise from exercises in affective politics.

Extending Agamben's ideas, political anthropologists argue that exception is not simply about legal recognition but also about affective recognition. Denying public recognition for sacrifice arguably places the donor of the sacrifice in a state of exception by erasing from public view an expression of love.[31] This idea, that migrants' expressions of love had been erased from public view and thus their sacrifices refused recognition by the nation, underpinned Contemplacion. In accounts of the case, the bureaucracy had presumably decided not to extend all available resources to assist a lower-class migrant woman, and it was this decision that marked the Philippine government as sovereign. Bureaucrats were accused of denying contract workers citizenship rights because backward, working-class migrants were an embarrassing hindrance to diplomacy. Through the public outcry the nation told the government that the bureaucracy was not the site of sovereign will. The Contemplacion case returned sovereignty to the people—the erupting, furious mob. Demonstrators, activists, and journalists all demanded that migrants be effectively restored to the bayan through their public claims that Contemplacion's corpse was the national body. The government acknowledged this claim, revaluing migrants as citizens by attaching to them a new kind of extraterritorial and cultural citizenship. The performances and eruptions of affect around Contemplacion enabled the ideal of sacrifice as a religious offering and that of migrants' practices of self-denial to bleed into each other and blend, creating a new, collective understanding of migration.

Practically, at the national level the Contemplacion case initiated profound changes within the governance of migration. The legislative arm of the Philippine government quickly passed a bill to establish migrants' rights (1995) and, later, a bill that enabled overseas workers to vote in national elections (2003). Departments introduced programs to allow workers overseas to make payments into the national social security system and to set up special immigration channels dedicated to migrant workers at the airport. Extending voting rights to migrants overseas brought visits to workers from local politicians and increasing public recognition, attaching public acclaim to migrants' civic contributions. Symbolically, the new OFW (Overseas Filipino Worker) immigration control channel at Manila's Ninoy Aquino International Airport was given a plush red carpet to greet returning workers in the style they deserved. Migrants and their families were offered programs through which they could apply for prizes, scholarships, and development funds to start small businesses. The result was not only broader public awareness and sympathy for migrants but also a global Filipino bayan that imagines its intrinsic character to be defined through migrants' experiences of suffering and success.

Contemplacion revealed how embodied, sensual affects—packed streets, public mourning, emotive outbursts on radio and television—linked people and government to form the nation-state. As Rafael describes in his account of necropolitics, Contemplacion's corpse became the site across which Filipinos tried to reconcile everyday experiences of governance with their ideals for the state.[32] Contemplacion herself was thus turned into a sacrificial offering made by the nation to secure a change in the way the bureaucracy treated individual migrants. Activists and media commentators deployed rumor and credulity to provoke government response, working within the gaps between the government's new migrant welfare rhetoric and existing policies. This proved to be an effective strategy to bring about some reform in the workings of the labor export program. In its wider effects, however, Contemplacion produced contradictory outcomes.

In Haliap, Contemplacion's migrant housewife / sacred martyr persona was much different from the self-interested, exchange-oriented businesswoman initially signified by the ways villagers appropriated the concept of "housewife" to their own ideas of progress and status, but it was a compelling figure nonetheless. As a global kind of woman, the ideal attached to the migrant martyr offered Haliap villagers an entry point into both the bayan and the global realm that lay beyond. Angelina, Rachel, and several of her friends began to seek overseas work themselves, shortly after the Contemplacion furor died down. In this their decisions were perhaps influenced not so much by the examples of their neighbor's successes—as, other than Nora, these were still few and faltering—but by the wider public outpouring of grief over a stranger's execution. They had witnessed the intimate, affective political power that came to female migrants when the public recognized their sacrifice and saw that this power was something they could append to themselves.

Going Abroad

After Contemplacion I found myself fielding an increasing number of requests for advice, contacts, and placements in overseas jobs. Angelina and her friends reasoned that a woman's absence from the house should be no novelty in Haliap. Some men had always done at least part of the child care while women farmed and worked outside of the village. Eva, recently married, explained to me that finding any kind of work in the lowlands would mean living away from the village for most of the week anyway. Thus she was asking herself why she should not try to go abroad, because she could earn far more overseas. Young women like Rosa, whom I had initially interviewed in 1992 as an aspiring local professional—proud of their modest dress style and faces without makeup—transformed themselves from distinctively Ifugao women to something closer to the Filipina ideal, anticipating their eventual migration. By the late 1990s, Angelina, Rosa, Eva, and Rachel were keenly aware of how consumer goods, clothing, makeup, shoulder bags, and high heels could be deployed to look housewife-like. Rather than teaching me how to become proficient in the techniques of Haliap-style domestic tasks (admittedly a frustrating exercise), my friends now wanted me to share my knowledge of global consumer femininity.

Traveling to Lagawe to buy stock for her store, Angelina would walk to the jeepney stop barefoot and chewing betel nut, then rinse her mouth and put on high heels for the ride into town, wiping away the overt signs of her ethnicity in favor of a more globally feminine appearance. Coming from Haliap, she knew that lowland Filipinos saw her as a brown-skinned salt-of-the-earth, if not as a primitive. In her dreams, working overseas would transform her into a *napudaw* (pale-skinned) Filipina. She began to collect details about recruiting agents and jobs abroad. She saw migration as extending from her study and work experiences in the lowlands. Working abroad, she imagined, would require the same virtues and capacities that enabled her to mix with non-Ifugao people and complete her schooling. First among these was *pakikisama,* the Tagalog virtue of being able to have smooth relationships with others, being solicitous, agreeable, and yielding when politic to do so. Thus Angelina talked to me about her ability to "go along with" and "adjust" to others' styles of interaction and expectations, the very skills and reasons she had for cultivating me as a friend and participating in my research as a regular interlocutor. This ability to get along with others, she thought, suited her to migration. She knew the habits, dispositions, and cultures of other places were different from her own, but the challenge of adjusting to them was one she could surmount with adaptability and a common humanity.

When I asked if she was worried about the dangers of migration, Angelina was optimistic that her *fate* or *luck* overseas would be different from Contemplacion's. In this she was not alone. Despite a temporary ban on the deployment of OFWs to Singapore, there was little decline in the overall numbers of female new hires departing the Philippines in subsequent years, with 1997 departures being virtually identical to the numbers of women leaving in 1995.[33] Since it took would-be migrants up to a year or more to secure a contract and process their papers, and since in 1997–1998 new hires were affected by the Asian economic crisis, it would be difficult to demonstrate that the Contemplacion case had any long-term dampening effect on new female departures. In fact, Haliap respondents suggested that much the opposite had occurred across the rural Philippines.

When I returned to discuss women and murder with Angelina, Edna, and Lourdes, the three young women who had argued vociferously that Domonyag had indeed killed the thieving priest had a very different understanding of this second putative case of murder. They did not really want to entertain the possibility that Flor Contemplacion had committed the crime for which she was executed. When I suggested that their argument that any woman could kill, which they had put forward to explain Domonyag, extended to Contemplacion's being capable of killing Maga, they fell silent. They understood the Contemplacion case was something special, a watershed moment.[34] Participating vicariously in the public outrage had offered them a chance to subscribe to a wider social imaginary for progress and to take on Filipina identity themselves rather than merely remaining indigenous (i.e., backward, rural, unsophisticated) women. The events of the case showed them that migrant women mattered to the nation when they worked beyond its formal borders in a way that indigenous women did not seem to matter when at home.

Thus, while the 1996 parade I was witness to excluded women from anti-colonial struggles and overseas migration, it would be fair to say that its story does not really seem to describe gender in Haliap nor modify it effectively. It would not be terribly helpful to think of Haliap women here as silenced subalterns, unable to voice their resistance to colonialism because Spanish patriarchy and local gender norms had coincided to restrict feminine agency. Indeed, where restrictive accounts of woman—specifying self-understanding and feelings delimited by a narrow set of domestic concerns—have emerged, people have quickly transformed these accounts and their key words into something else entirely. By combining and reworking apparently contradictory notions—*housewife* and *professional*, *sacrifice* and *self-denial*—villagers build their own coping strategies for engagements with the global world.

CHAPTER 3 ◆ Failing to Progress

DEVELOPMENT ITSELF NEVER SEEMED to arrive in Haliap. Instead, its precursors—exercises of classifying, researching, and training—occupied villagers along with a revolving cast of local officials, national agencies, and international donors. These development engagements required villagers to learn a new language and to identify and think about themselves and their village in new ways in order to communicate with government officers and development donors. Villagers made explicit the transformations required of them through the ways they used the Filipino English phrases that described their interactions with development initiatives. To enjoy development's benefits, people first had to bring themselves *in line with* (take on the priorities of) government policies and donor programs by *conforming to* (adopting the language and categories of) their requirements and *accomplishing* (filling out) forms. Doing so, they *attended offices* (visited, often waiting in line) and *coped up with* (struggled to meet) preconditions that they donate labor and goods to project activities, at the same time affixing their signatures to a stream of attendance lists, application forms, surveys, and other paperwork. Committing their time and labor, villagers anticipated that development should reciprocate by delivering progress. Balancing livelihood activities with meetings, working bees, and seminars, villagers found that participating in project activities demanded changes in how they thought about themselves. Their Filipino English idioms stressed the verbs—*aligning, conforming, accomplishing, attending*, and *coping*—that marked the ways development tried to make the village a legible field in which governing institutions could operate. These same words also suggested that development was largely about form rather than substance.

Luis took a leading role in Haliap's 1990s development activities, working with two internationally funded projects. He juggled his commitments with farming a rented field and doing day labor on relatives' farms. He spent his free time hanging out at Angelina's store and decided to court her. Their son, Oscar, was born in mid-1996 and they married a year later. Having left the Iglesia in his twenties, Luis rejoined the church, and Angelina, a Catholic, converted. Upon their marriage Angelina inherited a quarter-hectare rice field from her parents.

Luis and Angelina, land-poor but educated and ambitious, made ideal project beneficiaries. Their land was kurang (insufficient), producing only enough rice to feed them for eight or nine months. That was, of course, Luis observed, if they did not "entertain guests." The strain in his voice when he made this comment suggested the implausibility of restricting one's household stores from circulating in Haliap. To grow rice, Luis and Angelina needed cash to buy seed and fertilizer and to pay workers. Sustaining the exchange-labor relations needed to plant and harvest their small field conflicted with Luis's development project activities. Luis sought ongoing work and status through development, but the couple needed to balance the two, because their rice alone would not give them a secure livelihood, yet development activities could not guarantee money to buy food. Luis explained to me: "Marriage . . . , a child . . . this makes you plan. Plan for each day, next month, next year. Before I had my son, I would dream, but not really plan for it. Now I plan for my dreams." All three of them were living in Angelina's old store, which she had finally closed in late 1996. Luis called it "the house of a chicken." It was a one-room wood and galvanized iron shack with a dirt floor, no running water, and no toilet. Seeking assistance from relatives and looking for paid work farther afield had not given them security. "There's nothing here for us, no jobs," Angelina told me. They hoped that by participating in development as a volunteer and casual laborer, Luis would eventually find secure paid work.

Luis and Angelina defined *progress* very simply: "permanent jobs." For them, regular salaried work was necessary to found any stable livelihood they could reasonably hope to attain. But the improvements that government programs and donor projects offered the village had not been designed to provide people with ongoing salaried work. Instead, these projects and programs were directed toward inculcating civic virtues and creating *progressive*—meaning more strategic, better-informed—independent farmers who inhabited a bounded place where, by producing commodities for national or global markets, they could become self-sufficient. Mid-1990s development programs actually heightened the sense of insecurity among land-poor households like Luis and Angelina's.

In Line with Development

As villagers understood development, they exchanged their political support—through a mediating hierarchy of individual leaders, extending from the president down to the congressman, governor, mayor, and, finally, their barangay captain—in order to have development delivered to them. In Haliap drawing people in line with this hierarchy was more than simply a spatial metaphor.

In 1996 government employees decorated the main road, whitewashing rocks for six kilometers along the route from Haliap to the Asipulo municipal hall. Their efforts were in aid of Asipulo's unsuccessful bid for a "Clean and Green" municipality award that carried a cash prize to support municipal development projects. Lining the road with rocks aligned the municipality with government. But instead of being based on actual development efforts, the award recognized what people called closeness—personalistic, patron-client ties that operated not just between villagers and local politicians but also between mayors, governors' offices, and congressmen. The wobbly line of rocks, with their chipped paint, representing weeks of person-hours sat on the roadside for years. These rocks were a material reminder that even high-status, big people with salaried office jobs did menial and ultimately rather pointless work in pursuit of development.

Haliap needed development because households could not sustain themselves by farming alone. People had terraced Haliap's most fertile land—the black soil that could support native rice varieties—by the 1950s. During the 1970s and 1980s, villagers began depleting the forest on the upper slopes, clearing new swidden, and cutting logs for housing and for sale in the lowlands. Clearing the forest above the springs that fed the terrace irrigation reduced the water available for wet-rice farming. Water shortages saw farmers convert more forest to plant cash crops that could be sold to purchase rice on the national market. At the same time, Haliap's previous engagements with global markets were changing. Much of the forest had been underplanted with coffee during the coffee boom in the 1970s. When trees aged, the coffee frontier shifted elsewhere, coffee incomes declined in the 1980s, and logging became a primary livelihood activity.

Development, people hoped, would assuage intra-village disputes over land tenure. Forested land had been customarily communal, but villagers began to dispute the ownership of the trees themselves. In the 1980s, facing increasing pressure to find cash income to pay for school fees, health care, and transportation, as well as food, the more secure households began to claim parts of the forest as private property. These households marked out claims by planting coffee trees and then declared the land parcels to be taxed under individual names in the local land office. These plots were never working coffee plantations. And nobody I spoke with actually reported paying any tax. Instead, the claims to forest ownership were preemptive attempts to privatize land, but the process faltered. By 1992 many of the people on the list of landowners were deceased or had left the village. Other villagers disputed the legality of such claims and publicly challenged inheritance arrangements that passed the land on to claimants' children. But intra-village squabbles proved the least of their problems.

Viewing the land registry, villagers were shocked to discover that a provincial official had declared several taxable hectares of forest adjacent to the road for taxation, effectively claiming it as his private property. People were unsure how to respond. Without recognized ancestral land rights, villagers were unable to challenge the title. Instead, they created shifting cultivation plots downslope from his claim and then, my respondents said in voices dripping with irony, somehow "forgot" to build a fire line. In 1992 the main road offered a vista of charred, burned-out forest edged with plots of corn and vegetables, drawing the village in line with the predominant stereotype of Adyangan people as destructive shifting cultivators.

Meanwhile, the rice fields farthest from the springs feeding the irrigation canals, the newest fields, were not receiving their fair share of water. Villagers who already had sufficient rice land began to use these dry fields to grow commercial vegetable crops in so-called gardens.

NEW LOCAL FUTURES

Row upon row of beans took over the rice terraces as *gardening* came to Haliap. From the late 1980s to the late 1990s, the common bean (*Phaseolus vulgaris,* the common green bean), known locally as the "Baguio bean," was the major cash crop. Twenty-three percent of Haliap's rice paddies were converted to fields of green beans between 1992 and 1997, with rice almost vanishing along the road.[1] The English term *garden,* introduced by the Department of Agriculture (DA) extension program, emphasized both the novelty of producing commercial vegetables on such a large scale and local links to national markets, where the agricultural *medicines* were labeled in English.

Gardening was itself promised as development. Gardens were introduced following the DA's mandate to diversify rural agriculture and disseminate progressive farming techniques. In 1986, DA extension officers helped two teachers at the Haliap elementary school to plant a garden to demonstrate the new agricultural techniques and medicines. Growing beans soon offered villagers wildly fluctuating farm gate prices. Some gardeners enjoyed large windfalls; others fell into debt. Gardening was a risky business with a certain machismo attached to it, thus it initially attracted young single men. Being unmarried, they had not yet inherited land, had left secondary education, and were working for daily wages. Gardening gave them something progressive to do and was thus a welcome supplement to their households' portfolios of livelihood activities.

The typical gardener was still partially dependent on either his parents or married siblings in 1992. In exchange for subsistence, he helped with household expenses when, and if, he took a profit. Most gardeners were saving to establish themselves as potential husbands. Other producers of beans fell into two categories: those who were affluent enough to afford the risk and those who were desperate enough to brave the odds. Gardening involved either a large capital expenditure or a sizable debt incurred against an uncertain return. Gardeners who prospered usually inherited or borrowed a good field, rather than renting, and used their own capital. If field owners did not have the labor to do the gardening, they rented land to others or hired day-rate workers.

Unlike the household exchanges of ubfu, daily wages in gardens were paid to individuals. Following the practice in the lowlands, men were paid 20 percent more than women. Landless gardeners borrowed *packages* of inputs (seed, pesticides, and fertilizers) on credit from dealers at usurious rates. Gardeners were obliged to sell their harvest to the same dealer at a fixed price, usually well below the market price. This arrangement, called *contrata* (contract), allowed dealers to refuse beans produced outside their input-credit arrangements when supply exceeded demand. Independent gardeners could usually sell their harvest at the best price when supply was low, but struggled to sell at a fair price when supply was high. Contract gardeners, however, had to pay their debts to the dealers regardless of the price of beans. These debts were often compounded by their attempts to grow a second crop to make up for a loss on the first. A contract gardener would thus see a substantial profit from his beans only if the storms of the July-to-September typhoon season or a plague of pests destroyed his neighbors' crops. Because of these risks, only a few of the fairly secure married households were engaged in gardening in 1992. Instead, almost everyone in Haliap was involved in gardening indirectly, renting fields, providing wage or exchange labor, and supporting younger gardening siblings.

Luis was one of the first to take up gardening. He took on packages and planted on land borrowed from his older brothers. Luis compared gardening, unfavorably, to gambling. But he did enjoy the way that gardeners embodied and performed progress. They wore white T-shirts emblazoned with agrichemical logos, giveaways (promotional gifts) from their dealers. Gardeners thus stood out against a background of older farmers, male and female, in their dark-colored tattered shirts. Luis's group of gardeners was regularly invited to meet with development project proponents as representatives of Haliap's progressive farmers. Servicing ongoing debts established with their non-Haliap dealers, they began to dream of having their own operating capital, which they called *pohonon* (Adyangan; Tagalog: *puhunan,* meaning planting stock or *kapital*). Unlike the small amounts of money that featured in most villagers' plans, gardeners dreamed big, imagining large fields with bean crops valued in the tens of thousands of pesos.

While virtually all of the 163 households I surveyed in 1992 agreed that "gardening is for men," women worked on their husbands' beans and as exchange and wage labor on others' crops. Women prepared the field and weeded the crop, activities villagers called *cleaning,* suggesting an extension of their domestic responsibilities. As wives, they had little control over the proceeds from the sale of beans. Men carried sacks of beans from the fields and transported them to the point of sale, so they held the cash. The money was not enough to meet the needs of their households, so they frequently took their cash and went to the local drinking spots to gamble, hoping to make their money grow. Villagers were philosophical about this behavior. Money was not exchangeable and objective, but held by particular individuals who described how they *prepared* funds for specific purposes: investments in crops, home improvements, school fees, medical care, and transportation being the most common. The villagers believed that people in particular roles should contribute specific things and flows of value to their relationships. Because gardeners were trying as best they could to become the main cash earners for their families, it was best that their wives said nothing and looked elsewhere for their own cash earnings to supplement household budgets instead.

Several dealers who sold agricultural inputs and bought beans came from outside the community and were female. These women paid day wages to male porters and drivers doing the heavy lifting. Recognized by villagers as housewives, female dealers controlled their own economic affairs, operating in a realm of agribusiness rather than as producer-farmers. Dealers' households were prosperous, and they were able to pay the bribes necessary to transport trucks of beans to the buying station in the lowlands. Successful dealers could amass enough money for family members, both male and female, to run for elected office. Dealers became important local patrons, as they were able to contribute to politicians' campaign funds and mobilize their clients, the gardeners, to vote for particular candidates.

By 1996 the gendering of gardening had changed. Younger single women began to plant their own crops of beans, using their earnings from day labor on others' gardens as capital. Gardening had by then become a temporary remedy for them, intended to ready them for a life beyond farming. These new female gardeners did not consider themselves particularly progressive. They dreamed of the kind of progress that would see them become housewives, but gardening meant they had to remain farmers for the time being. For them, gardening was simply a means to an end, a step along their route toward higher-earning jobs in the lowlands or overseas and, eventually, attaining the *housewife* lifestyle.

Planting beans eventually led villagers to become disillusioned with innovating in agriculture as a pathway to progress. With hindsight, widespread indebtedness made villagers reconsider the government's reasons for introducing beans in the first place. Luis and his friends observed that the only people who ever made steady earnings from the beans were dealers who were closely linked to local government officials, not ordinary gardeners like them, who were even mortgaging their own land to stay afloat after a poor harvest.

During 2001 and 2002 the market price of rice began to increase. People converted the gardens back to rice fields and started to open new fields in areas of red soil. Red soils lacked the natural fertility to support native rice, but hybrid rice could be grown on them with the assistance of new medicines. By 2005 the vista along the main road was again dominated by rice fields, with only one small plot of beans remaining. There was a short boom in the building of *kiskisan,* rice mills, with two appearing in Haliap in the early 2000s. The problems posed by the beans—the lack of capital, the cost of the medicines and transportation, and indebtedness—were now problems of rice, but a much greater number of households were directly involved in producing the rice crop. People understood they would need capital more than ever. Seeking salaried jobs, they imagined migrants' cash remittances could be the answer to the ongoing scarcity of cash.

ALIGNING THROUGH EXCHANGE

The brief efflorescence of gardening revealed how efforts to govern the village contradicted themselves. Development, as promoted by the national government, required the local agents of governing institutions to encourage villagers to become producers of agricultural commodities for exchange rather than for their own subsistence. Thus the DA had introduced first coffee and then beans to Haliap. To be successful, such endeavors needed the support of a coherent bureaucracy in which various agents and activities worked together to regulate the emergent local agricultural economy. This governing required defined village territories to be administered through transparent, universally recognized regimes of private property. But land ownership in Haliap did not work like that. In 1992 my research had enumerated thirty-seven different routes by which an individual might gain temporary or more permanent access to land on which to plant. Routes of access depended on kinship, wealth, and the nature of the crops to be grown; whether intended for subsistence or sale; planted temporarily or for a longer term. Governance could not encompass this diversity, the constant challenging and rearranging of local norms, and how previously established agreements were continually opened up and renegotiated. Thus, instead of encountering a bureaucracy that functioned smoothly and found their tenure system legible so that they might align themselves to the government, Haliap people experienced development as a series of incoherent and conflicted exercises that attempted to rearrange local norms without first understanding how the rules of tenure operated. Development became a piecemeal and conflicted activity, inevitably reshaped by corruption and sometimes leading to the village being abandoned by its frustrated development donors.

On a day-to-day basis, villagers found themselves unable to hold government departments and programs accountable for the ways their representatives acted and the promises they made. Individual government workers were already caught up in reciprocal exchange relationships with their own relatives and neighbors and usually owed their jobs to alliances they had forged with more senior bureaucrats or wealthy sponsors. So, rather than requiring villagers to align themselves with well-defined and publicly accessible rules, development necessitated villagers' engaging government by negotiating nepotism and factionalism. Sometimes this meant offering bribes or reciprocal gifts, either in cash or in kind—usually in the form of votes. This kind of reciprocal exchange between village and government was easiest for villagers to navigate when it occurred within and between institutions active in Haliap. The same pattern of political ties on a larger scale tended to make interacting with institutions outside the village almost impossible to manage. Villagers solved this problem by extending their personal exchange networks. They expended much effort in attempts to build reciprocity with staff in government offices and development projects. They built close relations, making these staff into personal partners through whom they were transacting with the government more broadly, positioning themselves as the *beneficiaries* that staff were required to attract in order to justify their own ongoing employment. Villagers felt they had already donated votes and offered their consent, support, time, and labor to government projects. Thus, in return, they expected projects and programs to work and believed those holding political office or posts where they administered development activities should extend to villagers the more personal and adaptable kind of care due to them from patrons—jobs, livelihood assistance, and gifts. The result seemed to be a corrupt and inefficient approach to delivering development.

The mayor's office, for example, was continually caught between explicit government rules on transparency and accountability and informal, but no less compelling and far better established, norms for redistributing wealth to which locals expected good patrons would conform. In 2005, Jeff, one of the municipal employees, explained to me, "Other places have more voters and businesses, so we get almost nothing here," referring to the funds his municipality was allocated from central government coffers. The mayor nonetheless needed funds to meet the demands of the many villagers petitioning him for assistance. "When people need school fees, hospital expenses, money to pay for a funeral, a job, they go to him," Jeff said. "If he doesn't help, they won't support him, work for his projects, or reelect him." Project and program funds were often the only available monies from which to borrow. Villagers did not see the mayor's redirecting project funds to address desperate villagers' personal emergencies as corrupt or a misuse of government money per se, but instead necessary to enact the kind of social security they desired. It was right that their mayor was a big person on whom they could rely. He, in turn, could access more resources from further up the hierarchy to fill in the gaps left in the municipal accounts, including turning to international donors. Jeff laughed about this, saying, "It's our poor Filipino values, really." I laughed along but thought that Jeff's tone and choice of words—describing local coping strategies as "poor Filipino values"—suggested that his comment was intended to be ironic. Jeff actually seemed quite proud that his mayor could meet local needs and that he had chosen to give priority to how villagers expected their elected officials to show a good patron's "care" for clients over the obtuse rules of government departments.

Development was thus only ever a partial success; failing to meet the dreams of progress it nonetheless helped shape them among villagers. A case in point was the breeding pair of piglets Jenelyn's household received from a local Department of Agriculture distribution program. In 1997 this project was intended to provide the poorest households of the poorest barangays in Ifugao with productive assets. The barangay requested DA assistance, then individual households had conformed to a survey and accomplished forms detailing their poverty in order to be identified as suitable participants. Jenelyn and her father fed and washed their pigs and built a small enclosed pen to keep them out of the neighbors' fields. They could not afford to purchase new building materials, and the boards they recycled were too flimsy to contain the growing pigs. The pigs continually escaped to eat the neighbors' swidden crops. Their neighbors' complaints saw the case go to mediation with the barangay captain. These neighbors, who had applied but failed to be identified as target recipients for piglets themselves, eventually killed the pigs. They gave one to Jenelyn's father and kept the other themselves to cover the damages. Jenelyn's fury over this perceived injustice was directed at the government.

Jenelyn believed the government should compensate her father for his loss, including piglets in perpetuity. The DA extension officers had approved the application, provided the pigs, and visited Jenelyn's house to give veterinary care and advice. Village administrative rules, however, clearly stipulated that any stray animals were the responsibility of the owner, and the Haliap barangay council refused to compensate her father. Jenelyn blamed this outcome on the council members' close ties to her neighbors and turned to the DA instead. The DA extension office also refused to pay. Jenelyn thought they had been influenced by council members who were close to the government staff on the DA extension program. She began to talk about joining the New People's Army guerillas so that she could bring down the government, by which she meant the barangay council and the DA extension office. Jenelyn had understood the overarching development goal all too well. The DA piglet distribution program clearly intended its beneficiaries to have a secure income stream on an indefinite basis. Jenelyn's household had entered into exchanges with the DA to receive just that: an ongoing stream of benefits from generations of pigs in perpetuity. She was furious that the government had then decided that they had lost the equivalent value of only the first two pigs.

Politicians recognized outbursts like Jenelyn's as symptoms of rising levels of envy and insecurity within the village. Villagers' dreams of progress were being frustrated. To address rising ill feelings, Haliap's councilors tried to realign new and existing development initiatives with local desires to distribute secure, longer-term streams of benefits. Workers in donor projects and government programs were encouraged to create as many opportunities as possible for casual labor or temporary contracts. Meanwhile, municipality government continually promised that a much bigger program or more permanent jobs would be arriving in the not-too-distant future. Redistributing temporary work and promising future gifts of jobs on development programs comprised the local social safety net, keeping politicians in office and villagers busy. To see this network of material and symbolic exchanges as corrupt would have required people to distinguish local government from local people, abstracting themselves as a village community from government in order to constitute a separate realm of civil society. Like Jenelyn, most Haliap people tended to refuse to distinguish these realms, seeing instead familiar kinship and patronage ties that shaped close intra-village relations. If the rules delimiting local governance were difficult for villagers to understand, the relations that sustained local households were almost equally difficult for governing institutions to comprehend and engage through the general regulatory frameworks that development programs made available to them.

Conforming to a Village Ideal

One key problem for development was that Haliap did not take the form anticipated by surveys and project activities delimited by the barangay's administrative boundaries. Much of what actually sustained Haliap villagers lay elsewhere.

Cash transfers and in-kind gifts from outside the barangay supported a significant number of Haliap households. This was true for much of Ifugao. In 1990 the National Statistics Office in Lagawe estimated household income sources to be wages (10 percent); entrepreneurial activities, including agriculture (43.2

percent); and other activities (46.8 percent). This "other" category included remittances received from waged work and agricultural activities outside Ifugao Province.[2] Of 167 Haliap households I surveyed in 1996, 17 percent reported income remitted in cash by kin who had migrated. This data comes from a 1996 survey that began with a field census to establish the number of inhabited houses, 267, in Haliap and Panubtuban. This figure differs from the National Statistics Office Census data for 2000, which reports 310 households.[3] My survey identified 30 sitios (hamlets). With field assistants, I guesstimated the wealthiest and poorest households, based on locally recognized indicators such as roofing materials, appliances, livestock, and harvested crops. We then interviewed inhabitants in the wealthiest (representing upper income), poorest (lowest income), and a target of 50 percent of the remaining houses in each sitio, for a total of 167 surveys, or 62 percent coverage, spread across the community geographically. Five percent received income from kin who had migrated to other rural areas; 10 percent from family members working overseas; and 2 percent from relatives working in urban areas. (And these were just the recent cash transfers people were willing to report to me, someone they identified as affiliated with a previous development donor.) Remittances of goods and food were also evident across Haliap. Approximately a third of my respondents regularly received a share of rice harvest, transported in fifty-kilogram sacks from kin living in the lowlands or from fields beyond the village. About a fifth of village households surveyed held mortgages on fields elsewhere as investments; others arranged for their more distant inherited plots to be farmed by sharecroppers. The total cash value of the goods and services circulating in Haliap was difficult to estimate. Most people did not consider money for school fees, vegetables, fruit, casual work for young people, pigs for rituals, and rice shares for rent as remittances but as what they called *sharing*. Sending things, money, and people back and forth was an expected and thus unremarkable part of their livelihood, not progress as promised by development. People in Haliap considered the term *remittance* to refer exclusively to cash they received from migrants working overseas and thus to be much more like the progress they envisioned.

Villagers led mobile lives, even before overseas migration really took off. Migration within the region had long been their answer to the shortage of irrigated rice fields in the village. Parents would leave the village when their eldest children married and inherited their best rice fields. As middle-aged migrants they would move to other rural areas along the lowland frontier, creating new fields for their younger offspring to inherit. Eighty-seven of 132 households I had surveyed in 1992 indicated they would leave Barangay Haliap when their eldest child married. These out-migrants were usually destined for Kasibu, Nueva Viscaya, or Maddela, Quirino, or points in between. These were lowland areas opened up to pioneer Haliap settlers when commercial logging and mining interests built roads into previously inaccessible forest. The Haliap settlement in Maddela, Quirino, is known as Scaling, where the logs were scaled. Here, Haliap migrants established swidden, intending to grow commercial vegetable or fruit crops. They were also engaged in logging, wood carving, and work in small-scale mining.

Along this agrarian frontier, migrants established their claims to land by *improvement* and initially did not have secure or recognized tenure. All the Haliap settlements, save the commercial rice area of Cordon, Isabela, villagers described as "squatted" or "pioneered." Haliap migrants drove other indigenous groups, particularly Ilongot shifting cultivators, off of their traditional lands. On a 1996 visit to Maddela, I met five Haliap men known as *Texas,* a reference to the U.S. Army's Texas Rangers, who were reputed to have driven away the previous Ilongot residents by intimidating them with threats of physical violence and *fahi* (ritual).

On the frontier, informally recognized individual private property was the norm. Plots claimed and cleared here could be sold onward without the seller's being obliged to consult a wider kin group. Such transactions were fast, simple, and difficult to overturn. In Barangay Haliap kin could challenge sales, demanding to be compensated for not having been offered a chance to purchase the plot even years after the initial sale agreement. Thus these frontier areas rapidly became part of a regional land market, with purchases funded by and sought for overseas workers and urban professionals by kin remaining behind in rural Ifugao. Frontier investments led to further socioeconomic differences emerging within Haliap. Households that already had secure livelihoods—meaning wide rice fields and permanent salaried jobs in Ifugao—were able to invest in the most productive lands and to buy lands that already had formal title. The less well-off often had to try their luck in two or three sites before finding a sufficiently productive and secure plot. Sharecropping was common. Wealthier families put up the capital while poorer relatives cleared and farmed the land; from my 1996 survey, I estimated that 22 percent of 167 Haliap households belonged to the upper-income group. Only 4 percent of all Haliap households owned lands outside the province in 1997. All of these households reported that their rice fields in the lowlands were being farmed by sharecroppers, and they were selling the bulk of their rice harvest to the national market for profit.

Haliap out-migrants usually lived in frontier settlements that were ethnically mixed and politically contested. Migrants competed for land with each other, with locals, and with nationally and transnationally funded mining and logging companies. Where the government defended commercial interests against those of locals and migrants, there were active NPA cadres and a military presence. Most Haliap people thus did not leave their Ifugao village site permanently. Instead, they circulated to and from the frontier in response to the agricultural calendar, job opportunities, and outbreaks of violent conflict. In the mid-1990s younger men dominated these flows to and from the frontier because they were the key laborers farming commercial crops and clearing land. Their female counterparts, meanwhile, were sourcing the capital used to invest in land, crops, and mobility by moving into and out of urban labor markets in the Philippines and on to jobs overseas.

Urban areas drew an important group of Haliap migrants. Haliap villagers were latecomers to a much older tradition of rural women seeking urban work.[4] But only a very few of Haliap's female urban migrants became domestic workers, breaking with the expected trend. Upper-income households typically reported at least one member living in the city, usually someone practicing as a professional in either Baguio City or Manila. Urban remittances added to the capital available to invest in frontier land. However, only 12 percent of households reported regularly receiving cash from family members in urban areas. These funds usually represented an as-yet-unmarried college-graduate daughter contributing to her natal household and were considered a temporary flow, likely to be reduced in the future, rather than a permanent livelihood strategy.

This pattern of mobility made the national census and regular development project surveys into thankless tasks. Individuals circulated between village, frontier, and city, seeking work, helping out in farming, and attending family events such as weddings and funerals. Even counting households posed a conundrum. Households, locally understood as people who "ate together from the same pot," did not necessarily correspond to houses enumerated as separate buildings. Zeny, Haliap's barangay secretary, explained to me that her census had counted only inhabited houses. When it came to reporting numbers of inhabitants, she had taken the names of those who usually stayed in the house, leaving it up to the residents to decide who to report and who to omit. Since her census data would be fed into the bureaucracy's various activities of registering voters and controlling access to government programs, including the identification of target groups for distributing development benefits, everyone had good reason to report as many names as they could.

Few villagers working and earning outside the barangay put down permanent roots elsewhere. In cities they lived in boardinghouses or shared rented houses with relatives. Rural migrants tended to build relatively temporary buildings called *campos*, or rest houses, on frontier farms. Sojourning villagers often resumed residence after five or ten years of living outside the administrative boundaries of the village. Even while away, most sojourners returned to

Haliap fairly regularly to arrange schooling for children boarding with village relatives, to vote, and to access the comparatively wider range of government programs and services available to them through their status as members of the village. Though Haliap was considered a remote barangay, the frontier areas where migrants opened their new farms were even more remote and thus had fewer services and benefits on offer. So it was especially important to villagers, while they sojourned beyond the village, to maintain the kinship ties supporting their claim to residence.

Mobility had an important cultural valence for villagers here. Mobility has always been a characteristic part of Adyangan life-cycle events and livelihood strategies, produced by kinship and inheritance. Practices of adopting and creating fictive kinship help people access land and labor and redistribute child rearing across generations and sibling sets. I noted that Haliap children were regularly moved across extended family networks so that they could access better schools. After age eleven or so, these children would become working students, doing part-time domestic work for distant relatives who would pay for their education. Younger adults then studied in cities or worked in frontier settlements as a rite of passage that would equip them with new skills and social networks. Even when married and raising their own children in Haliap, villagers continued to work outside the barangay. New parents entrusted the care of their children to grandparents, aunts, and uncles while earning for themselves and their extended families. Although their primary duty was to their children and spouse, wage-earning adults were expected to continue to contribute to their natal household, often by supporting their younger siblings or aging parents.

Particularly close ties of exchange between adult siblings give shape to Adyangan extended family networks. Anthropologist Fred Eggan considers sibling relationships to be the primary site of obligation in Ifugao society, with siblings obliged "to consult each other on all important occasions . . . to present a united front, looking after one another's interests and helping to educate each other's children."[5] Older children are thus expected to express their gratitude to their parents by taking on an almost parental responsibility for younger siblings that extends into later life. Since the eldest sibling has usually inherited the bulk of the family's land, sibling care provides a long-term lifeline for landless households. Giving more-remote fields or frontier farms to younger siblings as tenant caretakers sustains lateral family networks. Thus, rather than simply having aging parents in Haliap and adult children working in Manila, Haliap households typically support adult siblings spread across the rural frontier too. It is from these extended kin relationships that village-ness emerges rather than the enumerative activities of local officials and development agents.

INTERVENING FOR PROGRESS

In Haliap, development projects were usually launched with a community survey and a series of organizing meetings attended by heads of beneficiary households or members of target groups: unemployed youth, mothers, progressive farmers, and so forth. The administrative requirements of these projects demanded a kind of *conforming to* that could not encompass villagers' practices of kinship, exchange, and mobility. Project surveys continually enumerated people who were later discovered not to be current residents of the village. Project meetings often collapsed when beneficiaries failed to attend or sent family members as delegates. Project activities, once commenced, could rarely find the budget or flexibility to incorporate recent and unanticipated returnees into training and extension activities, nor could they cope with their beneficiaries' regular, temporary absences. Project officers thus spent a great deal of time visiting house to house, tracking beneficiaries' movements in the faint hope that they would eventually return to the project, which could then proceed as planned. Projects wanted villagers to make their activities a priority, but villagers prioritized the activities and relations already sustaining them. While Haliap people expressed feelings of being misunderstood and abandoned by their government, there actually seemed to be an excess of state-type practices in the village. Development projects continually required presence and, by recording and disciplining absences, were arguably creating almost a parallel to life in the old Spanish mission towns.

By the late 1990s both international aid donors and Philippine national planners had come to understand the appropriate role of national government in local development to be largely a supervisory one. Rather than redistributing resources themselves, government offices were now tasked with facilitating and coordinating the local activities of donor-funded projects and nongovernmental organizations. This approach to development posed problems for Haliap. In Ifugao few people had experience of the kind of consolidated governance that enabled them to distinguish between the activities of government proper and those of the donor projects that government facilitated. To villagers, all governance was development and vice versa, regardless of which agents claimed to be responsible for the ensemble of activities and policies people encountered in their village. In terms of impacts on villagers' self-understandings, the most significant projects were those that drew on foreign expertise and money. It was the lines along which these foreign projects intervened, rather than the tangible benefits they provided, that gave people their compelling image for a global world.

Projects put a great deal of effort into classifying households and lands on the basis of wealth and livelihood security. As a consequence, development inscribed new identities on villagers. To become a project beneficiary, villagers had to submit to surveys that documented their failings and poverty, meet in planning groups, and provide the *counterpart* labor (the community's in-kind donation to the project). Counterpart served as the community contribution to project activities or services, ensuring people did not receive the benefits of development for free, but were actively engaged and invested in it. People who had signed up to become beneficiaries cleared roads, dug ditches, weeded fields, and cooked meals, among other activities. It was not always evident to them how their work helped the project to progress, simply that work was required for funds to be released.

At the same time, projects' community organizers tried to shape their beneficiaries into the new social groups, people's organizations, anticipated by their donors' programs. Development required the community to reform itself by reordering the ways people thought about themselves and lived their daily lives. Villagers thus needed to demonstrate unity at a time when they felt jealous, competitive, and found that religious conflicts were straining relations between them. People saw their efforts to comply with the plans of project staff as a kind of client patronage. Villagers could secure access to an ongoing stream of resources by portraying themselves as the unified group of beneficiaries the project staff required to meet their organization's own targets for program delivery.[6] Project staff would then owe them a debt of gratitude.

Villagers were really most interested in the ultimate origins of the project funds rather than the logics for their classificatory exercises. If they could just circumvent the middlemen and the tedious exercises in counting and organizing that they undertook to meet institutional targets, villagers imagined they could ask the patrons for donations directly and then do what they saw fit with the money. Ultimately, they imagined this would be a far more efficient and satisfactory approach than participating in the endless cycles of counterpart labor and the inevitable infighting in the beneficiary groups.

Most projects brought in their own permanent staff, usually Tuwali speakers with ties to the Ifugao provincial government in Lagawe, hiring a few villagers on a casual basis. Haliap project staff complained it was almost impossible to work in their own village because they were obliged to so many people; staff from outside the village complained that they could not connect with, or "gain the attention" of, the local people unless they gave something away. Those projects that followed donor rules rather than meeting local demands for sharing and exchange found their workers accused of having a superior attitude and distancing themselves from their fellow villagers. Each donor project struggled with this in its own way.

Canada

From 1991 Haliap was one of the research sites of a Canadian International Development Agency project hosted by the University of the Philippines. The project was a capacity-building initiative intended to train academic research teams from the University of the Philippines Los Baños and the Ifugao State College of Agriculture and Forestry. The project's overall goal was thus to train Filipino academics and institutions to carry out applied development research, working together with Canadians in three field sites. For the project planners and managers, the Haliap site exemplified a community of swidden farmers who could be induced to relocate from the forest to the lowlands to conserve the nation's forests. Project activities included a comprehensive household survey and studies of the amounts of soil being eroded from swidden. Villagers saw this approach as a threat to their tenure and quickly put forward a discourse of indigenous stewardship: "we improved the land; we made the rice fields" and "this place was empty when we came here." The proposed land survey went ahead, without addressing the question of how to compensate villagers to relocate elsewhere, while the erosion-measuring tubs quickly disappeared from the selected farmers' swidden. Villagers were relieved to find that the exercise had been a kind of training and would produce academic reports rather than practical development plans to be implemented in the village. But they were annoyed that the efforts they had put into conforming to interview schedules and attending meetings did not produce resources or benefits flowing either into their own households or into the barangay council and its projects.

As part of this larger project, I was trying to learn about local land tenure. Respondents helped me to draw up a typology of tenure showing how different kinds of land—forest, fields, rice paddies—could be accessed through a variety of arrangements. These included inheritance, borrowing, sharing, renting, mortgaging, two kinds of sharecropping, and squatting (using land without permission). The kinds of land that could be accessed through each specific arrangement were disputed, and so were the boundaries of many of the plots. I documented thirty-seven different possible ways of arranging access to six categories of land. My project colleagues were disinterested, as this was far too complex; they wanted to know what was communal and what was individual property. Many of these access arrangements were viewed as illegitimate by at least some of my respondents. Inheritances rules and boundaries were disputed, as were the proper mechanisms for resolving conflicts. The barangay captain dissuaded me from doing mapping exercises. He foresaw that any boundaries

I described or any transfers of ownership I documented would be perceived as having donor support, and thus my activities would heighten simmering conflicts. At the time, villagers were reworking their ideas of customary property and creating new rules attached to producing cash crops to cut the networks of traditional inheritance and exchange.[7] My interest in establishing boundaries or assessing disputes inevitably would have been understood as my own personalistic approach of taking sides.

The shift in national government policy on indigenous groups and land tenure represented by this Canadian project worried local elected officials. For years the national government had opposed communal land tenure for indigenous groups, seeing such arrangements as inevitably hindering development. Shared tenure did not allow people to borrow capital for cash-crop farming, and complex extended-family purchase arrangements required by customary law restricted the emergence of a local market in agricultural land. Some villagers had accepted the idea that a market in land was inevitable and were pushing to privatize; others advocated retaining customary practices. By the mid-1990s it became clear that ancestral domain would be implemented. People who had convinced themselves that individual title was in their best interest learned that they would now be asked to seek communal title for the entire land area occupied by their tribe. Villagers were critical: "We do not have shared properties. In Ifugao we've always been more individualistic." My respondents here were referring to differences between the corporate group forest tenure found elsewhere on the Cordillera and the Adyangan practice of *pinusu,* where individual households would cultivate saplings of high-value tree species in the village forests. They were concerned that norms from elsewhere might be imposed locally and found that various arms of the government were giving them conflicting messages. While some legislators, politicians, and scholars advocated what would become communal ancestral domain, a series of agricultural development projects were simultaneously trying to introduce crops for which people had to have rights both of use and disposal in land, requiring individual private property.

Europe

In 1989 a European-funded project had commenced activities in Haliap. The Central Cordillera Agricultural Program (CECAP) had its own office building and a team of field staff drawn from elsewhere in Ifugao. CECAP offered training in progressive farming, including integrated pest management, animal husbandry, and more. The team surveyed the village and mapped local land use. CECAP's efforts to introduce tree crops and encourage people to reforest former swidden were hampered by the tenure system. Planting tree crops equated to staking a permanent claim on land, so members of poorer households could not find land on which they could plant, and the land-rich were not interested in a crop that would not produce returns for some years. CECAP set up a youth group to introduce the village to cultivating papayas. The group's work was interrupted, however, when the Department of Agriculture, the Philippine cooperating agency, suspended staff salaries for three months in 1996. Most of their youth beneficiaries then left the village in search of paid work elsewhere. Suspending staff salaries also held up work on a village water system, CECAP's flagship project. Though it was eventually completed, the water system suffered from lack of maintenance, and the supply was regularly disrupted. The spring that filled the CECAP reservoir tank was already in use as the source feeding the rice fields of one of the up-slope sitios. During the growing season, farmers there would climb into the tank and block the outlet with a drinking cup, causing water to overflow from the tank and flood their rice paddies. Fair enough, people thought, because these farmers had been using the spring first.

Other CECAP initiatives were impeded by religion. In 1995 staff began holding charismatic Christian prayer meetings in the CECAP offices, sometimes during office hours. Haliap people began to ask if they should join the church so as to qualify as beneficiaries. At the time, Haliap was divided into three Christian subgroups as well as those who defined themselves as pagans. These were Catholics of a syncretic bent in both Panubtuban and Haliap, and "the Protestants": Pentecostals in Barangay Panubtuban and an Iglesia ni Cristo congregation in Haliap. Each group had its own place of worship. When CECAP appeared to be starting yet another church, people anticipated it would operate along the same lines. Fely, who ran one of the sari-sari stores, despaired: "We'll never develop here. Not like other places. There, they can progress because everyone can agree: they follow the same religion." Like many Haliap people, she saw churches as offering *kapatiran* (Tagalog: brotherhood), new networks of mutual support and exchange, that worked against village customs.

Villagers were confused about the appropriate place of religion in development. To them, religion seemed to be simultaneously a separate realm of social action and a legitimate part of the state and a development agent in its own right. Professing Christianity, at least by bearing a Christian first name, had always been necessary to secure government services and benefits. Even so-called pagans used their Christian names in government offices, though they described themselves as having "reverted" to practice their old faith. In the 1980s and 1990s, people noted that new Protestant churches were springing up across Ifugao and were seeking Catholic converts. An influx of Protestant missionaries attacked Catholics' syncretic approach to the older pagan traditions. To reform such backward villagers, the new churches offered converts comprehensive ways of explaining and reordering village lives. They advocated

a radical break with pagan rituals and practices of reciprocity that they identified as obstacles in people's efforts to become small-scale commercial farmers.
People thus understood the public religious observances of CECAP's Haliap
to be part of this same move away from paganism toward a faith that would
enable agricultural progress. Rumors spread through the village that the director
of CECAP had eventually left the project to join a missionary group based in
Manila, largely because he had become convinced that the route to development in the region lay in faith-based groups.

The new churches found in Haliap were based in the United States and
in Manila. They connected villagers to a wider global community of the faithful, offering them spiritual guidance and new avenues to prosperity. Financed
by gifts from lowland Filipino and international congregations, these churches
supported missionaries and local pastors, trained lay preachers, organized prayer
rallies and prayers for the sick, and put forward development plans for explicitly
Christian communities. Worshippers in Haliap's Pentecostal services were "slain
by the spirit" and spoke in tongues. They read their English-language Bibles for
themselves, developing their own understandings of the text. People in the Iglesia
services sang Tagalog hymns and followed their pastor's interpretation of the
Bible, as well as voting along the lines set out by their church in the local elections. Both of these new churches emphasized saving individual souls. Despite
this, villagers' approach to faith remained stubbornly transactional, being less
about belief in divine salvation in the world to come and more about finding
themselves within immediate church networks and resources. Villagers believed
that donating labor or money to these churches would beget luck, seeing the
specific value donated returned in a greater sum. They expected that God's mercy
would provide spiritual comfort along with jobs, housing, food, and money.

Though Catholics had enjoyed access to long-standing educational and
charitable networks, these networks seemed to have been largely captured by
Tuwali speakers. Catholicism had not offered Haliap people much movement
toward centers of power. If you were lucky and did well in your studies and were
religious, my friend Rachel observed, you might get as far as the Dominican
convent in Solano, Nueva Viscaya. In contrast, the Protestant churches were
more interested in Adyangans and offered them more immediate links to
Manila and the United States. The Pentecostals enjoyed irregular visits from
American missionaries and promised that their trainee pastors could visit the
United States. The Iglesia had its own education and charitable initiatives based
in Manila. By the mid-1990s several Haliap youths had already received Iglesia
scholarships to support study in Manila.

CECAP projects made explicit the ways religion shaped development. Both
the Iglesia and the Pentecostals forbade their members from having anything to

do with paganism. Thus, if their members were to participate in any traditional rituals, they could be excommunicated. Iglesia members were also forbidden from joining any group that was not sponsored or sanctioned by their church. When CECAP tried to set up producers' and consumers' cooperatives in 1992, the one in Barangay Panubtuban (Catholic/Pentecostal) succeeded, but the one in Barangay Haliap (Catholic/Iglesia) failed. Rather than cooperating with CECAP and their Catholic neighbors, the Iglesia group had formed their own competing co-op, dividing the barangay. Villagers were already using faith-based networks to interrupt obligatory reciprocal exchange networks. Iglesia members were withdrawing from ubfu and changa' events where pagan chants were sung or sacrifices of chickens took place. By recasting economic progress as delimited by personalistic relations among faith-based social groups, CECAP's attempts to establish cooperatives had intensified intra-village conflicts.

CECAP also organized a brief visit from a UNICEF-funded mother-and-child nutrition program in 1996. Program officials arrived during the May planting season and were upset to find that the mothers, their intended beneficiaries, were almost all out planting their swidden. In beneficiaries' homes, fathers were caring for the children, but no one suggested a father-and-child nutrition seminar. Instead, the visitors departed. According to Steve, the visitors did not think men were either knowledgeable or interested in child nutrition: "The UNICEF [representative] . . . she only liked to talk with the mother, and was dismayed that she was gone to the kaingin [swidden]. She did not like to talk with me, even if I am the one cooking then." This encounter convinced people that respect and resources would flow most frequently to households with housewives: women who did not farm.

Laudably, CECAP has maintained long-term engagement in the village. In 2005 CECAP was supporting the municipality in preparing Asipulo's submission for ancestral domain, assisting in social preparation and boundary conflict resolution, before the process stalled.

United States

It was a health care project, funded by an American faith-based charity and delivered by a Manila-based NGO, that had the greatest impact on the village. In the mid-1990s the Asipulo municipality had no doctor, nurse, or hospital, so any initiative offering health services was welcomed. This project hired Haliap women who were qualified professionals—midwives—as barangay health workers. The project converted one of the elementary school outbuildings into a clinic. During 1996 the health workers trained by the project surveyed the community. Their survey was required to justify the release of project funds, so everyone wanted to comply with it. The health workers visited and evaluated each house in the community according to six indicators: nutrition, whether residents had been immunized, the source of their drinking water, what kind of toilet they used, maternal health, and their acceptance of family planning measures. For each category they assigned the house one of four colors: red (for dangerous), yellow (indicating some problems), green (for okay), and blue (for excellent). They recorded their data by coloring in boxes on a palm-sized cardboard card that they then stapled to the front doorpost of each house. Another identically colored card was then stapled to a large map on the wall of the newly converted barangay health clinic.

The cards on their houses upset villagers. Anyone passing by could see how their domestic circumstances and compliance with global public health norms had been evaluated. Luis and Angelina's house bore a card of red and yellow squares. This card told passers-by that they lacked clean running water and a toilet, did not accept birth control, and their child was malnourished. During their assessments, Luis explained, he had refused to answer some of the health workers' questions. His neighbors, he observed, had answered incorrectly, or had even disputed their assigned categories and, if the health workers had refused to change them, had changed them themselves after the health workers left. The cards, however, presented a material truth. Their project role had enabled the health workers to publicly represent their fellow villagers as objects of lack. Some villagers felt the whole exercise had simply allowed the health workers to reinscribe their own personal prejudices onto their neighbors, noting that the assessors had not given their relatives' households the low scores some thought these houses merited. The resentment of their fellow villagers created a good deal of discomfort among the health workers. When I asked Maria how she felt about the uproar over the cards, she sighed and said: "How else will we progress? No clinic . . . means no nurse visiting, no medicines . . . nothing. If the people would not conform to our questions, we had to guess. If our forms were not accomplished, they do not like to release our budget."

The cards were intended to render the households and bodies of villagers legible to the projects of development. The cards' colors signaled levels of progress, making villagers subject to the project's discipline and control through public shame or praise. This approach to development as social control is one we might have expected to instantiate a classically modern mode of governing— a kind of governing that works through people internalizing the hygienic gaze into their individual psyches and thus disciplines their bodily actions. This project should have created healthy villagers by engaging people's innermost desires for their own progress. In an exercise of governing with this design, the data the health workers had collected should, like the census, have generated new stories of village realities. These stories would then have shaped the approaches of government officials to providing resources and recognizing rights. But recruiting village residents themselves to deliver the project produced problems. Most villagers saw the possible personal benefits of conforming to the questions asked in this activity as remote and unlikely. Instead, they expressed resentment toward the health workers themselves. Who did they think they were to govern? Why were the houses of their close relatives assessed as blue and green regardless? Why should their guess be recorded as fact? The cards remained in place for only a few weeks and then vanished.

Villagers resented the status afforded the health workers by their salaried role. Unlike Angelina, who had had to drop out, all of these women had been able to afford the cost of college midwifery degrees and been able to fund their review for the board exams that had certified them as professionals. All were married to the few men with permanent jobs, either in teaching or local government. Like Sarah, they publicly identified themselves as a proper kind of stay-at-home Filipina housewives and cultivated what they called *home gardens* rather than traditional swidden. They could do so because their household livelihoods were largely secured without the supplement of selling cash crops. Their livelihood security meant they could afford to cultivate extra-nutritious foods for their families around their large house lots rather than grow for market in up-slope fields that were more remote. In public gatherings they put themselves forward as women of proper feminine virtue: they cared for their children and their community. They explicitly contrasted themselves to overseas migrants, women who had left the village in search of employment elsewhere. In a public meeting on village health, Maria explained, "Instead of looking everywhere for money, we are the ones who sacrifice to stay here and care for our children."

Debating the Family

The health workers and their American-funded project took up a family values discourse on women's migration. This discourse was one consolidated around the Contemplacion case and circulated widely in the media and among aid donors, academics, and migrants who considered themselves professionals in the mid-1990s. Here is a longer example of it, drawn from a public address by an indigenous Filipino academic. In his framing of it, women's migration entails:

> a role reversal in our family system . . . instead of menfolk leaving home in the off season to work elsewhere, it is now our womenfolk who leave home on extended periods to find work as domestics in faraway places such as Hong Kong, Singapore, and the Middle East. Please note that I am not leveling any criticism here. Our beloved

sisters, just like us, are willing to make a sacrifice in order to help their families attain higher living standards and to provide resources for the future education of their children. . . . there is now an increasing incidence of crimes against children such as incest and child abuse and crimes by those neglected children themselves . . . the consequences of moms leaving children in the care of overburdened grandparents and husbands who may be good providers but are poor substitutes for mothers.[8]

The family system he describes was one to which the majority of Haliap villagers, other than the health workers, could only aspire. Though a recognizable pattern, it was neither easily attained nor widespread.

By generalizing the Filipino family system, talking about migration and gender in this way reinforced the role of the family in defining a Filipina identity. This argument then attached a particular kind of self-sacrificing and middle-class Filipina femininity to an equally specific account of the nation. We saw earlier how the Contemplacion furor had placed the nuclear family at the moral center of an affective bond between citizens and their state, enabling the family to work as an ambiguous—and thus very practical—political symbol.[9] Haliap villagers, being indigenous people often left out of the imagined nation, understandably wanted to be part of this bond between citizens and state. When the health workers' project introduced this discourse on gender and migration in public debates over the proper conduct of women, it provided an opportunity to transform village gender norms to better fit the national story and make Adyangans more Filipino. Perhaps the chance to take up this national version of family—one that reflected metropolitan middle-class norms, not rural life or local, indigenous culture—was the most powerful development tool offered to the village.

Villagers knew from their experiences with UNICEF and the health workers that their household level and personal inabilities to materialize this vision of nuclear households in their daily lives had placed them in the category of "project beneficiary" rather than "project staff" in the first place. Even though taking on this family ideal seemed to be the key to unlocking the reciprocal exchange of development, villagers like Luis and Angelina stubbornly refused to accept the health workers' ideas about what constituted a worthwhile form of family life.

In 1996 underemployed men like Luis experienced this discourse and the way it turned absent mothers into a national, public problem—first from UNICEF and then from their health workers—as humiliating. At the same time, news reports were describing cases of Filipino men abusing their own children, attributing their behavior to male "culture shock . . . brought about by . . . reports on the crimes of foreign pedophiles in the media . . . and mothers away from the home . . . as OCWs."[10] Luis and his gardening friends found the underlying logic deeply disturbing: as Filipino men, they could not be trusted either to earn a household wage or to care for children. Without realistic hopes of finding salaried jobs locally and facing the limits of local agriculture, young men like Luis responded to being humiliated by performing a kind of hypermasculinity—drinking, gambling, and getting into public disputes.[11]

As each of these development projects and programs failed to deliver the jobs and security villagers wanted, their anger with the government grew. Each different initiative revealed that the ways villagers understood and practiced the very things that defined them as persons—gender roles, kin relations, family life, owning land, working together, ritual, customs, religious faith—impeded government plans for development. Were villagers themselves inadequate to the projects of development? Or had development failed their village?

Coping Up with Development

Villagers coped up with developments' failures by recreating their global imaginaries through a variety of performances and personal changes. In this the barangay health workers themselves led the way. They contributed a comic skit to the evening program for the 1996 municipal fiesta. The skit began with the entry of several women dressed in satiny evening wear and sunglasses. They sashayed across the stage with a few disco dance moves, striking poses at one side, like fashion models. Next, a group of women in new kinds of native uniform, the tapis and blouse, crossed the stage, moving with arm gestures taken from traditional Ifugao dance. These women joined with the first group and struck similar poses. Then all the performers moved to center stage, dancing in the disco style of the first group. Suddenly, another person appeared on the stage, clad in a men's tennis outfit, accessorized with a racket and a heavy (shoe polish) beard. This white-clad woman, Maria, posing as a man, sauntered to center stage and put her hands on her hips, surveying the scene. She then chased the would-be models around the stage, making lascivious motions with her pelvis. The assembled audience greeted this performance with cheers and riotous laughter.

As a fashion show, this skit stitched together the feminine future—new fashions being what women will soon be wearing—and the indigenous past. The health workers had borrowed dresses from returning overseas migrants, supplying their own tapis. Juxtaposing the clothes to suggest they were both local girls and OCWs at the same time, the health workers' skit portrayed village women as globally desirable. Theirs was a future where locality and globality were successfully blended together in stylistic terms. The performance suggested that a Haliap woman could be glamorous, wealthy, and in control of flows of foreign money and, perhaps, foreign sexualities. Since Maria played a man but was still recognizably female, the skit also showed local women in the role of white men—coming and going as leisured and rich.

Blending the Ifugao woman who knows what to do (wearing the tapis) with the simple housewife and her professional qualifications (the real-life health workers) and the OCW (wearing satin dresses) blurred the categories used to delimit women and the meanings attached to these styles of presenting feminine selves. The skit undid the prevailing critique of absent female migrants by revealing that the health workers also desired their audience's imagined future of female travel, glamour, romance, and material goods. The skit worked as an exemplary event where both performers and audience effected a change in their lives, a change expressed in the blend between the performance and the everyday world. The blend happened in a prolonged moment of suspense in which the affective intensity produced by the performers' embodied actions sought an outlet. This desire found its release in the audience's laughter as the village collectively realized that the health workers aspired not just to be exemplary, progressive local women but also to be migrants and even foreign men. Theirs was not simply a performance of a rather conventional femininity oriented to the narrative of the Philippines as a global nation, but it was also a reworking of that same femininity to incorporate elements of more egalitarian Adyangan gender norms.

RETURNING MIGRANTS

Returning migrants embodied this blend on a daily basis. Returnees moved within a heady atmosphere of independent economic power and glamorous, consumption-based femininity. Rather than accepting that development would arrive from elsewhere, they had gone out to secure it for themselves and bring it home. Their progress was defined by locally recognized ideals, and they sought to use global things and ideas to innovate in village lives, blending them together with traditional ways. Migrants returned to a village that was well aware of the personal changes enabled by overseas work.

By the end of the 1990s Haliap respondents identified villages with many workers abroad as "progressive" places, having already "developed." "Because they've got OCWs there, they have no problems—they have money" was a common refrain. Because development was made visible through intensified patterns of consumption, my Haliap friends pointed out again and again how those receiving remittances from abroad had development, meaning they owned better houses and distinctive clothes, did less agricultural labor, could afford to own cars or jeepneys, and had "complete appliances." They saw this as progress through migration.

Cell phones were added to the list of development essentials by 2002. A cell phone tower indicating network coverage had by then become a key indicator of remittance-led development. The more easily people could contact their absent kin, the more easily they could appropriate, redistribute, and invest migrant earnings. While popular enthusiasm for cell phones enabled Filipinos to generate a whole new popular culture of text messaging in the 2000s, it has also linked villages to expatriate workers overseas, creating more prosaic but no less radical changes in household communications and economies.[12] Haliap people longed to be part of this and they got their wish. By early 2003 there were two cellular networks in Asipulo, with both towers located behind the new municipal hall.

In 1997 I learned of sixteen Haliap OCWs, all women. They were in Hong Kong (eight), Singapore (three), "Saudi" (meaning the Arabian Gulf region, two), Taiwan (two), and Malaysia (one). Villagers had told me of only two OCWs—one in Hong Kong and one in Saudi—in 1992, so fourteen migrants five years later was a significant increase. Costs for migration varied, but estimates from my respondents ranged from P45,000 (US$1,710) for Singapore or Hong Kong to more than P180,000 (US$6,840) for Canada.[13] These estimates included expenses related to the contract itself, including airfare and a medical exam, as well as agency fees for placement and possibly training, travel expenses to and from government offices, possible gratuities for government officers, and the fees of expediters who shepherded applications through the bureaucracy. Though many villagers wanted to seek overseas work in the 1990s, the costs deterred them. A much lower number of Haliap women—16 women out of 167 households surveyed suggested that roughly 2 percent of Haliap's working-age women were overseas—had migrated in 1997 than women from towns in nearby lowland provinces where households already had larger cash incomes.[14]

Villagers with migrants in their families were eager to reflect on migrants' movements, plans, and the changes their migration had enabled. "Migrants are our new kadangyans [elite]," was how my friend Evelyn explained it. Describing his niece, returned from Singapore and planning to go to Taiwan, Saturnino then said, "How can we keep her here, now that she has seen those far places? There is no more for her to do, except more adventures there." His niece, Rosalie, was a twenty-seven-year-old mother of three. Though married, she had migrated as a single woman, without mentioning her spouse or children in her employment application or travel documents. According to data gathered at POEA predeparture seminars, Rosalie's story is fairly representative of the 1990s trend: female migrants were typically single, comparatively well educated, and in their early twenties at the time of their first contract.[15] Rosalie's remittances from Singapore provided the capital for her husband's gardening and supported her extended family while they looked after her children. Coming back on a break between contracts, her fellow villagers recognized Rosalie as a returned OCW before they saw her face. Evelyn had pointed Rosalie out to me as she got down from a jeepney; her designer jeans and T-shirt, large sunglasses, high heels, and authentic Chicago Bulls baseball cap all shouted OCW.

Lydia, another returning migrant I met in 1997, had just finished her first contract in Singapore. Her family had migrated to Kasibu, Nueva Viscaya, when she was a baby, so she had grown up in Haliap's extended village. On a break before taking on a second contract, she had come to Barangay Haliap to recruit girls for her "auntie's" maid agency in Singapore. She explained the lure of overseas work for young women in these terms: "What's left for them here anyway? They get married in high school, have their babies. . . . There's no money, there's nothing here. What can they do? They are already wives, mothers, but it is still kurang [lacking]. Always looking somewhere for food, for money. No nice things, no respect. So they like to go abroad. It is something new for them. There is money . . . but there are also new friends, new places to learn." Attending a Haliap wedding, Lydia wore red leather heels and flashed her Lancôme lipstick. Angelina and her sister Tricia discussed Lydia's shoes and lipstick at length. She had captured the attention of local bachelors, not with beauty and virtue, but with these global things. That Lydia was recruiting more workers and would receive a commission for her efforts seemed unremarkable to Angelina and Tricia. The woman Lydia called her "auntie" was fictive kin, clearly her patron and business partner in Singapore, and if Lydia recommended good employees to her, Lydia then deserved a share in her profits.

None of Haliap's sixteen migrants had yet been able to return permanently in 1997. The growing needs of their households kept them abroad or sent them back again. These migrants met the criticisms of the family values discourse and the health workers head on, reframing their own migration as evidence of the ways they were oriented to maternal care and domestic concerns, despite what anyone else might say. Sabel, visiting kin in Haliap while on her first vacation from Hong Kong in 1996, explained her migration in terms of her provisioning responsibilities: "When I see our rice pot is empty, I'm the one to find for our needs, so I went to Hong Kong." With the cooking pot as a metaphor for her household budget, Sabel described overseas work as part of a woman's domestic responsibility to make ends meet and identified herself as a housewife. She explained that rather than looking to her husband alone to provide, an Adyangan woman should do what she can to share the household burden, even sacrificing to go overseas for work. Describing herself in terms of household budgeting and self-denial, Sabel distanced herself from how some of the younger, single migrants tried to perform a global femininity by consuming in order to enhance their own appearance and status, like Lydia did. With her modest self-presentation and successful college-student children, Sabel set another kind of example for not-yet-migrant married women.

In the mid-1990s migrants and their families did not (yet) seem to be the targets of development projects in the village. They did not need handouts of cash, distributions of pigs, casual work, or free meals, and their families did not have to go the mayor's office in emergencies. Returning women had truly become housewives. They planned to go into business or manage their investments in land rather than go back to farming themselves. Virtually all of them declared that they would go overseas again if their plans did not succeed rather than going back to planting rice. Seeing their new clothes and things and listening to tales of their overseas success, my friends Angelina and Rachel quickly forgot the boring, repetitive, and isolated nature of the work that migrants said they had been doing abroad. My friends likewise discounted media reports of abuse and suffering among migrants abroad and did not ask returnees too many personal questions about their employment experiences. In turn, visiting migrants rarely spoke about feelings of isolation, the drudgery of their work, and their exploitative working conditions, fearing they would be shamed as not having been able to cope up and thus somehow held responsible for their own bad luck.

By 2000 it seemed there was always someone from Haliap traveling abroad; someone working there to receive them; and someone on the way back home to bring news, money, and gifts that circulated in community exchange. Villagers now imagined themselves as moving in an extended community space with an international purview, even if they were not currently migrants. It was now just as common for both young unmarried women and those in newly formed households to plan a future based on contract work in Singapore or Hong Kong as it was for them to seek jobs in Nueva Viscaya or Manila.

Left by the Wayside

Luis and Angelina were among those villagers without land or overseas remittances who became increasingly indebted and vulnerable during the late 1990s. Luis's interest in making a success of "progressive farming" led him to attend the CECAP seminars and training activities. He more or less single-handedly maintained the CECAP-installed water system, combining extensive counterpart project work as the representative of village beneficiaries with his bean farming. His project ties were also personal. Before marrying Angelina, Luis briefly romanced one of the CECAP staff. In 1992 she had recommended him for casual work as a research assistant with the Canadian research training project on which I was working. He had declined. He didn't think he would like working for a foreign woman but ended up becoming a key respondent and a casual research assistant on my project.

After their marriage, Luis focused on farming, but he and Angelina struggled. Angelina's store had been closed as a result of her customers' unpaid debts. They had no steady source of cash, so Luis reduced his project work to seek a permanent job that would allow him to improve their house and provide adequate food and clothing. He trained with the Ifugao electrical company as a linesman, helping to install electricity throughout the municipality. The work was paid at casual rates and never materialized into the salaried job he had initially been promised. Luis then found some casual carpentry work and went back to gardening, taking on another package of beans. In 1997, a disastrous year for the bean crop, he ended up P4,000 (US$152, the average monthly income of a Haliap household at the time) in debt. Feeling desperate, Angelina had mortgaged the plot on which the former store, now their house, stood. Neighbors took the mortgage at a price far below the plot's market value. Angelina spent the money on daily living expenses before Luis found out. Luis was despondent and furious with his wife and neighbors. "If only I had capital," he said to me, ". . . then we would not suffer like this." His solution was to find work overseas himself. He approached me to see if I could find a job for him in Canada. He did not want Angelina to go overseas, he explained, "because they do horrible things to our women."

Luis dreamed of a job with a steady salary. Some of his acquaintances had apparently found secure work overseas. Frank, a man from nearby Kiangan, had migrated to Vancouver, where I was living in 1997. I had met Frank when, after five years as a marine engineer on Liberian-flagged boats, he had come ashore and married a Filipina Canadian. He was working as a delivery driver for Kentucky Fried Chicken. When I told Luis about Frank's work, he disputed my account. I must be wrong, Luis told me, because nobody from a wealthy Kiangan family would ever take a low job like delivery driver. In Luis's global imaginary, success was assured and local social hierarchies maintained. Luis considered he had *opened a problem* to me, breaching his own privacy and expressing a heretofore repressed affective state as an emotion with particular intent. By laying open his vulnerabilities and feelings for me to see, he was obliging me to assist him by activating my own personal networks. He understood my inability to help him find a job abroad as refusing a legitimate claim on my friendship. He was then angry and distant with me for several weeks.

Luis's earnings from his casual work were insufficient for the kind of progress he wanted. He tried to make his money "grow" by gambling, usually with neighbors and while drinking in the local stores. Luis explained that his "vices"—drinking, smoking, and gambling—released tension and expressed what he called his "not nice" feelings with his lot in life. Unable to provide, Luis felt himself to be an emotionally distant partner and father. He felt, he said, small, humiliated by his continual failures to change his circumstances. His household depended on his siblings, including his younger sister Sarah, for ongoing small gifts of financial support. He resented his dependence very deeply. These gifts reversed the expected flow of resources and advice from older to younger sibling. His family and neighbors treated him with pity and more than a twinge of contempt, despite—and perhaps even because of—all his community development work. Combined with the messages he received from development projects and the radio about being less ethnic and more manly, Luis felt put upon but never accepted the idea that he was too inadequate to progress.

To mend relations I offered Luis more casual work as a research assistant. I wanted to learn about the native varieties of rice, but my field assistants were college graduates and devout members of the Iglesia ni Cristo and thus could not undertake research involving the pagan rituals for planting and harvest. As would-be professionals they had never even planted the old varieties in their family fields themselves. Luis, I knew, was curious about the traditional rice varieties and had experience with planting and harvesting. He had already done some independent preliminary research on local knowledge of native varieties funded by another researcher on the Canadian project. When I raised the topic with him, Luis prevaricated. After the mortgage crisis, he finally explained that he had burned the data he had collected.

Luis resented the casual nature of his research job. He would decline day labor and delay planting his own field as he waited for his employer to arrive. He had continually received a message rescheduling their research meetings. After three or four deferrals, in 1996 he decided to reschedule himself. He traveled to a Haliap friend's funeral in the Kasibu out-migration settlement. His friend had been murdered in a land dispute. The funeral was emotional, and Luis came back to Haliap three days later, still reeling from drink. His employer had arrived two days before, so Luis stepped down from a jeepney to be scolded in front of his neighbors. In response to being publicly humiliated, he had thrown his notes and completed surveys into a garbage pit and set them alight. He reasoned:

> Those questionnaires, all those stories, it was all for them at the university, not for us here. It is over. It is gone now, the old rice and our way of planting it. It is only good for research but no more for us. Why do I want to help the research? The researcher got angry to me, and I think, I am also human. So I quit. And I burned it all. Do you think

someone like me has anywhere to put all that paper? It would just become destroyed. . . . Even me, I don't like my wife to plant the old rice. It is better that she finishes her college and finds her profession. That needs money. There is no money in the old rice.

Luis's claim—"I am also human"—drew on widespread Filipino ideas of what it means to feel and regard oneself as human and to be treated as such by others. Norms marked by the Tagalog terms *pagkatao* (to have dignity) and *makatao* (to be treated humanely) are fundamental to maintaining social relations. Luis's was not a rights-based model of interacting with others that asserted all people were inherently equal, but a more individuated claim that asserted he was equal to others. Luis did not want development if it did not give him the human dignity he sought as an equal. His experience of development was of having his dignity undermined. Repudiating a past he had been quite knowledgeable about, he was willing himself into a progressive future where he dreamed he could find the equality he sought. His feelings of disappointment and being excluded also led him back to his Iglesia church. He wanted to see if religion could offer him the progress-with-dignity the government had failed to deliver.

Angelina bore all of this with patience. She did not criticize her husband but tried all the avenues she could find to augment their income. She worked as a casual laborer in planting and harvesting. She made and sold snack foods. Eventually she began to suggest, softly and persistently, that she was the one who should seek work abroad. Angelina made inquiries with Haliap friends, Nora and Sabel, who were already in Hong Kong, and sought out an employment agency there. She arranged for her parents to help Luis care for their son. She began to save the money she would need to apply for her passport and buy a ticket. Luis decided to support her efforts, pragmatically putting aside his qualms about women's migration and deferring his own plan to become the major breadwinner. In 2001 Angelina flew to Hong Kong.

Lacking Value

From the perspective of villagers like Luis and Angelina, development projects reflected other people's self-interested visions for village futures rather than villagers' own dreams. Such projects required would-be beneficiaries to represent themselves as kurang. Villagers had to show project developers that their lack was not simply poverty but a lack of dignity and human value. As they sought to recreate their personal relations within government institutions and development projects into satisfactory and familiar patron-client ties, it seemed to villagers that it was precisely by agreeing to present themselves as unworthy that they could then be dismissed, cast aside, and passed over when it came to developers redistributing patrons' goods and favors. At the same time, villagers could see what they considered to be huge amounts of money circulating through the plethora of agents who were producing developments' rules and plans, conducting surveys and delivering reports, while driving project cars and motorcycles and attending apparently important meetings and seminars beyond the village. This evidence of links to wealth outside the village motivated people to keep trying to engage the projects and to move closer to development's apparent source.

That Haliap villagers were not the ideal subjects of development programs did not convince them of their personal inadequacy to the broader project of progress; it merely showed them that they were people who found themselves in the wrong circumstances to actualize their capabilities. Villagers saw that the rearrangements of maps, censuses, and ethnic categories made by developers were inaccurate. They knew that the new peoples' organizations being set up did not fit into the village's existing social patterns. They did not even really expect that the infrastructure of a regulated agricultural commodity system could be effectively built and administered in Haliap. While project developers tended to assume that villagers needed to learn how to think of themselves as composing civil society and demand things from their government more effectively, people saw this kind of organizing in order to demand as a dead end. People knew that they were already quite good at getting what little local government offices and their officials had to give and that they could not do so any more efficiently if they followed the official rules of development projects.

Haliap villagers wanted something more. They wanted to become *big* in village terms, to use the global realm to enact their village dreams: secure ownership of rice fields, investments in cash crops, a modern house, complete appliances, a car, and a professional education for their children. They wanted to make their village and the wider world conform to the ideals they already held for dignity and humane treatment, ones based on reciprocal obligation. They did not want development to reorient their values, reformulate their kinship, criticize their gender roles, introduce new religions among them, or impose a new tenure system on them. But these shifts in how they thought about themselves in the world seemed to be just what development projects in Haliap had to accomplish before progress could occur. Villagers thus sought to escape being intruded on by development. *Abroad* became a utopia where the transformative powers of movement would allow villagers to make their own dreams reality.

CHAPTER 4 ✦ New Territories

BY 2008 HALIAP MIGRANTS in Hong Kong included Angelina as well as Nora, Darcy, Elvie, Priscilla, Sabel, and Maritess, and, finally, Luis himself. Their presence extended Haliap along the MTR (mass transit railway) stations of Hong Kong: Wan Chai, Admiralty, Shau Kei Wan, and the New Territories. Like Angelina and Luis, each of these migrants was able to secure a contract in Hong Kong by drawing on the dense ties of indebtedness and affection between themselves and their Haliap kin.

Angelina asked their neighbor, Jane, to contact her sister Nora, who had already been in Hong Kong for nearly a decade, and asked to be recommended to a Hong Kong employment agency. In 2001 this agency found Angelina a job as a domestic for a wealthy Chinese household. Angelina and Luis needed P70,000 (US$1,369) to pay her passport fees, security clearance, medical exam, agency fees, and airfare.[1] Luis's younger sister, Sarah, and her husband, Brandon, helped them with the finances. Sarah had received a loan from a government program to assist schoolteachers, and she re-loaned the money to Luis. Luis supplemented this with the proceeds from the sale of four of Brandon's pigs, secured through a Department of Agriculture distribution program, but Luis "borrowed" this money without first asking Brandon. Angelina repaid the outstanding amount to Sarah and Brandon within four months of arriving in Hong Kong, but relations between Luis and Brandon remained strained. Sarah and Brandon were partially responsible for Angelina and Luis's shift from living in poverty to relative economic security. Because Luis and Angelina could never truly reciprocate, their relationship combined economic calculations of debts owed while at the same time expressing familial intimacy.

Angelina then paid for Luis to visit Hong Kong as a tourist in 2004. Her employer interviewed him, offering him a contract as a gardener and houseboy. Luis would plant and weed the garden, cut the grass, care for a fishpond of valuable ornamental carp, and feed and groom guard dogs, as well as run errands. In 2004 the Philippine Overseas Employment Administration reported 197,345 Filipinos in Hong Kong, including 194,241 on temporary working visas; 2,700 irregular migrants; and 404 permanent residents. Of these, 95 percent were female, making Luis one of a very few men.[2] Luis and Angelina had become a rarity among Filipino contract workers: a couple who migrated together.

Luis and Angelina's employer lived in a luxury home in the Victoria Peak area of Hong Kong Island. The employer's part of the house had stunning views over Hong Kong Harbor, a terrace with a large fishpond, large airy rooms, and lovely marble floors. The servants' quarters, located off the laundry, had low ceilings and tiny rooms. Luis and Angelina shared the servants' quarters with another Filipino couple, a single Filipina, and a Thai cook. There were also three Hong Kong Chinese workers—a cook, a driver, and a security guard—who lived outside the home. In 2005 Luis and Angelina each earned HK$3,640 (US$468) per month under Hong Kong's Foreign Domestic Helper program.[3] This amount was more than the government-mandated HK$3,240 (US$417), because their employer had decided not to follow an official change in the rules governing Hong Kong's domestic worker scheme that had reduced mandatory pay in 2002. They shared the bottom of a twin bunk bed made of unfinished wood. Their top bunk stored Angelina's growing collection of soft toys and their clothes. The room had one tiny window, barred but unscreened. They could not open the door of the room more than two feet before it hit the bed. "We're lucky we still love each other," Luis told me in 2005, gesturing to the cramped, dark space.

To get to Hong Kong, both Luis and Angelina had filled out forms and signed papers in government offices and attended the POEA's mandatory pre-departure seminars. When they recounted the process step-by-step, they each remembered people's names in various offices but not their institutional roles. It all seemed a bit of a blur. They were not really sure whom they had been dealing with and why and when they had visited which offices.[4] This impression may have been heightened by my own lack of firsthand knowledge of the system, but it also reflected their understanding of bureaucracy. Rather than describing encounters with an abstract whole, a system that processed migration in a logical way, Luis and Angelina described a series of interpersonal encounters, offering me not accounts of people's roles but their first names, along with comments on how friendly or unapproachable each individual had been.

Even in Hong Kong, Luis and Angelina thought of themselves foremost as villagers. They were first *Ihaliap sa Hong Kong* (people from Haliap in Hong Kong), or "us, the Haliapian guys." Scaling up, they were OCWs, or "us, the Filipinos here." On Filipinos in Hong Kong more generally, they had two things to say. The first was that many women they met had come to Hong Kong for financial reasons in the aftermath of broken romantic relationships at home. For these women, Hong Kong represented a site of freedom and release. Many seemed to be conducting affairs and enjoying themselves by shopping. Second, Luis and Angelina saw that most Filipinos were taking on high levels of debt. Filipinos borrowed from Hong Kong finance companies and from one another to send money home. Because of debts and broken relationships, some Filipinos had committed suicide. Even in their own workplace, some, like Soledad, the senior Filipina housekeeper, had huge financial woes. She pressured Angelina to take out a loan with a finance company and turn the money over to her. Luis continually had to explain to Soledad that their church did not permit them to make personal loans.

Luis and Angelina spoke Tagalog at work so that their coworkers could understand them. Angelina joked that Hong Kong had improved her Tagalog more than her English. She and Luis rarely spoke Adyangan. If their coworkers heard, they explained, it might create "a bad impression." They clearly did not wish to disclose their indigenous ethnic identity and region of origin. Feeling at least partially excluded from the imaginaries of bayan in the Philippines, migration allowed them to experience themselves as Filipinos. At the same time, their ethnicity was occasionally an advantage in dealing with Hong Kong employment agencies and employers. Luis explained that Ilokano-speaking Filipinos "from the north" were considered humble, modest, and hardworking by Hong Kong employers. Employers expected that northern Filipinos would be diligent and financially responsible in contrast to Tagalog-speaking Filipinos, who some employers considered unreliable.

Central

On Sundays the business district of Hong Kong Island, known as Central, fills with Filipinas. Beginning mid-morning, small groups put down picnic blankets around the Star Ferry terminal, on Statue Square, under the headquarters of the Hong Kong and Shanghai Bank, and in the Chater Gardens park. As the day goes on, their ranks swell with more women emerging from churches and public transit. They sit and exchange news, gossip, food, and money late into the evening. Mobile Chinese vendors arrive to sell them food and drink. The word *Central* describes both the gathering and its location—the two are simultaneous.

Central recreates Hong Kong's financial district into a site of Filipino sociality and exchange. Here, NGOs representing migrant groups, Philippine municipal mayors looking for the overseas workers' vote, consular officials, and researchers all visit workers who would usually be inaccessible. This is the time when workers meet up with friends and fellow villagers and communicate with their kin and friends in the Philippines. Filipinos doing domestic work in Hong Kong command some of the highest salaries in the global market for domestic labor, but the costs of living in the city are also high. In Hong Kong domestic helpers are required to live in their employers' homes and cannot apply for a residency card. Other migrants can apply for residency after seven years, but domestic workers are specifically excluded from this immigration route. Living in, they receive board and lodging in kind, keeping their cash salaries low. Migrant domestic workers do unskilled, low-status work and are unable to become permanent residents. Filipino domestics are not generally welcomed into Hong Kong's public spaces, but at least they are tolerated. It is in the throngs of Central that Filipinas are thus at their most anonymous and most comfortable.

Central offers shops and services to meet migrants' needs for banking, shopping, socializing, and eating Filipino food. The landmark site for these services is the World-Wide Plaza shopping mall. World-Wide Plaza has Filipino banks and international remittance companies, package-sending services, telephone cards, telephones, cell phone cards, and food to eat in or take away. Being able to become permanent residents only by marriage to a local or a skilled migrant, Filipino domestic workers in Hong Kong dream of, prepare for, and invest in futures that will happen at home. Businesses in World-Wide Plaza advertise a wide variety of products and services to outfit these futures. Migrants can buy house-and-land packages, agricultural equipment, furniture, and cars on installment, all for delivery in the Philippines. Nearby churches—Catholic, Anglican, Iglesia ni Cristo, and more—offer worship, fellowship, and outreach programs. On any day of the week there are Filipinas running errands in the mall. Sundays are the day off for the majority of Filipinas, so the halls of World-Wide Plaza are jammed as soon as church services end.[5]

As relations with people and institutions at home occupy migrants' thoughts, Philippine government programs try to convince migrants and their households to make productive investments that will revive the ailing national economy. Development aid donors and migrant advocates have campaigned to reduce fees charged by banks and finance agencies to handle remittances. The idea is that more money arriving in the Philippines will produce economic growth. Thus migrants earn money, but it is not quite their own to dispose of as they see fit. Posters in World-Wide (the Filipino nickname for the mall) suggest how migrants can honor claims on their earnings made by both their families and their government. Migrants' experiences of Hong Kong are thus shaped by an assemblage of three intimate concerns: (1) family ties, what those at home expect to receive, and their relationships with fellow migrants; (2) institutional structures that comprise the programs, laws, and regulations of the Philippines and Hong Kong and the activities of the bureaucrats, recruiting agencies, and employers that implement them; and (3) working conditions in employers' households.[6] In private homes, the circumstances of migrants' work are difficult to regulate. Some migrants are able to build *understanding* with their employers;

others find them too *strict* and demanding, making it difficult to build social networks and earn the extra money they need to send home. Migrants' unpredictable circumstances abroad often lead to dreams of return home as a kind of solace.

Managing unpredictability ties migrants to ongoing exchanges with the spirit world, often mediated by those they have left behind. Filipinos consider migrants' success to be a matter of luck (in Tagalog, *suwerte,* but my respondents tended to use the English term) and migration as a kind of gamble, a testing of one's fate. Filipinos tend to believe that luck is proportionate to one's own innate value but can be influenced by good deeds and sacrifices. A successful migrant is a winner (Tagalog: *panalo*) in migration's game of chance, having invested his or her good deeds in the spiritual realm to produce money in the material realm.[7] To ensure that this luck will hold, a migrant must share his or her good fortune with others. Migrants who cannot redistribute their earnings feel anxious. Being stingy (Ilocano: *kuripot*) opens them to the ill will of others. This could cause their migration luck to sour and their earnings to dwindle.

SERVICE HUB AND SENSUAL EXPERIENCE

Central is noisy. Buses roar by and vendors hawk their wares. Cell phones are ubiquitous, though few migrants take voice calls in the din. Sunday is the day that many workers call home, usually organizing their calls by texting first. World-Wide offers several long-distance calling services. Its stores sell SIM (subscriber identity module) cards and "load" (prepaid) cards so that migrants can access Philippine cellular networks. This reduces the cost of sending messages to Hong Kong for their family and friends at home, shifting the bulk of the charges to the migrants themselves. Philippine mobile networks offer *pasa load* (load to share) for Philippine cellular networks. Pasa load is electronic value sent directly to numbers in the Philippines to fund incoming and outgoing calls and messages. Growing numbers of Filipino migrants use e-mail, Internet chat, Skype, and Friendster or Facebook, but these services were not yet widely accessible in rural areas like Ifugao during my 2005–2009 fieldwork.

Most migrants thus remained "texted in" to home, living in Hong Kong and the Philippines simultaneously. Their cell phones made migrants virtually present, moment by moment, across distance. Just the potential for this connection was a comfort. Luis and Angelina kept their phones in their pockets while working and by their bed as they slept. By creating this kind of long-distance copresence, cell phones opened up ways to extend and enrich villagers' understandings of and feelings about themselves in the world. Sending text messages just to say hello initiated and sustained villagers' affective ties.[8] Migrants abroad thus developed a self-awareness shaped by the continual emotional demands of being recognized, sharing goods, and expressing caring feeling across the virtual village. These patterns of connection emerge and persist through exchanges and gifts.

STAYING CONNECTED

In sending money home, most migrants I interviewed preferred to use bank-to-bank transfers. They also used specialized remittance agencies and informal channels, usually friends and fellow villagers going home on vacation, either for emergencies or when they proved to be cheaper. Hong Kong remittance agencies offered benefits such as free text-messaging cards or phone cards as well as confirmed receipt by text message when the money sent had been paid out in the Philippines.

Because of their numbers and the sophisticated nature of the Philippine cell phone market, Filipino migrants in Asia are offered services that are not widely available elsewhere. These services address the long-distance struggles in which migrants must engage, such as allowing cash value to be remitted directly to the cell phones of people who cannot afford the cost of initiating phone contact. Since almost twice as many Filipinos—over 30 million—had cell phones as had ATM bank cards in 2005, texting value home to be paid out through local networks is an efficient, though still costly, way to distribute remittances.[9] One service called "G-cash," set up by Philippines-based communications provider Globe, sells migrants cash value cards that then allow them to transfer balances to other Globe cell subscribers. The transferred value can be spent only at certain government agencies or businesses—bookstores, pharmacies, and so forth. G-cash charges a premium to allow migrants abroad to restrict the ways those at home can spend remitted money.

Sending goods home is another way migrants sustain their ties to kin and neighbors. Shipping services in World-Wide send *balikbayan* boxes to addresses all over the Philippines, charging a premium for remote areas. These are large cardboard containers filled with household items, packaged food, cosmetics, novelty products, towels, linens, and clothes. Their contents are either used or redistributed by the receiving household.[10] Receiving balikbayan boxes is so ubiquitous in the Philippines that people talk of the contents as "typical," "the usual stuff overseas workers send."[11] Storefronts on the top floor of World-Wide provide space to store and pack goods. The contents spilling out of these bags and boxes appear to be the stuff of daily life at home. Staples such as tinned meat, jam, coffee, milk drinks, and biscuits (the dry, hard, sweet British kind) are sent in bulk, in containers intended for long-term storage. The added cost of shipping these goods seems to undermine any savings on the items sent when compared to their purchase prices in the Philippines.[12] With the balikbayan box, though, it is the thought, not the cost, that counts. Most things sent are not souvenirs of Hong Kong. Instead, the items in these boxes replace things that migrants themselves would have bought to provision daily domestic life, as if they were still at home. Though some of the objects, like cosmetics, no doubt try to tell stories about cosmopolitan spaces and sophisticated personal tastes, much of each box is made up of utensils, tools, food, towels, soap, and linens. Carefully collected through migrants' frugal shopping over several months, these things speak about sustaining households and quotidian living. Sending goods reproduces migrants' identities as household members who share domestic concerns with those at home. By sending items for daily use, migrants remind their households of their long-distance affections and demonstrate, in a material way, how they continue to participate in those households.

The combination of texting, making phone calls, and sending boxes engenders a sense of immediacy. This sense of closeness sustains neighborhoods in terms of both emotions and economies. It allows migrants to remain engaged in everyday rituals that create a village sense of place. Text presence facilitates what anthropologist Raul Pertierra calls the "temporal structure of expectations," sustaining trust between kin and neighbors, making settlements into communities.[13] Through regular dealings with each other, villagers build a common pool of shared experiences, creating a common local world. With cell phones, the ability to text several times a day and call weekly allows migrants to remain, at least partially, within what Pertierra calls "village-time." Migrants communicate with those at home about value in the form of cash sent and spent as it intersects with the value of mutual displays of feelings of caring. The text messages and calls received by migrants are typically requests for funds to cover the expenses of school fees, weddings, funerals, unexpected medical costs, debts to neighbors, and livelihood emergencies. Sending funds to meet such requests constrains migrants' abilities to save their overseas earnings for future investment, but their prompt responses to crises at home renew trust and intimacy.

To meet unanticipated requests for large amounts, my migrant friends negotiated loans from Hong Kong finance companies against their salaries. When they had borrowed the maximum HK$30,000 (US$3,861) in 2005–2009, they could turn to their employers for advances or borrow additional funds from other migrants who had savings in the bank. Demand for loans to be sent back to the Philippines had created a secondary market for credit. Migrants became moneylenders, borrowing from credit agencies, then re-loaning to fellow Filipinas at higher rates of interest.

Migrants had also taken on a community-development role, often in partnership with the local government or an NGO. Place-based groups of migrants who met each week in Central often organized themselves to give back to their communities. The Asipulo–Hong Kong Benevolent Association first provided funds to build the new municipal stage and basketball court cum rice-drying pavement in 1995. In 1999 all the municipal mayors of Ifugao visited Hong Kong, funded by the congressman (who had judged the ethnic parade). The Ifugao Association of Foreign Workers in Hongkong (IAFWH) in Hong Kong had donated P25,000 (US$622) for the purchase of chairs for the waiting room at the Ifugao General Hospital in Lagawe and planned to donate another P116,000 (US$2,886) to build a home for people with disabilities.[14] The mayors met villagers in the Central gathering. They picked their way through the crowds, looking self-conscious in their informal uniform of satin baseball jackets and Ray-Ban-style sunglasses. Their visit recognized in a very public way that gifts of cash from migrants were an increasingly important source of money for Ifugao municipal government projects.

A Global Village

Acting as the material site for the reflexive practice of migrants' collective dreams, Hong Kong becomes their global realm. Just as the village emerges through engagements with nonlocal processes, this global realm is necessarily built on very particular sites. Central is structured as a fluid series of mini-meetings. While the gathering shifts and changes each week, it is laid out as a series of neighborhoods, grouped by province and municipality, working as a kind of ethnopolitical map of the Philippines. I found that I could navigate through Central by asking women in the crowd for directions to the spot occupied by particular language speakers, and from there establish coordinates for province-of-origin groups and, finally, municipalities and villages. In 2005, Asipulo, including Haliap, congregated near the "Black Man" statue in Statue Square.[15] Haliap villagers spent most of their days off with fellow villagers but also met up with other people from the Adyangan side.

On their picnic rugs, villagers talked about remittances. In 2005 all of the Haliap migrants were sending their household—typically an extended family—a monthly "allowance" via bank transfer. Other studies have indicated that Filipino migrants typically remitted a maximum of 75 percent of their monthly salary, with 30–50 percent being more common, and as Hong Kong salaries then ranged from between US$200 and US$500 per month, most households in the Philippines were likely receiving about US$150 per month from family members in Hong Kong.[16] Once my respondents' transfers home had been processed, they alerted the recipient, usually a sister or daughter, by text message. In 2005 my Haliap respondents reported that these monies sent home to Haliap were running between P7,000–P8,000 (US$124–142) per month. Household allowances were calculated in terms of Philippine peso needs rather than their absolute cost in Hong Kong dollars earned. These remittances covered regular family expenses such as electricity bills, rice purchases, transportation costs, cooperative fees, local school fees, clothing, health care, and children's schooling. In 2005 the average household income in Ifugao was approximately P4,500 (US$80) per month for a farming family of four, so a P7,000 (US$124) allowance provided a reasonably comfortable living by local standards.[17] University students, who were all studying nursing or accounting in either Baguio or Manila, received additional money to cover their individual fees, housing, clothing, and allowances for transportation and food. When the peso rose against the Hong Kong dollar, migrants looked for additional sources of income.

Central is also where important parts of Haliap's village exchanges took place. When a family required a pig to sacrifice for a particular ritual or life-course event—an engagement, wedding, baptism, or funeral—kin at home negotiated a price with their neighbors. Both families then sent text messages to Hong Kong to arrange payment between the migrants. Eventually the equivalent value would be either deducted from the regular amounts remitted home or absorbed into a generalized household reciprocity. Migrants also negotiated sales and mortgages on lands in the frontier settlements, sourcing lands through Hong Kong networks or following leads from kin at home.

The negotiable boundary of Haliap villagers in Hong Kong remained the ubfu, or exchange labor, group. In Hong Kong, though, it was cash rather than labor that people exchanged. In 2005, Nora, the most senior Haliap migrant, was setting up a rotating credit group described as "money ubfu." This was my chance to finally meet the much-respected Nora, and I was not disappointed. Not only was she a powerhouse in organizing community meetings and activities, but she was also the driving force behind the Haliap village network in Hong Kong. In 2007 each member was putting in HK$200 (US$26) per rotation into her rotating credit fund. With five members, each used the HK$1,000 (US$129) for a month before handing it on to the next. At the end of the rotation, each person got her initial HK$200 (US$26) back. Luis and Angelina did not join, because they did not have the money to invest. They were tithing to their church from their salaries and had already committed the rest to their family. Nora and the group did not entirely accept their explanations of their priorities and faith. Luis and Angelina took Thursdays—the Iglesia holy day— as their official day off. Although they could rarely join the rest of their fellow villagers for the full Sunday gathering, they nonetheless turned up each month for an hour or two. Nora told me, "They say they cannot join us, but really, if you observe them, they are joining when they need us. It is their Iglesia, it makes them . . . talk one way, and not share money, but really they still act the same. We just say nothing and do not call their attention to it. After all, they are our barrio-mates. They come when we call them to eat."

Angelina and Luis were less interested in pursuing regular financial exchanges with the Haliap group than they were in exploring their church relationships. Luis saw his intensified relationship with his church in terms of exchange, participating in tithing, prayers, and blessings. He explained to me that regularly attending worship and donating the appropriate thanksgiving gifts were conciliating him to God in a way that saw his prayers answered. "God gives me remedies," he explained. "The things I need, I just pray for and I will receive them." Their church discouraged borrowing and lending money, but this seemed impractical to Luis, and he preferred not to dwell on it. However, when Luis and Angelina needed to borrow small amounts of money, or learn about finance companies, they turned to Nora first.

Nora was lending money, working with capital she had borrowed from a finance agency and from a non-Ifugao migrant friend. She was lending at 4 percent—2 percent more than the 2 percent per month the finance agency charged her—but only to relatives and fellow villagers whose families she knew, as she could find her debtors or their families in the Philippines should they default on their loans. Most of her clients were Haliap people or from other Asipulo and Kiangan villages where she had kinship ties. Nora also sent money home to her husband to lend out at the prevailing local rate of 10 percent per month. Nora was a migrant who knew what to do. After fifteen years with one employer, she was earning more than HK$12,000 (US$1,558) per month by 2007. The bulk of her work was no longer child care but supervising construction workers who were renovating her employers' investment properties. Nora's own investments in the Philippines were suffering in comparison, however, since her husband was an inconsistent manager. Ironically, the longer Nora stayed away and the more she earned, the more she needed her extended family and village social networks to help her invest at home.

Coping by Remote Control

Other Haliap migrants like Nora become benefactors and patrons through their remittances and gifts. Their families and wider village networks look to them for leadership, innovative ideas for development, and assistance in emergencies. However, their investment and caretaking relations with those at home are never unproblematic, but simply the best available option. Because the Philippine government cannot afford to provide widespread social benefits, investing in personal networks is the one strategy that may entitle migrants to reciprocal aid in the future. Thus migrants' transfers home act as an informal and personal insurance policy to provide for their eventual retirement, care from their kin should they meet an accident, and to cover any emergency medical assistance their kin might need in the interim. This makes maintaining good relations with those at home a paramount concern.

The risk of borrowing from finance companies to invest or to meet emergencies was one that almost all migrants eventually took on. Finance companies required the borrower to give them his or her employer's landline phone number. Should the borrower fall behind in payments or the debt not be repaid in full, the company would call the employer's home repeatedly. A series of calls almost inevitably led to the employer's immediately terminating the migrant's contract. Angelina herself borrowed money to bring her neighbor Dulcie to Hong Kong, only for Dulcie to find her job intolerable. Dulcie returned to Haliap, and Angelina was left to pay off the loan. Dulcie was unlikely to repay her, but if she fell behind on the loan, Angelina would then lose her own job.

Migrants thus spent much of their time worrying about things at home. Ideally, they wanted their transfers of money to open up into shared stories and shared judgments of how to spend, what to invest in, and what the outcomes of their gifts should be. They used phone calls and text messages to create a shared narrative that did not exclude those left at home from progress or themselves from securing their investments for the future. Migrants talked about kinship and intergenerational obligation, but people at home often attached different meanings to migrants' cash gifts and allowances. Those at home often thought of cash received as entitlements or attempts to compensate them for the opportunities they themselves had forgone or work they had completed. While they worked in Hong Kong, migrants were often simultaneously involved in text message exchanges in their roles as sibling / parent / wage earner / investor / advisor / friend. When they met up together in Central, migrants would compare notes. Talking about their remittances and investments, they evaluated their relations, both emotional and economic, with the households that sent them to Hong Kong and with their kin and neighbors in the broader Haliap locality, shaping new sets of priorities and judgments.

People across Haliap—in Hong Kong, Barangay Haliap, and the outmigration areas—made it a priority to invest both time and money in keeping communication constant. Angelina and Luis calculated that they spent one-sixth of their combined Hong Kong earnings on cell phone load. This expenditure covered not just the costs of calls and text messages to their son, sister, parents, and in-laws but also communications with neighbors and friends in the Philippines and Hong Kong. Luis and Angelina estimated that each of them sent and received a minimum of fifteen text messages a day. This constant communication opened up new ways of understanding and practicing long-distance intimacy. Failing to answer the phone or text back promptly was interpreted as indicating emotional distance and displeasure or, if people were being generous, lack of load.

WHERE THE MONEY GOES

During my visits to Luis and Angelina in Hong Kong between 2004 and 2007, I found it difficult to secure time with Angelina on her own. Her employers required her to be constantly present in their home, while Luis was able to roam around the city, running errands, often with me in tow. Thus I developed a much clearer idea of Luis's experiences of Hong Kong and often learned about Angelina's experience through the lens of Luis's thoughts rather than directly from her. Much of what I learned is thus not typical for the majority of female migrants in Hong Kong who are there on their own and work for less elite Hong Kong employers. Nonetheless, Luis's and Angelina's personal experiences illustrate some of the key features of migrant experience in the city.

In 2005 Luis gave up his weekly day off. In return he earned an extra HK$1,000 ($129) per month working night shifts as a security guard. Luis initially described how this brought him closer to his employer, who seemed to appreciate that Luis was giving up his official free time for running personal errands, visiting friends, and worshipping. But Luis still needed to absent himself from work to remit money home, pay his loans, attend Iglesia ni Cristo worship, and buy groceries and sundries for Angelina and his employer. Running these errands gave him a chance to visit with other Haliap migrants and members of his church. Despite being boring and onerous, working nights allowed Luis to pass more or less freely through Hong Kong on most afternoons. His employer agreed that he could go out as long as his other tasks were done and he was contactable on his cell phone, and provided he reported on time for his 7:00 PM shift. Luis had some freedom but also a large debt.

Angelina and Luis initially borrowed against their salaries to buy rice fields that were farmed for them on a sharecropping basis by Angelina's parents. Angelina and Luis paid for the rice seed and medicines for the crop. They split the proceeds from the two harvests each year, keeping one-third for themselves. In 2005 the second harvest was sold for P12,000 (US$213). Together, they sent P7,000 (US$124) each month for the care of their son, Oscar, who stayed in the new house Luis and Angelina had built, also with their borrowed funds. The allowance for Oscar included P4,000 (US$71) for household expenses such as food and schoolbooks and P3,000 (US$53) for his principal caregiver. From Luis's 2004 migration to 2006, Angelina's younger sister, Tricia, took care of Oscar. Tricia was assisted by Luis's sister Sarah and Angelina's parents.

In mid-2006 Tricia married and started her own family. Luis and Angelina then transferred Oscar to the household of William, Luis's younger brother, who was helping Luis to buy land. Oscar moved to Nueva Viscaya to live with his uncle while Tricia and her family remained in Ifugao as caretakers for the house.

By 2006 Luis and Angelina believed they had made enough improvements to their Haliap house—adding two rooms, a kitchen, and an indoor bathroom/toilet—and they wanted to invest in productive assets. Such investments required a relative, usually a younger sibling, to forgo some of his or her own life options to care for crops or property in which he or she would not have an ownership interest. In 2007 Luis's brothers Samuel and William arranged for Luis to buy a citrus plantation near Kasibu, in Nueva Viscaya. Purchasing the farm was the first part of a strategy to expand their landholdings outside Barangay Haliap. Jerome, another younger sibling, became the first caretaker. Sometimes such investments became more like donations to family, who expected generalized reciprocity, than profitable activities. This was the case with Jerome. After Jerome's departure, Luis speculated that the ideal caretaker would be a second cousin. A cousin would be less likely than a sibling to resent his requests and waste his funds, but would also be close enough that he or she could not simply abscond with the monies sent.

Luis and Angelina also made a number of special payments, usually gifts and loans. Between September and December 2005 Luis sent money to his sister Amy, working with a foreign-owned call center in Manila. Amy had been training, without salary, in Manila for the previous two months, making cold calls to overseas brokerage firms to sell them investment packages in the Philippines. In December 2005 she had just been treated for dengue fever and typhoid, and Luis sent money to pay her hospital bills. With Luis coordinating by text message from Hong Kong, Amy and I met up at a food court in a shopping mall. Amy was with two people she called "sisters" who were from her new church: she had become a Mormon. Luis was reaching the end of his patience with Amy. Her sister, Sarah, had refused to help her out again, having sent her money the previous month. Instead, Sarah had reiterated her offer to pay for Amy to come back to Ifugao and baby-sit Sarah's three daughters. Amy, however, wanted to stay in Manila. Luis's second special payment went to an older brother, Randy, also in Manila, intended to cover his agency fees for a job as a carpenter in Dubai. Luis also funded the wedding expenses of Samuel, the younger brother who had found him the citrus plantation, and sent money for his father's remarriage and move to Nueva Viscaya. He then sent some money to Jerome, who had migrated to work on a farm in Malaybalay, Bukidnon, a frontier province in the uplands of the southern island of Mindanao, but found himself struggling. (Luis would soon have to help him return to Haliap and get back on his feet by offering him caretaking work, but Jerome had other ambitions.) Angelina, meanwhile, directed her earnings to servicing their bank loans, paying her mother's pension plan, saving for an upcoming vacation in the Philippines, saving for their son's school fees in a new school near his uncle's home, and giving a gift of cash for her sister Tricia's wedding. For all of these they had planned, yet unexpected requests continued to arrive.

In late 2006 Luis received a request for emergency funds from William, the brother who was caring for Oscar. William's car had collided with a motorized tricycle and injured a small child, who then needed extensive hospital treatment. To meet these costs, Luis again took the maximum loan of HK$30,000 (US$3,856) from JCM Finance, a financial services company in Central.[18] Reflecting on his dream of pohonon, or capital, Luis mused that he had considered P100,000 (US$2,004) a vast sum of money before he came to Hong Kong. He had imagined that such a sum would be sufficient to fund a secure livelihood. From Hong Kong, however, that amount seemed tiny. In the last four months of 2005 he and Angelina had remitted that much already, and he had borrowed P500,000 ($10,020) in total between 2004 and 2006. He calculated that he had redistributed more money since he arrived in Hong Kong than he had ever seen in Ifugao. Doing so, he considered, had transformed him into a different person.

The Cost of Redeeming Oneself

For Luis, Angelina's 2001 departure from Haliap made the difference. For the three years Angelina was on her own in Hong Kong, Luis was a single father. During that time he gave up drinking and worked diligently. He wanted to be a better father, to administer Angelina's remittances well, and to regain some respect in the community. He welcomed all the requests for help he received from their kin. Luis was thus able to use Angelina's migration and her remittances to renew relations with relatives who had forgotten them when they were poor. Later, when he had arrived in Hong Kong himself, Luis considered that his own migration had allowed him to respect Angelina properly, provide for his son and offer him good advice, and engage with his siblings as both equal and patron. Luis explained that although he and Angelina now expressed care for their son through phone calls, text messages, and gifts, their premigration circumstances had not allowed them to be nurturing parents. Angelina, too, described Luis as being "redeemed" and a much-improved partner and husband.

Angelina and Luis were very concerned about what impact their migration might have on their son. They were more than familiar with the "family values" account of women's migration. Together, they ensured that Oscar had access to his caregiver's cell phone and regular additions of cell phone load sent from his parents in Hong Kong by pasa load. Oscar sent them two or three text messages each day, to which his parents always replied. They had a thirty-minute voice call every Sunday. At his new school, Oscar socialized with several classmates whose mothers were also working in Hong Kong, so Luis hoped that his son did not feel his circumstances were unusual. Angelina knew that a mother's absence could produce emotional distress and maladjustment in children, but she judged that the alternative—a life of poverty and malnutrition with quarreling parents—would undermine whatever emotional advantages her presence might bring. Both Luis and Angelina had spent their adolescence living with relatives while pursuing education outside their village, and they considered such an arrangement to be a valuable part of a child's development toward young adulthood. Living with his aunt and uncle was a chance for Oscar to become close to extended family and build ties to provide him with practical and emotional support in later life. The high point of 2007 was when Oscar graduated from elementary school as valedictorian. Angelina attended the ceremony and returned with photographs and samples of schoolwork to share with Luis. The ways Luis and Angelina live across the virtual village opens up more profound questions about love and money.

CONSIDERING CARING WORK

Angelina did caring work. Her job as a maid required both physical and emotional labor as she "cared for the needs" (her words) of her employer and two teenage daughters. Her employer regularly sent her to her elderly mother's home to assist with elder care. While Angelina was in either house, she was always on duty and constantly available to the members of the family. Alongside cleaning and ironing, she provided emotional support and advice, listening sympathetically to dilemmas of clothing choice, social relations, or other personal concerns. Making humble, helpful suggestions, Angelina built emotional bonds. These bonds secured good working conditions and sustained her sense of self as someone who knew what to do and could cope up. Her employment relied on her pakikisama, her smooth relations with others. One of Angelina's prized possessions is a heart-shaped gold locket that her employers presented to her at Christmas in 2004. She pointed to it as evidence that her care for them was reciprocated. It was what she called an *extra,* a gesture of concern and reward toward her, and a *remembrance,* something she carries with her as a mark of her success in Hong Kong.

Angelina described how her job involved emotional work. As a maid in a Cantonese-speaking Hong Kong household, she had to conform to a new set of emotional norms and performances. Angelina had to *swallow* her feelings and not show affective responses to the work or to the ways her employers spoke to her. Angelina had to follow her employers in using the correct words and gestures and suppressing any inappropriate feelings that might be made evident on her face or in her body language. She thus learned a new set of gestures of deference, affection, and gratitude to display the appropriate emotions of a maid to her employers. This learning and performance—"the mundane emotional labor of the workplace"—secured her employment.[19] Angelina's emotional expression and suppression occurred when she translated her experience and feelings between Haliap and Filipino cultural frames and those of her Cantonese workplace. This meant Angelina's rather bounded daily life in Hong Kong required sophisticated techniques of self-management. She explained, "I'm not just a maid here, I'm a mother and I'm sending money, all together. So even if I'm not liking how my work is that one day, I can be happy that I'm advising my son or helping my mother."

One way to explain Angelina's work is to think about care as a commodity, using the concept of care chains. Care chains posit care as withdrawn from Third World households for export into global labor markets. The concept describes the linked relations that transport women like Angelina to developed economies in order to perform not merely physical labor—"caring for"—but also emotional labor—"caring about."[20] *Caring about* is "having affection and concern for the other and working on the relationship between the self and the other to ensure the development of the bond."[21] Care chains feature in a feminist political economy analysis that connects female workers, recruiters, agents, and employers. The concept describes labor as a commodity and theorizes that the agents in the chain appropriate the surplus value produced by migrants through physical labor and emotional labor. Care chains are described as extracting "emotional surplus value" from families in one place and delivering it to another, usually in the embodied form of a female migrant worker who performs emotional labor for a wage.

Though it seems an elegant concept, it is difficult to quantify emotional labor in an empirical case study. In the case of Angelina and Luis, it is challenging to specify where Angelina's emotional labor is performed, who benefits, and how much it is worth. Thus, while it is possible to measure the number and movements of migrants and the amounts of money they remit fairly accurately, emotional labor cannot easily be either quantified or contracted. If emotional labor is finite, the worker performing it must be redirecting care from kin to employer. Care chains should thus result in "care drains," localities or households where children and the elderly suffer from a deficit of parental and filial care. This analysis seems to anticipate that the intimate domestic sphere from which care is withdrawn will not be a space that has previously been penetrated by the redirected flows of value and new identities that support capitalism. The care chains analysis, like the "family values" critique of migration, predicts that substituting other carers for mothers will produce an "emotional void" within the family.[22] Yet the migrants who would leave behind this void seem to be rather mechanical, divorced emotionally from home by the institutions and discourses that shape their migration.

Considering how Angelina and Luis lived, the care chains account seems to be a poor fit. Luis also did emotional labor in his work and caring for home. And their extended family networks do not reveal an "emotional void" opened up by their absence. Instead, Angelina's and Luis's experiences of migration in Haliap suggest a different approach to emotions and economies.

DESCRIBING LONG-DISTANCE ATTACHMENTS

When Angelina talked about her feelings for those at home, she used her Adyangan vocabulary. The emotion saturating her relations with those at home was *iliw* (roughly, homesickness, the verb form being *mailiw,* to be homesick)— the same word used by Luis and by their families in the Philippines. The narrative below comes from my notes on a December 2005 visit to the Philippines and Hong Kong. Initially I met up with Angelina and Luis's extended family in Barangay Haliap before traveling on through Manila to board a plane and visit the couple in Hong Kong.

One December evening I sat with Luis's sister Sarah on the front steps of Luis and Angelina's house in Haliap. Sarah was waiting for a jeepney to take her back to her own home, husband, and children, about forty minutes down the road. It was dusk, and clouds were rolling down the mountains around us, rain falling in intermittent sheets. We were huddled under my umbrella, chatting, when her phone rang. Luis was calling from Hong Kong. He wanted to know when I would arrive and if I could carry some packages for him. Sarah and I answered together. We handed the phone back and forth, switching from English to a mix of Adyangan and Ilokano. "Can you bring some yeast?" Luis asked me. He was planning to brew Ifugao rice wine for his Hong Kong employer. Then he asked about my trip, the weather, the food. I started to worry about how much the call would cost and begged off, telling him that we would catch up when I arrived. Afterward, I asked Sarah if I had been rude. "No," she said, "he is having mailiw now and wants to talk about home."

Mailiw is an emotion. It does not really have a good, firm equivalent in English. When I asked Sarah, she said, "It's your feeling of homesickness. That feeling in your stomach you get when you are away for too long and it feels . . . wrong to you. And you want to see your place, your family, and your friends again." To illustrate her point, she told me about her thirteen-year-old cousin.

He had come to live in Sarah's household from his sitio outside Banaue to complete high school as a working student. His iliw grew so strong that he had to go home. "He never showed it to us," Sarah said, "but he tells me that at night he used to cry, by himself. He missed his place." I asked if you should be ashamed to show mailiw to other people. Sarah paused, then replied, "It's natural . . . but if it is too much, then you are not adjusting to your companions now. If you are mailiw, you are not enjoying your new place, so you cannot show them that." I asked if she was offended that her cousin left. She said, "No, we understood. His feeling was too heavy to stay." About her brother Luis and his feeling, she observed, "When his feeling is heavy, he must call!"

People feel iliw, a state of longing for place and people left behind, as a heaviness in the body. The word labels their feeling of a body out of place, a dis-emplaced corporeality. Geladé's Ilokano dictionary defines *iliw* as longing, homesickness, or nostalgia. *Mailiw,* the verb, means "to remember with affection (as in an absent friend, relatives, etc.); to long for, to long to see; to visit (an absent friend, etc.); to be homesick, nostalgic."[23] Though it weighs one down, mailiw is a state that one can choose to some extent to reveal or conceal from others. While Sarah, Luis, and Angelina speak fluent English, they rarely translated mailiw for me after this. Iliw was something they expected me to understand as the key to explaining their shared experiences, because it works as the ground of the intersubjective long-distance field in which they interact. Identifying iliw in Luis let Sarah create empathy and sustain intimacy across the village. The extent to which one feels iliw marks one's adjustment to new circumstances. Extending iliw to Luis in Hong Kong brought him into alignment with village life. Just like their cousin, if Luis could not contain and manage his iliw, he might have to come home. Identifying iliw in Luis and helping him to assuage it with talk of plans and tastes of home sustains the village by making it virtual.

A week after his phone call, I was in Hong Kong with Luis. I asked him about iliw. Luis told me that the feeling of iliw is in the heart and in the head and that he feels like crying when he is "having mailiw." But he can soothe himself. "When I'm mailiw, I'll take a picture and look at it—a picture of my family—it makes my heart feel better . . . and I'll call home. Now that we have cell phones, it is much better. Before, when I could not call, I felt very mailiw, but now just a little. Because every time I have that feeling, I can call."

Luis thinks all Filipino migrants share this feeling: "In general, Filipinos here get mailiw when they are hard up [struggling] with work. When they remember their purpose in the Philippines, and the situation there." For Luis, work takes his mind off the mailiw feeling. He does not share it with others, but keeps it to himself. "I just control my feeling and say, 'Oh, I'll be going home soon, the time will come,' like that. And I take a Hope [cigarette] and a coffee and say, 'I'm here.'"

Mailiw motivated Luis to contact his family and friends in the Philippines. "We feel close by calling them and saying hello, or by sending texts. We are no longer sending letters; it's too slow. Sometimes we send tapes when people are going home. Speaking on the phone, mostly, is what keeps us feeling close." The content of his telephone exchanges expressed intimacy: "I show my feeling for my family by giving my advice and asking them what is happening, if there are any problems . . . things like that." Luis admitted, however, "Sometimes I don't want to talk to them, because they only talk to us when they need money." After making this comment, he quickly moved on to explain how sharing money was also a way of sharing emotion: "Sending dollars shows feeling! I am happy sending, because I know they need it and that's my obligation. I am here in Hong Kong to send money so they'll have some money for food, clothing, things in the house, and medicine. . . . I'm happy if I send dollars to them, because I know that they are also happy. We share the feeling."

While Luis and I were sitting together in Central's Statue Square with my voice recorder running, he received a text from Tricia. His sister-in-law asked him for money to pay for his mother-in-law's health plan, the costs of renovating the kitchen of his house, and some seed capital for her to set up a sari-sari store. We read the message together and began to laugh, Luis sputtering: "feeling close is . . . also feeling like a bank."

Evaluating Intimacy

Ifugao iliw rather than English *love* is what connects Haliap migrants to those at home. The most frequent translation of the English word *love* into Adyangan Ifugao is *penpenhod,* intense liking. The root verb, *penhod,* can describe both liking a meal and person, so my respondents often preferred to use the English term *love* to talk about their intimate, interpersonal relationships. Though Adyangan Ifugao does not have quite the same detailed vocabulary describing emotional states that is available in English, this clearly does not mean that people do not reflect on their feelings. People tend to use English emotion words—*ashamed,* in particular—except when the nuanced cultural differences are very important to them. This should not be understood as suggesting that Adyangan social relations lack intimacy. Instead, "sharing" and "showing" "feeling" describes an intimacy of affective alignment and exchange rather than the verbal, emotional self-disclosure that English tends to shape. This intimacy is not a special feature of long-distance ties but arises through a variety of other everyday ways of interacting too. With migration intimacy is built, renewed, and sustained by exchanges of value that can be expressed as work, cash remittances, and phone load or objects such as household things, mementos, and photographs.

Research on intimacy between Filipino migrant mothers and their left-behind children has been the basis of the care chains analysis.[24] Studying migrants' families in an urban center in the Visayas, sociologist Rhacel Parreñas described the ways global economic structures restricted the intimacy possible within transnational families, particularly those in rural areas in the early 2000s. In her study, long-distance communication between family members was not always smooth or equal. Children and migrants' other dependents lacked access to call credits needed to initiate emotional exchanges. Instead, they had to wait for displays of caring from abroad. Parreñas concluded that mobility and distance meant that intimacy in Filipino transnational families was not "full." Larger systems of global inequality denied the members of the transnational families she studied the emotional benefits and security enabled by physical presence. Instead, migrants' remittances and phone calls became ultimately unsuccessful efforts to generate the kind of familial intimacy her left-behind respondents desired. While the transnational family is a contested emotional field, the yearning that Parreñas reports among left-behind children for a present mother reflects an idealized middle-class urban family life. From a 1990s Haliap perspective, this family seemed desirable but remote, part of the village of abstract institutional plans, of UNICEF and the health workers, not yet the world of day-to-day village lives.

By universalizing and thus promoting what is a more particular account of intimacy, the care chains approach reflects contemporary, commonsense understandings of gendered family roles that predominate in the middle-class, northern European West. Care chains assume a universal understanding of intimacy as a quality that emerges from intense, long-standing interpersonal ties. What is popularly considered to be true intimacy typically requires long periods of face-to-face contact; reciprocal sharing of affective states; and the mutual disclosure of a person's emotional self-understandings, desires, dreams, and individual life story.[25] These ideas about intimacy rely on what are relatively recent norms for heterosexual, middle-class romantic relationships and nuclear-family households. Intimacy's antithesis, alienation, is associated with the global, urban, and technologically mediated world of the marketplace, a sphere where the nuclear family is under threat.

Intimacy in Haliap is characterized by creating shared narratives rather than physical proximity. This is a kind of intimacy that cultural theorist Lauren Berlant describes as having "at its root an aspiration for a narrative about something shared, a story about oneself and others that will turn out in a particular way."[26] This intimacy arises from emotional labor, the work of connecting, sharing, telling stories, listening, responding. However, shared stories now also emerge from long-distance and technologically mediated forms of closeness rather than simply interacting face-to-face. Luis and Angelina's extended family exemplifies how acts of practical care build and sustain this intimacy. It requires a certain material security and minimal level of provisioning to enable people to express emotion in appropriate ways, through redistributive gifts. Thus Luis and Angelina actually feel closer in Hong Kong to each other and to their kin, because they can do the things they are obliged to do as son, daughter, parent, and sibling. Sarah, Luis's sister, said much the same thing in 2005. She feels closer to Luis since he has, she said, "remedied" his life. He now behaves like a good husband and has taken on his proper role as an older brother, so Sarah is more demonstrative toward him, and vice versa. Indeed, Sarah and Luis both suggested their entire natal family actually feels much closer since they have spread out across the Philippines, Dubai, Singapore, and Hong Kong.

Luis and Angelina's story challenges the universal emotions and family forms that underpin care chain accounts. Their extended family and village networks are not simply another rent-seeking actor like the finance companies or employment agents, appropriating the surplus generated by migrants. Migrants' family and village ties and emotions are not just personal choices and their consequences merely personal and individual problems. Instead, migrants' judgments balance conflicting demands and values, performing selves that remain embedded in a collective, reflexive village practice.

STRUGGLING OVER VALUE

Angelina and Luis also experienced iliw as constraint. Because of the strength of the feeling, they could not save as efficiently as they might wish. "Everyone always has their hand open, so Luis's money becomes scattered," Sarah said of her brother. To forgo expressing this caring through sending value home would undermine Luis's new self-identity. In the Philippines, Luis's siblings compared notes on the amounts he sent them and the purposes to which these would be put, trying to figure out with whom he currently feels close and with whom he is *dismayed* (meaning fed up with or has had enough of). But Luis did not consider all of his family's claims on his money to be reasonable, and conflict and tension resulted. Luis reflected on his premigration ideas: "I used to think migrants had no problems. Now I know . . . there are many debts . . . Many broken relationships . . . broken because of money and separation."

Luis's younger siblings expected gifts from their older brother without being obliged to reciprocate. However, Luis expected them to follow his advice in return. Luis observed how his Cantonese employer managed his economic dependents and expressed a wish that his own siblings would show a similar kind of deference. Over the phone, his sister Amy rejected his advice, saying, "You are not our father." She also complained to me about Luis's attitude to her requests for cash in the same terms. She thought Luis should be grateful that he had people who appreciated him, because his donations to them would maintain his good luck in Hong Kong. His siblings' attitudes dismayed Luis, but he felt he could not refuse their requests. His role as older brother and his *iliw* obligated him to demonstrate his care. At the same time, Luis observed that his Hong Kong Chinese coworkers could rely on their government, rather than kin, for assistance.

The caring aspects of the Hong Kong state intrigued Luis and Angelina. Their coworkers told them about the various services and benefits available to citizens. Luis and Angelina compared these—insurance, health care, subsidized housing—unfavorably to the very limited services on offer in Haliap. They were aware of Philippine government initiatives to assist migrants abroad to prepare to return home and participate in development. Both Luis and Angelina contributed to the government's Social Security System (SSS) and health care plans (PhilHealth) and paid their Overseas Workers Welfare Administration (OWWA) levy. They opened special *pangarap* peso accounts with the Philippine National Bank, where they would save Hong Kong dollar deposits in the Philippine banking system in pesos to prepare for their eventual return. However, they rarely made deposits, because their other financial needs were more compelling. Like other migrants, they found their dreams of economic security threatened by rising familial expectations and the continuing financial and political crisis in the Philippines.

Rather than planning for eventual returns, many Filipinos in Hong Kong planned to move onward to seek permanent settlement elsewhere. The most popular destinations were English-speaking liberal democracies with welfare states and temporary migration programs—Canada, Australia, and the United Kingdom—where there had been strong demand for workers in the health and social care sectors. In World-Wide in 2007 Luis showed me a Philippine government poster that asked migrant workers to remit through the banks, rather than informal channels, to increase the Philippines' gross domestic product. Contemplating the fine print, with its encouragement to contribute to the Philippines' national standing in a global contest measuring the formal economy, Luis was skeptical. "This government," Luis observed, "just wants our money but won't give us anything in Haliap. It will just scatter it instead." As Luis explained of Filipino migrants collectively, "What we are seeking, really, is a government that cares for its people."

Angelina and Luis considered their lives in Hong Kong to be an improvement on their premigration circumstances. They longed to return home but were concerned they had not yet secured their livelihood. Luis had variously planned to farm organic rice or start a piggery in Haliap. Angelina planned to start a vegetable buy-and-sell business from their citrus plantation in Kasibu. While waiting for their trees to mature enough to produce fruit, she planned to grow tomatoes and perhaps squash for sale. Yet they had other dreams too. One was to move onward to another overseas future. Angelina imagined them all living together in Canada, with Oscar becoming an Iglesia pastor, a spiritual guide for future Haliap migrants. Deciding what their next move would be became an ongoing research project. During 2007 and 2008 they were corresponding with an Adyangan-side friend, Jojo, who had left Hong Kong for Canada's Live-in Caregiver Program in 2006. Assessing her reports of life as a domestic worker there, they debated the merits of Angelina's taking a lower salary for three years against a chance of becoming a permanent resident and being allowed to seek nondomestic work.

By working in Hong Kong, Angelina and Luis had become not only a maid and a gardener but also patrons, investors, and long-distance parents, children, and siblings. They struggled to shape the behavior of those at home and to save their earnings. They found new ways of socializing, sustaining relationships with text messages, voice calls, and meetings at church and in Central. They developed new ways to judge what they expected of each other, family at home, and of employers, moneylenders, finance companies, remittance agencies, and governments. They shaped a shared village sense of placeness that came increasingly from text messages, conversations, and gifts linking home to away, but they also remained strongly characterized by affective connection. Here, emotional nurturing and economic provision are not separable, nor is emotional labor exclusively feminine. Instead, both nurturing and providing are elements of the care—in their words, "sharing" and "feeling"—within which people cultivate the new personal attributes they need to attain their dreams. These long-distance exchanges of goods, gifts, and communications become the ground for their thoughts and feelings about themselves in the world, and the pressure to sustain and intensify these exchanges both pushes and enables them to explore further afield.

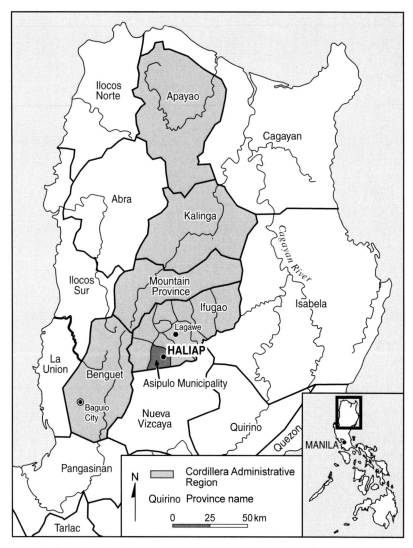

MAP 1. Haliap, Asipulo, location

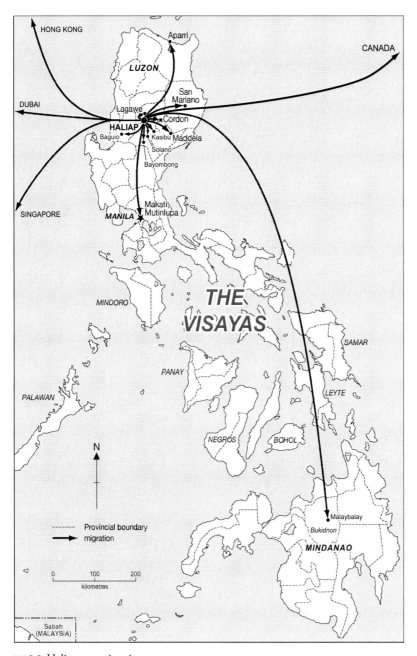

MAP 2. Haliap out-migration

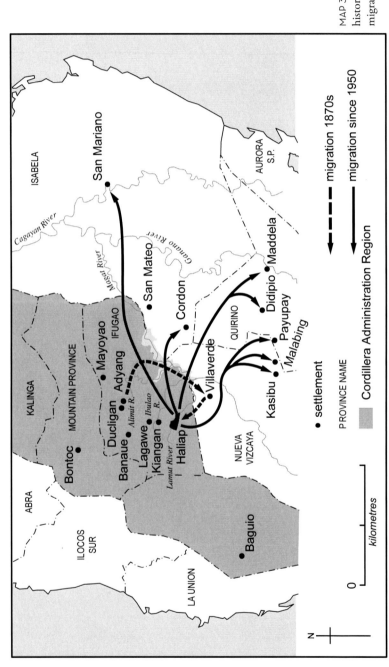

MAP 3. Haliap historical migration

- - - migration 1870s
——— migration since 1950

● settlement

PROVINCE NAME

Cordillera Administration Region

ISABELA

San Mariano

AURORA
S.P.

Cagayan River

Magat River

Gurano River

San Mateo

Cordon

Maddela

QUIRINO

Didipio

Payupay

Malabing

Villaverde

Kasibu

KALINGA

MOUNTAIN PROVINCE

Mayoyao

IFUGAO

Adyang

Ducligan

Banaue

Alimit R.

Ibulao R.

Lagawe

Kiangan

Haliap

Lamut River

NUEVA
VIZCAYA

Bontoc

ABRA

ILOCOS
SUR

LA UNION

Baguio

0

kilometres

N

FIGURE 1. The Hagalap (Lamut) River and upper Haliap valley (2005)

FIGURE 2. Luis, Angelina, and coworkers, Hong Kong (2005)

FIGURE 3. Luis at Stanley Beach, Hong Kong (2005)

FIGURE 4. Luis and Angelina on the Star Ferry, Hong Kong (2005)

FIGURE 5. Luis in Statue Square, Hong Kong (2005)

FIGURE 6. Nora's money-ubfu group, Chater Gardens, Hong Kong (2007)

FIGURE 7. Luis photographing the Rockies, Alberta, Canada (2009)

CHAPTER 5 ◆ Haunted by Images

PHOTOGRAPHS AND VIDEO MESSAGES moving across the village reveal how migration shapes Haliap personhood. This is because photographs help migrants create the shared stories that tie them to those at home. But perhaps the most important thing about photographs is that they do not circulate alone. Photographs move alongside the text messages, phone calls, e-mails, letters, and boxes of goods, all of which form part of the "migrant archive." As Arjun Appadurai describes, this archive is "a continuous and conscious work of the imagination, seeking in collective memory an ethical basis for the sustainable reproduction of cultural identities."[1] The archive contextualizes and makes material people's experiences of migration. It thus offers marginal people opportunities to dream their own global dreams. Because the archive is formed by private messages that accrete as they circulate through an extended public, it exists both alongside and beyond the media debates on the Filipina and migration I described in chapters 3 and 4. Though its content is personal, Appadurai describes it as a politically contested space: a site of "voice, agency and debate, rather than . . . mere reading, reception and interpellation."[2] In Haliap, migrants' photographs locate persons within a dense network of affective and obligatory ties as well as exchange, gift, and redistributive relations. Photographic prints serve as reminders, promissory notes, and preemptive displays. Exchanging photographs condenses and expresses the affects attached to the borrowing, indebtedness, and economic care that sustain village placeness.

Sending photographs home is a material act of showing and sharing feeling, supporting both family claims on migrants' earnings and migrants' claims to make investments and have these managed by kin and community. Photographs circulating in Haliap thus have particular themes, showing a "finite and well-defined range of subjects, genres and compositions."[3] These photographic genres are shaped by the work people want their photographs to do, the limits of the technologies they can access, and the material fragility of the images themselves. This chapter begins by exploring what migrants' photographs can tell us about the ways they feel and think about themselves in the world, then moves on to consider how best to describe their emergent global subjectivities.

Kinds of Photographs

Cell phone photographs form an important aspect of the archive. Photographs attach meaning to text messages that, on their own, are difficult to share with others and hard to store. By 2007 all the Haliap migrants in Hong Kong owned cell phones with built-in cameras that they used to store collected photographs. In 2005–2009 none of my respondents could afford the cost of services that would transfer images directly from phone to phone. Their electronic albums include pictures taken with the phone in both Hong Kong and Haliap, as well as images created by rephotographing prints in other migrants' personal collections. Migrants often composed text messages after looking at a photograph stored on their cell phone, carried in their wallet, or displayed on the wall of their room. When they displayed or read to their friends the messages they had received, they frequently showed them their most recent photograph of the sender too.

Displaying photographic prints in domestic spaces makes migrants present in the daily life of the village. As material objects, these photographs impel migrants into intimate relations among their left-behind kin.[4] Photographs in Haliap houses keep people talking about and thinking of those in Hong Kong. Likewise, when those in Hong Kong circulate photographs from home, they allow the village to encompass the spaces in which they are sojourning. Families usually display prints of the most recently received photographs in the room from which they text or call. The images provide material evidence that the migrant is doing well and that debts at home will be repaid. A current photograph of a migrant is both a source of prestige—a display of their global links for visitors—and of comfort, reminding them of a relationship they can turn to in a crisis.

Photographic prints also travel from Haliap to Hong Kong. These are fewer in number but just as important. Migrants circulate photographs on Sundays in Central, exchanging information on relations at home. The photographs they receive document life events that migrants have funded, such as graduations, weddings, funerals, and village festivals. These tend to be images of large groups of people against a background decorated with paper flowers and strings of lights. Another genre of photograph shows the happy outcomes of the receipt of migrants' funds, documenting new fields, repaired houses, new agricultural equipment, new clothes, DVDs and CD players, or commemorative banners for community events, recording migrants' names as sponsors. Such photographs are of landscapes and objects rather than people. These images provide migrants with evidence of their gifts, further materializing a sociality shaped by reciprocal exchange, and they are produced to intensify that exchange. Luis once complained to me that "sometimes they only send pictures when they've spent my money, because they want more; otherwise, nothing."

The veracity of photographs creates anxiety for everyone. In Haliap relatives are anxious that the progress and gratitude migrants expect to see will be shown to them by the images sent from home to Hong Kong. Migrants abroad express concerns that photographs from home may be staged or faked. They worry that their kin have not managed their investments properly nor made the kinds of substantial improvements that the photographs might suggest. They want independent photos. When Luis bought his citrus plantation, he was not satisfied with the few landscape photographs sent on by his siblings. Angelina returned from her vacation with photographs that documented the farm more thoroughly. Luis examined them to assess how his family members were managing and showed them to his fellow migrants to discuss their own experiences by way of comparison.

The last genre of photograph is the *solo* photographic portrait. Though fewer in number, portraits of individual subjects do a familiar and important kind of work. Part of the reason we are attracted to our own photographic images lies in the ways they allow us to play with time. Our pictures offer us a chance to shape ourselves by letting us reinvent ourselves the way we would like others to see us. Pictures of us can suggest to others that features of the context or environment are somehow the result of our own personal capabilities. Experimenting with our photographs can allow us to establish our presence in a social space where we feel uncertain. Photographs freeze, frame, and fix us as their subjects. By being simultaneously immediately present and showing us what has already happened, photographs blur our usual experiences of time and space. Pictures can suggest that an event their subjects intended to occur in the future has already come to pass.[5]

Migrants' photographic portraits shape future selves by informing the things expected from them by those at home. Their portraits challenge migrants to become (more like) the person who appears in their image. Sociologist Celia Lury describes this aspect of photographs as "prosthetic biography," a way of attaching a new history to the self through manipulating one's image that allows photographs to act with "retrodictive prophecy."[6] A migrant's success in manipulating her image thus depends on her ability to anticipate how her intended audience will interpret the photograph. The viewers of her portrait must anticipate the particular future biography her image suggests. Where image and biography coincide, migrants' photographic portraits create the shared stories that sustain long-distance intimacy.

Kinds of Persons

Solo portraits make visible the forms of social status that Haliap people describe with metaphors of social size. Migrants' solo portraits show them as (in English) big persons, meaning they are portrayed as being central to networks of exchange. "Big" is an emic category in Haliap. Big people are local figures, formerly kadangyans (elites) and now likely to be merchants or dealers or even returned overseas workers, who build their personal power through generosity, charisma, wisdom, and cultivating clients. They can sometimes even transform themselves into politicians by converting cash, goods, and goodwill into votes. This local Haliap use differs from the more familiar "big man" complex, where big men embody a mutant form of traditional authority made possible by their preferential engagements with the intermittent power of the state. In the Philippines, such big men would be the *warlords,* politicians who engage in high-level corruption and can afford to be rude and violent toward their clients, a category that is not evident in Haliap village politics.[7]

Of course, other kinds of photographs also make visible the shape of personhood, but it can be more difficult to see that shape in other genres. All photographs document, maintain, expand, and materialize relations that extend beyond the boundaries created by people's individual identities. However, persons in most photographs more often than not are represented as a set of social relations to others—their siblings, their household, their kin group, their neighborhood cluster, and their village of Haliap—rather than bounded, individual selves. This is why most of the photographs circulating across Haliap depict people within kin groups, shared projects, or labor exchange groups, and in community-wide celebrations. Villagers were often unable to give me the names of all the people pictured in the photographs they sent and received. However, they were unperturbed by this and described in detail the event where the photograph was taken, the economic exchanges underlying its sociality, and the village ties the images enacted for them, even if they could not name all the faces. Such photographs reminded everyone that people are constituted through relations with others and that these relations depend on values arising with feelings shown, amounts, and objects exchanged.[8] In this field a solo individual portrait stood out as a claim to individual status and important intimate connection.

Following Photographs Home

Not quite a year after Luis arrived in Hong Kong, in July 2005 he asked me to help him buy a camera. He wanted to join in the exchange and circulate his own print photographs alongside those of the other Haliap migrants. Together, we took a series of shots that Luis then had printed. Some, he decided, were suitable only as personal mementos; others he sent back to the Philippines. Tracking the fate of the photographs he and Angelina sent home shows how migrants try to transform themselves through their images.

One photograph showed Luis on the beach beside the Stanley Markets on Hong Kong Island. Luis had suggested we each pose for a photograph by the water's edge. Reflecting on the image I shot, Luis pointed out that he was wearing a turtleneck shirt as well as black Chinese cotton slippers. The photograph depicted him in the uniform of a helper and reminded him that traveling around Hong Kong in these clothes, he had been stopped by the police, on three separate occasions, because the police suspected he was an undocumented worker from Mainland China. Because this image depicted what he knew people at home would consider to be his *low work,* he decided not to send it but to keep it as a remembrance of my visit.

Of the photographs he did send home, one was of him with Angelina, sitting on a bench at Ocean Park. Ocean Park is a Hong Kong amusement attraction displaying panda bears, dolphins, and seals mixed in with Disney-themed areas. It is a popular middle-class leisure destination, on the Filipino OCW list of must-see sites. Angelina chose the bench featuring Disney's Little Mermaid for the picture. Their image suggests they participate in a global popular culture and consume leisure services as tourists. They deemed it suitable to share with kin in Haliap. Another similar image sent home was one I had taken of the two of them sitting on the Star Ferry.

The photograph Luis described to me as "most important" to him was a portrait of him taken by Angelina. This picture was taken just after Luis had remitted their Christmas gifts (of cash) to Haliap. It depicts Luis standing in Statue Square, near the World-Wide Plaza in Hong Kong's Central district. He is carrying a promotional bag from the Philippine National Bank. The bag indicates he has remitted an amount sufficient to merit a giveaway from the bank. Behind him is Santa's Village, a display of Christmas decorations erected to celebrate the season, blocking access to the benches and steps on which Filipino workers usually congregate. Luis is wearing his church-going clothes. Angelina told me his watch and shoes were purchased with money borrowed from a finance agency. Luis's image here speaks of success and affluence.

To stand in front of the camera clean, well dressed, and prosperous cites Luis's Ifugao ethnicity in particular ways. He is presenting himself in ways that are intended to convey messages about both his sophisticated tastes and his personal economic potency against stereotypes of backwardness and ignorance. His clean, leisure-oriented clothes, new shoes, and cigarette emphasize that he can afford some personal luxuries alongside the gifts he sent home. There is no sign that his apparent success depends on borrowing. The Luis in the picture looks more like a government official than a farmer—solid, secure, and worthy, a person who can offer assistance, guidance, and material help to others. In Haliap terms, he has had himself photographed as a big person. How his family in Haliap received these photographs was a subject we discussed on my return visit to Hong Kong.

Luis laughed as he told me the photos had generated a flurry of text messages and phone calls requesting loans. Since his status depends on reciprocity and the debts of gratitude, the number of requests indicated that people held him in increasing esteem. Luis's laughter expressed his relief that the photographs had worked. Circulating his image drew others into his project of remaking himself, distributing his sense of himself as potent and successful across a wide set of social relations.

HOW PHOTOGRAPHS BECOME CONSUMED

Visiting Barangay Haliap in late 2005, I followed the fate of Luis's prints. In Haliap houses very few photographs are framed and hung. Instead, people arrange photographs on shelves, tack them to doors, or store them in plastic-leafed booklets, keeping them easily accessible. Luis's photographs were shared with guests and handled regularly by Luis's and Angelina's families. Prints are inherently fragile objects, given the damp of Haliap's rainy season and their treatment by curious children. Luis's photographs had quickly become mildewed and covered in greasy fingerprints. Their time in the migrant archive was fleeting. About three months after they arrived, they were declared "consumed." His sister-in-law, Tricia, cut out the figures of people, including Luis's "most important" image, and added them to a large collage on the wall opposite the front door of his house.

Tricia's collage had as its background a huge (5'×3') poster of a waterfall and also featured clippings from glossy magazines. The collage was notable for its large scale and the way it dominated the room where visitors were received and phone calls and text messages were sent. The collage placed both Tricia and her boyfriend, Jesse, on a liminal landscape that seemed to be her own global imaginary. Luis's figure was pasted on alongside photos of office towers and the cutout figures of several Haliap neighbors, now also migrants. Tricia grounded her global imaginary in current kin and village relations. She explained that her collage was "just for fun," then elaborated, "and to remind myself that I have a dream to work abroad too." She seemed to be waiting for her own life to begin, mapping her dreams with this collage.

Tricia was then in the enviable but restrictive role of caretaker for the house and for Oscar, Angelina and Luis's son. It was what villagers called an "improved" house with several rooms, including an inside kitchen and bath, electricity, and a galvanized iron roof, but it wasn't hers. The kitchen was dominated by Angelina's brand-new refrigerator, but Tricia stored only margarine and oil in it. She bought most of the food on a day-by-day basis but found that the allowance Luis and Angelina sent was insufficient. Tricia was P4,000 ($US75)—more than one month's household allowance—in debt to the new Haliap cooperative store, largely for purchases of basic needs, including food and cell phone credits.[9] Tricia imagined herself elsewhere, but her sister and brother-in-law's need obliged her to remain in Haliap. Like other caretaker relatives of migrants, Tricia used the resources and information she received to shape her own dreams of migration. Her collage exemplifies how the migrant archive increases the capacity to aspire and the possibility of taking risks for people who are not (yet) migrants themselves. By adding bits of the photographs sent by Luis to her collage, she mapped into a network of relations that would enable her, too, to take the risk of going into business—starting a store selling home-baked goods—and to aspire to further success through migration. Tricia had responded to Luis's July 2005 photographs by texting him her own list of requests, including an oven for baking.

Photographs sent by migrants generally did not seem to spark much debate in Barangay Haliap. Villagers rarely considered how the images of relatives and friends in Hong Kong might be staged. Instead, the very materiality of the photographs seemed to support their faith in migration as the most effective remedy to local struggles for livelihood and development. Luis's neighbors, brothers, sisters, and sister-in-law considered Luis's photographs to document real increases in his material wealth, personal well-being, and potential to act as patron within the village. When I suggested that Luis and Angelina were struggling with finances, his neighbors were dismissive, referring me back to the images and talking about his abilities to meet most requests for assistance. Luis wanted to avoid sharing his own struggles; by doing so he could maintain his pride and feel he remained big in local people's eyes. Those at home offered him seemingly endless stories of bad news of their own, so he would send more money. Left-behind kin thus performed in what migrants described as a "pitiful" and abject manner, "opening" their problems in texts but more often in phone calls.

Migrants' self-portraits presented a version of the migrant's self that seemed less accessible than in real life, an absent presence that was smooth and whole. By making physically present a relationship in which the other party was not engaged in a dialogue, photographic images created an unusual moment of autonomy for their subject. Self-portraits enabled migrants to engage in a kind of monologue about their success in realizing their dreams. This kind of monologue, however, existed only when it had an audience. Thus the kind of relational personhood Haliap people shaped was self-scaling; migrants alternated between experiencing themselves as big and small based on the responses of others. Across Haliap, the desire for status and the desire to redistribute came together. People at home responded to migrants' photographs with requests, and migrants became the big persons of their images. But migrants then found themselves unable to save their earnings, so their continued success at home depended on further borrowing and the migrant thus remaining abroad. By 2007 Angelina and Luis were both borrowing from a Hong Kong finance company at 27 percent per annum, risking their employment contracts and thus their migration and the projects it was funding at home. It was, Luis reflected, as if they had found a new kind of gambling.

FAMILIAR ANXIETIES

Rather than providing stability, migration intensified familiar anxieties. Though Angelina had intended to complete only two contracts in Hong Kong and Luis one, in 2006 they decided to remain abroad. They did not yet have the capital they needed to realize their plans. Examining their photographic portraits brought this anxiety into focus for Luis. His pictures showed a redeemed and transformed self, but as he faced his debts in Hong Kong, these same self-portraits haunted him, showing him that he had not truly reformed his old ways. It seemed the longer Angelina and Luis remained abroad, the stronger their subjective experience of imposture and the associated feelings of anxiety and longing became. Because their photographs were material and were consumed, they continually sent home new, better, and more successful portraits to maintain their hard-won social position. In shaping a village sociality based on economic exchange, photographs thus showed a kind of inflation—each image of success had to somehow top that of the previous portrait.

When Luis talked about his size, he reflected on his affective experiences of being both recognized for and refused the identity he was trying to establish for himself. Luis explained that when he could not grant loans and make gifts, he felt he had failed in his plans and become smaller, losing status: "when they are disappointed in me, I feel small." However, when he could share his savings or bonuses or take on extra work or loans, he continued to be recognized—and to recognize himself—as the patron of his photographic portraits. Luis described how imagining the ways people felt when they had received his photographs and gifts made him feel satisfied and secure: "Then they cannot look at me as if I am become small." This sense that he is big to those at home enables him to cope up with doing low work in Hong Kong.

Considering how Tricia trimmed down Luis's most important photographic portraits for her collage, the material treatment of photographs is another way that those at home express agency in their relations with migrants. Cutting migrants' images down to size minimizes some of the resentments villagers feel toward patrons. Angelina and Luis knew that migrants who returned to the Philippines and squandered their overseas earnings on gifts were widely derided. People made disparaging remarks and treated them as small unless they continued to make gifts and redistribute their earnings. Returning migrants were thus cut down to size and removed from others' global imaginaries through everyday, face-to-face encounters. Luis worried about people judging him and Angelina as having failed if they returned without being able to start a new and successful business. Such a failure would represent an inability to be recognized by others for one's innate personal capacities—both individual attributes and abilities to create networks—and would be profoundly humiliating.

Photographs thus reveal that the ways migrants think of themselves are shaped by imposture and anxiety as well as ambition and hope. By renewing their photographs and inflating the success portrayed in their images, migrants sustain intimacy by remaining abroad. Though migration is itself often depicted as fundamentally a process of making people into individuals, that does not seem to be the experience here. Haliap migrants do not seem to be becoming the kinds of modern, Western-style individuals we might expect to encounter. To think about why this might be, I turn back to Appadurai's migrant archive and, to contextualize it, to debates on cosmopolitan identities.

A Transnational Pig

In late 2005 Sarah asked Luis to contribute a pig to a ritual she was planning. She sent him this request in response to his photos, asking me to film the message on my video camera. On a clip she intended I play for Luis and Angelina in Hong Kong, Sarah asked her brother to send money for the purchase of a pig. She was asking him to contribute to the Ifugao healing ritual of *fogwa*, or "the washing of the bones." Asking Luis to sponsor a sacrificial pig (typically, a cost of P7,000 [US$131] to P15,000 [US$281], depending on its size), Sarah anticipated how and why he might object. Because Luis's church, the Iglesia ni Cristo, forbids supporting what they believe is paganism, she assured him on the video that no prayers would accompany the sacrifice.

Sarah and Brandon lived in his Kalanguya-speaking village in Asipulo. Both were in their late thirties at the time. Sarah is a schoolteacher; Brandon, a police officer. Their marriage is not only interethnic but also interfaith. Sarah left the Iglesia ni Cristo and converted to Catholicism to marry Brandon. They were living near Asipulo's municipal hall, but she was teaching in Barangay Camandag, on the Nueva Viscaya border. She had a two-to-three-hour hike each way to reach the school, so she rented a room nearby during the week. She and Brandon depended on working students to help take care of their three children when Sarah was absent. Though considered a true housewife, she actually spent most of the week away from her family to maintain her household income. She found it difficult being married into a Kalanguya family and a Catholic, and she experienced her job as an additional mental strain. Sarah's posting was in a non-Adyangan area, the barangay that stalled the ancestral domain process when it was claimed by two provinces. Part of Sarah's teaching job was to count the votes during the contentious local elections.

Sarah had become ill in mid-2004. She had persistent fatigue and felt as if she was floating *in her head,* above the ground. An expensive series of consultations in the lowlands had ruled out ischemic heart disease. Beyond this, doctors could not offer a diagnosis. One of Sarah's sisters-in-law referred her to an Adyangan healing medium, a *munanap.* The medium told her that her dead mother was disturbing her. The cure would be to perform a fogwa, to ask a munfahi (native priest) to wash and rebury her mother's bones.

Sarah and Luis's mother had also belonged to the Iglesia ni Cristo, so Sarah was surprised to learn their mother was requesting *finogwa* (to perform fogwa). Brandon's Kalanguya Catholicism was syncretic, so he was much more enthusiastic. He disinterred his mother-in-law's bones, contacted a munfahi to chant the required invocations to the ancestors, and began sourcing the sacrificial animals to feed the visitors. Fogwa is a redistributive feast where the house is open to all. Brandon was planning to feed many people and was adamant that Luis donate a pig. Sarah thus followed up on her video message with text messages. Providing a pig, she told Luis, would "show my family has not abandoned me." By sending cash for the pig, Luis would convert the use-value of his money into the cultural value of Sarah and Brandon's social status and, by extension, his own.

After her medical treatment, Sarah asked for a transfer to the school in Haliap. Her manager promised to consider her request but seemed to be lingering over the decision. Holding fogwa for Sarah's health was one way she and Brandon could rally public support and pressure the local Department of Education officials to reassign her.

Sarah's request for a pig—or the money to purchase one intended for the ritual—challenged Luis's judgment. Although Luis and Angelina had repaid the money they borrowed from Sarah and Brandon, a sense of indebtedness still lingered. Previously, Brandon had asked Luis to send him some Merrell brand shoes as a gift. In her video message, Sarah told Luis to forget the shoes because Brandon was now insisting on the pig. Both requests demonstrated Brandon's ability to command resources across international borders and thus his social size. Brandon's desire had shifted from being oriented to a more generic consumer culture, the name-brand shoes, to globalizing his own ideas about the value of local cultural forms, the pig. While the shoes demonstrated his sophisticated consumer desires, asking for money to support the ritual demonstrated Sarah and Brandon's ability to divert Luis's Hong Kong earnings toward their own cultural values. Luis, however, did not want to be forced to bend his religious precepts by his brother-in-law. Sarah felt caught between her natal family and her husband and exposed to community censure. Her request was a public one, in which the relative sizes of Brandon and Luis and the meanings of debt and obligation were demonstrated and debated. This was why Sarah had asked me to show her video message to her Hong Kong friends. The pros and cons, obligations and claims behind the request for a pig were widely argued as the story played out through text messages and voice calls across Haliap.

RITUALS AND NETWORKS

After considering the message for a few days, Luis decided not to send Sarah funds to purchase a sacrificial pig. His reasoning for this surprised me. Rather than adopting a self-consciously modern or religious approach to the request, Luis still considered medical healing and social healing to be more or less one and the same.

Luis's sojourn in Hong Kong had strengthened his engagement with the Iglesia ni Cristo as a global and fundamentalist church. Iglesia doctrine is based on the church founder's reading of the Bible, as elaborated by the pastors. The Iglesia believes "unity is only possible when everyone completely agrees," and thus members draw themselves into line with the Manila-based church leadership. The church expresses a Filipino national fundamentalism that claims globality through superior access to religious truth and superior administrative skills, and it claims to be the "true church of Christ in the East," as foretold in the scriptures, with other Christian denominations having fallen into apostasy.[10] The Iglesia administers its congregations as a kind of parallel state, with a transparent bureaucracy that rewards moral and legal behaviors. It offers members spiritual governance and cultivates an aesthetic of uniformity. The church cannot adapt its doctrine in the same syncretic way as Catholicism had in engaging Ifugao communities. Instead, the Iglesia depends on principles of conduct based on a view of reality as unitary and unmediated, not open to interpretation: these principles are universal, predetermined, and nonnegotiable.[11] Luis enjoys belonging to a wider collective with clear chains of command, transparent finances, and an explicit set of practices to ensure one lives a daily life that leads to prosperity. His church is "not corrupt like the government."

In Haliap, Luis had been a church deacon. Deacons lead small groups of church members as their first point of connection with the church, providing

guidance on spiritual well-being and personal concerns and monitoring attendance and congregants' tithes. Luis had accompanied the Iglesia pastor to pray
over sick villagers and tried to dissuade his Catholic neighbors from seeking
out ritual cures. In Hong Kong he had been looking to take on the same role,
building personal networks among his fellow congregants. This strategy was
part of his plan to amass cultural capital abroad in order to return home with a
higher status in his church—at least that was his dream. Luis's engagement with
the church was less about becoming an individual and more about situating
his extended self within a new and more powerful set of networks. Most of the
members of his Hong Kong congregation spoke Filipino and knew very little
about Ifugao, so he did not openly identify himself as ethnic or IP. That did not
matter to Luis, because, he said, "God is the same everywhere," and he could
follow the church's teachings and rules just as well as anyone else. However, he
did not consult his church friends about Sarah's request.

Luis did not decline Sarah's request for the pig on specifically religious
grounds. He was concerned with the efficacy of the ritual rather than the pro-
bity of paganism. I had heard Luis describe pagan practices as spiritually wrong,
"prayers to the devil." But in this circumstance, Luis explained that even without the munfahi saying prayers, "Finogwa—it is really a pagan ritual. Before,
when everyone followed *fahi* and believed in it, it was medicine. Now it is just
feeding the people . . . and a way of scattering money." Luis considered belief to
reveal something about the identity and state of mind of believers. He thought
villagers "no longer truly believe" but "just like to be fed." And this fault in their
faith rendered ritual powerless. He was not concerned about faith in an abstract
spiritual realm populated by "devils" but about his wider community believing
that his mother's spirit and his sister's health were connected. Luis's claim was
that his fellow villagers lacked the proper intentions.

I anticipated that Luis would be most concerned about the possibility
of being excommunicated and focus on his own disillusionment with pagan
practices. Surprisingly, his concern instead was the effectiveness of the treatment. He texted his sister: "If you go to hospital, I can give money. But not
for finogwa." He offered to arrange for Haliap's Iglesia congregation to hold
special prayers for her health. He also suggested Western-style medical treatment, because he had already prayed for Sarah and said "it did not work."
Luis presumed that the most effective healing would come, not from either
superior scientific understanding or better access to God or divinities, but from
recruiting the widest possible spiritual and material networks of support. He
wanted to link his sister to spiritual realms beyond the limited scope of local
ritual. For him, social efficacy and medical efficacy remained the same thing:
a matter of the scope of one's networks. Luis did not focus on the specific
beliefs held by the Iglesia as opposed to the Catholics or the so-called pagans.

Instead, he evaluated the possibilities that interested him within these different belief systems, those for networks and exchanges. I asked him if he would have responded differently if the pig had been requested for a ritual to be held—and the meat redistributed—in Haliap rather than in the Kalanguya-speaking barangays. He demurred, explaining he would look for "a way around" so that he could avoid being sanctioned by his church but gain the additional prestige he would garner among his largely Catholic neighbors by contributing to the ritual. Such spirits did not disturb Haliap people in Hong Kong, he explained, because they remained at home "with their bones" and "in the surroundings."

Luis was not worried about what might happen if Sarah did not hold the ritual. He predicted that "nothing" would happen, meaning she would not recover, nor would her illness become more serious. This use of the word *nothing* led him to recall how, in the early 1990s, he had felled a tree in his family's rice fields. This had been the tree where the ancestral spirits lived and where his family had sacrificed chickens to ensure the fertility of their fields. Felling it had been an experiment with paganism; he had wanted to see if anything would happen. What occurred then, he explained, was also "nothing." This was a joke, referring to the years during which he and Angelina suffered. Laughing, he refused to distinguish between retributive justice enacted on him by Haliap's spirits of place and simple bad luck. Instead, he offered, "Sometimes nothing may really be something . . . , but I'm not yet sure." In Luis's view of the cosmos, the spirits of fahi could still have some effect, but his church would likely have more.

DEBATE AND CRITIQUE

Sarah's request for a pig—the pig and the money to purchase it being considered pretty much one and the same by villagers—provoked a villagewide response. In Hong Kong, Sarah's friends took up her cause. I watched Sarah's video together with Nora, Darcy, and Elvie in Central, and they described Luis's refusal as "hard-hearted" and "closed-minded." They also made these comments in text messages and voice calls to Luis, Sarah, and others across Haliap. They accused Luis of an un-brotherly kind of stinginess, an attempt to pull himself and his household away from Haliap community networks toward his church connections.

Sarah's friends made four points: First, there was no ritual held when Luis and Sarah's mother died. Even though she was Iglesia, neglecting Ifugao ritual disrespected her kin, friends, and ancestors who remained Catholic and pagan. This was a claim of the precedence of a kind of indigenous cultural value, funerals being for the living, over that of the new Protestant churches. Making this claim, Sarah's friends argued for the primacy of economic equity and kin obligations over nonlocal faith. Second, because Sarah had donated a pig for Luis's engagement ritual, as close kin he was obliged to give back in kind when asked, an obligation that came before his personal religious beliefs. Third, Sarah was asking Luis for money, and it should be up to Sarah to decide how she should spend it. This argument separated an exchange of economic value for a cultural debt from the ways a creditor might then choose to invest the repayments. And, finally, Sarah's friends observed that since the ritual would not be held in Luis's house, the Iglesia could not act against him, so Luis could not claim that he was really endangering his own stature within his church. Sarah's friends thus decided Luis's refusal could not be based on any reasonable self-interest but only because he had decided to create distance between himself and his sister.

Nora explained to me, "Here in Hong Kong, we learn that you do not have to be the same to go together. You just have to respect other customs and give them their place. That is how our thinking must be if we will join many peoples and faiths here, and how we should adapt if we will transfer again to a new place. Now, in Haliap, we should practice both Iglesia and fogwa." Nora's comments outlined a way of being a villager in a global world, one that did not depend on first becoming a modern kind of individual and distancing oneself from Haliap. Hers is a non-cosmopolitan approach to the global. It runs against the widely accepted idea that by using mobility to transform themselves, migrants become individuated, modern subjects. To better describe who these villagers consider themselves to be, we need to examine who they are not.

Becoming Cosmopolitan?

Cosmopolitan is more than just a synonym for a sophisticated or worldly person. Cosmopolitans understand themselves primarily to be citizens of the globe. Their identities as nationals of a particular state, adherents of a particular faith, or members of a family, and/or practitioners of a craft or profession, and so forth are secondary to their global belonging. Cosmopolitans think of themselves as sharing a distinct set of feelings and attitudes, priorities and judgments, and practices of self-shaping that constitute their global belonging. They self-consciously shift their senses of self away from the opinions of family, village, and nation toward a global imaginary where they are the authentic global actors, open to novel and different cultural experiences in ways that mere villagers are not.[12]

Sociologists suggest that cultivating such cosmopolitan identities will create a new, global ecumene. As expounded by Ulrich Beck, cosmopolitanism marks the process and forms of agency through which shared norms of autonomy and loyalty, and the identities of people and states can be established in the globalizing world. Creating cosmopolitans from diverse national and cultural backgrounds is how Beck imagines the hearts and minds of the postcolonial world can be won. He describes an epic struggle between cosmopolitanism and its enemies: parochial nationalisms and religious fundamentalisms. Becoming cosmopolitan is, for Beck, a form of globalization that happens from within national societies, a process of transforming both people's identities and their everyday self-consciousness. Cosmopolitans choose to take on the new identities inscribed on them by democratic politics, secular belief systems, and liberal values. They reject fundamentalist or ethnic nationalist identities. Beck's cosmopolitan subject thus emerges from and then replaces an earlier, individuated national subject; Beck's cosmopolitanism presupposes the individual. Beck thus suggests that the change in everyday consciousness and identities he describes simply articulates a universal kind of personhood with an already widely shared, well-defined, Western-oriented global imaginary. Beck argues that such a shift is the only logical response to a new global realm composed of entangled modernities. He then goes on to outline what he calls a "rooted" cosmopolitanism, one where "identities . . . are ethically and culturally simultaneously global and local." Beck's cosmopolitans thus differ from mere locals, not only because they attempt to open their locality to the world, but also because their personhood displays the internal architecture of the modern subject. But what Haliap migrants show us is that basing a theory of the global on the idea of the bounded individual is problematic.[13]

Migration has been posited as the definitive individuating experience shaping cosmopolitan identities. Experiences of international migration can certainly predispose people to prioritize participating in a global community above and beyond the claims of the family members and nation they leave behind.[14] Theorists of cosmopolitanism can thus argue that living in a country other than one's own places a person within an ontology of "oneself as another," producing an openness to others that offers a "conceptualization of justice, irreducible to the law."[15] But cosmopolitanism is something more than simply this openness to others. Cosmopolitanism is what my Filipino NGO friends call a "values orientation" that enables frictionless movement through the world.[16] A cosmopolitan is an individuated person whose values transcend his parochial, local roots and who thus subordinates his concerns for kin, locality, and nation to give priority to participating in an ethics of shaping the world as a whole. Most of my migrant friends in Hong Kong did not seem to fit this identity particularly well. The disjuncture between cosmopolitans and Haliap migrants suggested that the kind of person being shaped by the virtual village did not correspond to the person anticipated by cosmopolitan theory: the individuated subject.

Returning to the ethnic parade that opened this book, cosmopolitanism could quite easily describe the next vignette in the story. Consider the visiting

Filipino Canadian who appeared to be filming the parade to record a part of her own cultural heritage. We could imagine her to be someone who, secure in her new citizenship, can visit home as a heritage tourist and benefactor. In places other than Haliap, diasporic Filipinos themselves are increasingly being reidentified as agents of development, being consulted on project design and collaborating with donor agencies, church groups, and the Philippine government in development activities. As individuals, these emigrants seem to have the freedom to choose the ways they will acknowledge obligations to home. Their names appear on commemorative plaques and project signs, alongside politicians and members of the elite. Engaged in philanthropy, they even become patrons for places where they do not have close relatives. In contrast, Haliap's temporary contract workers must prepare to eventually return home for good or try to move on. They are obliged to channel their gifts through preexisting personal relations. Their few experiences of being consulted and included in planning as donors have yet to dull their painful memories of being reorganized and given new identities as project beneficiaries. When they form groups to give back in a way that can enable them to be recognized as patrons by a wider public, their members face a seemingly endless stream of requests from disgruntled kin. They share in norms of village exchange that limit the possibilities of identifying and practicing as cosmopolitans.

Recognizing that prevailing accounts of cosmopolitanism seem exclusive, other academics have attempted to shift the meaning of the term to better describe non-Western subjects. Cosmopolitan debates have elaborated on grounded, divergent, disparate, rooted, realistic, working-class or demotic, emancipatory, and despotic forms. Anthropologist Paul Rabinow argues for a "(self)-critical cosmopolitanism" that combines "an ethos of macro-independencies with an acute consciousness . . . of the inescapabilities and particularities of places, characters, historical trajectories and fate." Historian James Clifford describes a "discrepant" cosmopolitanism that includes servants and migrant workers, people excluded when the term *cosmopolitan* has been applied to Westernized global elites. Cultural theorist Stuart Hall describes a "vernacular cosmopolitanism" that marks the global, modern everyday that is made through the prosaic cultural encounters of diasporic lives. Anthropologist Pnina Werbner differentiates between an aesthetic, or prosaic, cosmopolitanism and a normative, or political, cosmopolitanism, but considers that both share a "faith in the necessity for open borders and the inalienable human right to move beyond one's own society," a faith she labels as Kantian. Beck himself distinguishes between the "realistic" cosmopolitanism—that of the social sciences and political theory—and a "philosophical" cosmopolitanism derived from the philosophies of Kant and Descartes, claiming that the former has developed after the collapse of the latter.

Proliferating *cosmopolitan*'s qualifying adjectives cannot quite conceal an anxiety that the term is inherently Eurocentric, with the prosaic use of *cosmopolitan* and the idea of the modern individual unavoidably collapsing into each other. For our purposes here, none of these terms really seems to describe how Nora and her friends approach their world.[17]

The strongest critique of cosmopolitanism's underlying ethnocentrism has come from the work of the anthropologist Bruno Latour. Latour argues that the term marks a striving toward a secular but post-Christian Western modernity, something the non-West lacks but can evolve toward. To evolve, however, the non-West must properly channel its dreams, modifying the objects of its desires and forms taken by its constitutive social relations to fit established Western norms. Latour thus considers cosmopolitanism to be yet another concept that claims to be a universal but actually acts as a surrogate for a very specific idea of Western civilization. However, he argues, the enabling assumptions behind this European modernity are decidedly not ones that are shared by the majority of the world's people. In his analysis, the cosmopolitan project, centered on the work of Beck, undermines its own goals, attempting to globalize the Euro-American ideas of the person as a route to negotiate ways of living together with the rest of the world. Rejecting this approach, Latour argues for a new, shared cosmos to be negotiated between worlds, worlds created from multiple and specifically situated worldviews, not all of which are modern.[18] The idea of negotiating a shared cosmos sounds more like Nora's approach.

"Cosmopolitics" is Latour's way of referring to how multiple and situated worlds negotiate with each other: "We perhaps never differ about opinions but rather always about things—about what world we inhabit. And very probably, it never happens that adversaries come to agree on opinions: they begin, rather, to inhabit a different world."[19] Cosmopolitics responds to the refusal of cosmopolitanism to see diversity and its tendency to hold on to the idea that one cosmos is indeed already known. With this concept, Latour tries to describe attempts to compose a different kind of world that does not require people to detach themselves from the divinities and spirits that make them persons.

Applying Latour to the story of the pig, the phone and text debates that resulted from Sarah's request for a pig can be understood to be exercises in cosmopolitics. In these debates, Haliap migrants engaged with plural religious norms in ways that were quite consciously designed to make themselves globally mobile, shaping their own situated ways of thinking and feeling about themselves in the world—in terms that were not those of modernity. If migration had made my Haliap friends cosmopolitan, following both Latour and Beck, they would then have already been modern individuals. This insight prompted me to go back to my data to seek evidence of modernity. The modernity literature suggested I should return to examine the conjunctures where I had been surprised by the ways my Haliap friends understood themselves in the world.

SURPRISE AND THE MODERN

Surprise is one of the pleasures and perils of ethnographic fieldwork; ethnographers should expect their fieldwork to throw up the unexpected and the puzzling. But surprises can be difficult to see when ethnographers are blinded by particular kinds of theoretical commitments. It should no longer be a surprise that non-Western respondents are familiar with global norms for gender roles or family models, or that they self-consciously consume global goods. But their sophisticated tastes and global understandings do not necessarily mean that respondents are modern individuals. Indeed, the theoretical framing of the multiple modernities approach—the approach that underpins Beck's ideas about cosmopolitans—draws on ideas about modernity that have been strenuously critiqued.

The multiple modernities literature theorizes the global as a universal sociocultural realm being produced by a series of non-Western vernacular variations of a universal form of modernity. This global but European modernity is characterized by disillusionment, a move to secular beliefs, and it legitimizes forms of political power that are exercised through the nation-state and its bureaucracy. For people who previously defined themselves through respect for divinity (or divinities)—a sense of engagement with a transcendent, spiritual realm and faith in intangible powers—modernity should mark an abrupt change, requiring them to very self-consciously reject their past.[20] This change should result from proliferating forms of technical knowledge and their growing dominance over everyday ways of knowing, a hollowing out of the category of the sacred and the emergence of a new set of myths that bring into being individual persons and new realms of endeavor—like the global.[21] The idea that modernity had taken on this universal form in multiple local places shaped a swath of ethnographies from the mid-1990s onward. These ethnographic accounts of multiple modernities have since been criticized for stretching their theoretical commitments beyond the remit of their ethnographic data.

In their reading of the modernities literature, anthropologists Harri Englund and James Leach found that the idea of the modern framing of these local multiples inevitably anticipated a Western-style individual. Englund and Leach made this argument by piecing together the organizing assumptions behind multiple modernities, not all of which appear in any single study.[22] They then examined how scholars applied the elements of this theory of modernity to their data and realized they had often done so regardless of how well it fit. The elegance of the theory had so entranced ethnographers that they had resisted being surprised by what their respondents were actually saying or doing. Englund and Leach found they could read the ethnographic data supporting multiple modernities arguments and conclude with a rather different view of the global world. The critique they produced resonates with Latour's criticism of cosmopolitanism.

The idea of a global modernity extends a sociological imagination that universalizes the Western individual. Debates on cosmopolitanism are thus reworkings of an earlier set of debates on modernity, without offering much progress toward conceptualizing varieties of personhood. As historian Timothy Mitchell writes, "staging the modern has always required the nonmodern, the space of colonial difference." Replace "modern"' with "cosmopolitan" and this fits nicely with Beck's idea of cosmopolitanism and its enemies. Mitchell characterizes modernity as having "an autocentric picture of itself as the expression of a universal certainty, whether the certainty of human reason freed from particular traditions, or of technological power freed from the constraints of the natural world." Similar autocentric tendencies appear in cosmopolitan theory. Englund and Leach argue that modernity comes about through people's self-consciously defining themselves as "modern" as they experience fundamental ruptures or discontinuities in their sociocultural forms. This sounds very much like Beck's ideas of people taking on new identities and refusing older ones rather than blending them together. Mitchell, too, finds modernity's local multiples a problem, because "the vocabulary of alternatives can still imply an underlying and fundamentally singular modernity, modified by its local circumstances into a multiplicity of cultural forms. It is only in reference to this implied generic that such variations can be imagined and discussed." The same can be argued for cosmopolitanism, with the logical requirements of different forms of cosmopolitan being a modern, individuated self whose desire makes a Western-style global. Here, I cannot find any compelling evidence that Haliap's global imaginaries are entirely individuated and Western.[23]

The theory of multiple modernities feeds into cosmopolitanism by suggesting that the ontological anchorage for a modern individual lies in the nation-state and its institutions: the government and allied projects and agencies. Here, individuals are made primarily by identifying as citizens. Finding their identity in the nation then shapes their individual personhood as self-consciously modern. From this being national, becoming cosmopolitan is the next step in progress. Citizens give up their primary attachment to a national identity to take on a global one—as the global Filipino, a citizen of a global nation. In Haliap I found there was evidence that some attempts to make people think of themselves as individuals and national citizens had been successful but also that the majority of such projects had faltered. Changes in land tenure, development initiatives, and the institutions and programs of government were frag-mented and contradictory in villagers' experience. Though these assemblages produced discourses that identified people with new categories and names, only a few of these new identities gained sway over the ways people thought about themselves. In the village the discourses and projects of governing were not always aligned with the government and were not always actually, recogniz-ably, about national citizenship. Often these discourses and projects were part of various churches or development agencies that, though apparently doing the work of governance, were also doing a whole host of other, contradictory things through their relations with villagers. Take Luis and his church, for example. I thought he would turn to his church for guidance or use church principles to defend his earnings from his relatives. Instead, he produced an argument about efficiency, comparing each approach—fahi or conventional medicine and/or Iglesia prayers—in terms of the likely size of the network of support it would recruit for his sister. Much as Englund and Leach argue, the ways people think and feel about themselves in the world are more often than not a surprise.

Returning to the story of the pig, cosmopolitanism does not emerge from within Brandon's and Sarah's requests for the shoes and the pig, despite the kind of sophisticated consumer knowledge expressed in the request for the Merrell shoes. Nor does it lie within Angelina and Luis's multiethnic work environ-ment in Hong Kong, though they interacted intimately with their Hong Kong Chinese, Thai, and Tagalog-speaking Filipino workmates and their elite Hong Kong employers. The ways of thinking about oneself that are required to handle consumer desires or family demands do not necessarily motivate a desire for a different kind of identity: global citizen. Luis and Angelina did not discuss the specifics of Sarah's request with their Filipino workmates, but with their fel-low Haliap migrants. Likewise, though Luis shared his church's concern with efficacy, this was not shared in a way that distinguished this concern from the concerns of Adyangan fahi approaches. Luis was trying to judge how best to manipulate the spiritual world to provide material goods and personal benefits: much the same concern that underpins fahi. And both Luis and Brandon now engaged this concern through different sets of self-consciously global practices. Luis explained that since the Iglesia has congregations among Filipinos in coun-tries around the world and actively evangelizes among non-Filipinos, his church could offer prayers that would recruit far more support than simply feeding the community through fogwa. In this respect, his engagements with the church allow Haliap to become more global but do not challenge the Haliap idea that the purpose of such ties is to translate spiritual networks into efficacy in healing.

If we seek to identify Luis as modern subject, we ought to be able to frame his responses to Sarah's request within themes of becoming individual, becoming alienated, and becoming disenchanted with the sacred. Luis should define the disenchantment of the pagan Ifugao landscape as one of his own modernity's key features and then describe how it has been re-enchanted by an Igelsia God.[24] Luis, however, has never described himself as "modern" to differentiate himself from those with pagan beliefs, though he uses the word, in the sense of contemporary, to talk about styles of farming, clothes, and vehicles. In evaluating Sarah's request, Luis's concerns showed that he remained within the familial and communal collective, still connected to its locality and rituals. Thus whatever Christian faith is doing for people in Haliap—and this is a much wider variety of things than I have accounted for here—it does not appear to be creating the individual, bounded selves we might anticipate. Rather than preparing the ground for the more powerful forces of global modernity that would then succeed it, creating post-Christian, secular cosmopolitans, religion is producing a plural cosmology within the village.[25] We can see this plurality in what Luis did not do.

Luis could have used this request as an opportunity to justify withdrawing from a broader set of obligations to his extended family, creating a rift with Brandon and Sarah and individuating himself. This outcome was what his Hong Kong friends were trying to preempt by talking about it, shaming him in advance. Luis, instead, found a kind of middle ground in which he acknowledged local ideas about networks and healing by offering his own, more global connections. Luis's approach to ritual across the virtual village is thus cautious, focused on unity and recruiting numbers for efficacy. His is a transactional model of bargaining with the cosmos, situated in a collective and enacted by persons who extend through their social networks rather than a discontinuous, individuated person inhabiting a secular, cosmopolitan world.

Luis, Sarah, and her friends in Hong Kong were not performing any self-conscious modernity through their own beliefs. Instead, their concerns with networks and efficacy blended the purpose of local ritual with the possibilities of global faith. This idea was extended by Nora's comments. Reflecting on what would be an appropriate response to such a request in a village divided by religions reveals something akin to Latour's cosmopolitical approach. Nora sees a cosmos in which her village is open to local pluralities, considering them at a global scale. She tried to make this dream real in very practical ways by intervening in village debates. Where the Iglesia idea of unity might be monological, what Nora advocates is closer to what Luis actually practiced: a kind of unity in diversity, to be applied to home rather than simply tolerated while sojourning in Hong Kong. Nora's comments did not offer evidence for any shared, global modernity being made over into local vocabularies of cause and effect. Nora did not speculate on what might truly be causing Sarah's illness. Instead, she allowed the Adyangan vocabulary of cause and effect—mother's spirit as causing sickness—to underpin her approach to local pluralism. She did not challenge the spirit basis of sickness, because she had reflected on her own experience of others' attachments to their particular beliefs. Her personal experiences of inter-connectedness in Hong Kong have led her to become familiar with the cultural complexities of Cantonese tradition in her Chinese employer's household. She finds that her sojourn abroad has motivated her to identify with humanity in its diversity. Nora identified as a villager rather than describing herself as a secular, post-Christian, individuated modern. She did not think of herself first as a citizen of the Philippines, but as a Haliap villager and an Ifugao. Nora's concern was to accommodate Haliap's local pluralities in a way that would not preclude moving on—"to transfer again to a new place"—to cope with globalism.

Coping through Connection

By sustaining and intensifying their long-distance ties, migrants remain intimately tied to local cosmologies. Thus, instead of taking on individuated or cosmopolitan identities, migrants continue to think of themselves as and feel themselves to be villagers. Abroad, migrants are haunted by their futures, as well as by ghosts from the past. They worry about their status within the village and the most effective ways to manipulate their fate or luck in the world. Even at a distance, they remain villagers in their hearts, working on themselves, bring-ing their identities and self-understandings into affective alignment with their fellow village migrants and those at home. Migration thus sustains and even strengthens a relational kind of personhood.

Here, photographs and pigs are exchanged to objectify and renew particu-lar village relationships and identities. Both are also consumed, but in differ-ent ways. Pigs move through established rituals and record—and are recorded by—their givers and recipients, embodying the care of kin and coming back to donors as other pigs. Pigs propitiate local spirits and ghosts, renewing kin-ship. Though obligations to exchange are negotiated, Ifugao tradition means that everyone has a fairly good idea of what those obligations ought to be and can engage in debate. Photographs, however, require a new set of rituals and generate a different kind of haunting. The images of selves that circulate in migrants' photographic portraits are not returned to their subjects. All that comes back is the response of others to the migrant's self-fashioning through the image. These images work on the migrants pictured in them, demanding that exchanges be renewed and new networks of exchange be brought into being. Migrants dream that these new exchange networks will become secured when they become symbolically tied to their receiving state as a citizen, hence the yearning to become a "permanent" elsewhere. In virtual Haliap the line between permanent residency and citizenship is a blurry one. Perhaps this is because both appear to offer the same stable economic base, and nobody really understands how the bureaucracies of host nation-states distinguish between the two. All of this means that for Luis to become the person depicted in his photographs, he must offer something more than the pigs prescribed by the munfahi. He needs to become a conduit to broader networks of exchange, relays of value that are more efficacious because of their global reach. Sending home his photographic portraits is the first step in bringing those networks and their efficacy into being.

CHAPTER 6 ◆ Moving On

ANGELINA AND LUIS LIVE as if the whole of Haliap has come along with them, observing, judging, expecting, and evaluating their day-to-day lives in Hong Kong. Their village ties continue to shape the ways they aspire to progress, motivating them to move in new and different directions. And, just like many of their migrant compatriots, Angelina and Luis find themselves at a crossroads several years into their sojourn. Should they go home or move on? Depending on their luck, some migrants will decide to intensify ties between Hong Kong and home; others will seek new horizons. From Hong Kong, migrants are constantly imagining life upon their return to the Philippines or are making plans to move on, so much of their time abroad is actually spent dreaming of life elsewhere. Migrants abroad can thus find themselves dwelling in a kind of reverie while abroad, anticipating the moment their dreams will come true and their circumstances will change for the better, always calculating their progress against village ideals. Yet migrants overseas assume—and returnees observe—that nothing much will have changed at home in their absence, and in important ways they are likely to be right.[1] The news from the village is that development, at least as initiated and facilitated by the institutions of national governance, has largely failed to gain much further purchase on producing progress at home.

In October 2007 I met Luis, Nora, Darcy, and Elvie in Central. We sat in Chater Gardens, eating *pancit bihon* (fried mung bean noodles) and *bibingka* (sticky rice cakes). We drank *fedjah,* a rice wine made with yeast from Haliap, brewed secretly in vinegar and soy bottles in their employers' kitchens with yeast I had brought back from Haliap on an earlier trip. We played Scrabble on a magnetic board supplied by Nora. This was her money-saving measure, distracting migrants from Hong Kong's consumer pleasures. Players limited their gambling to penny stakes. Some of Nora's friends from Kiangan joined us, members of her expanding money-ubfu group. Nora brought along her accounts book to take ubfu and loan payments and arrange new loans. As we sat and chatted, over the noise of Hong Kong traffic I heard someone singing a harvesting song, not quite under her breath. Each migrant was weighing up his or her options for returning home, staying in Hong Kong, or moving on, comparing experiences and swapping information as they did so.

Luis updated us on the movements of his family. His older brother in Dubai was doing well. His sister in Manila had left the call center. Luis did not know what her new job was. He was fed up with her continual requests for money. Not only had she refused to take his advice, but she also had remained in the Mormon Church. (To this, the group made sympathetic murmurs.) Luis had rescued his younger brother Jerome from his disastrous sojourn in Mindanao to manage Luis's farm in Nueva Viscaya. During her vacation in the Philippines, Angelina discovered he had made a mess of it. Jerome had subsequently moved on to a farm outside Baguio City to garden. (A sharp intake of breath and a slight shaking of heads accompanied this story.) Meanwhile, Luis's sister Linda had been deported from Singapore. Her employers had found surveillance video showing her hiding under the kitchen table chewing betel nut. (This elicited laughter from the sister's former classmates.) Her contract had been terminated. She apparently did a stint in a special center where addicts were rehabilitated and then put on a plane home. Linda was now managing Luis's citrus farm. (The group's second sharp intake of breath denoted this as risky.) Oscar was starting secondary school, staying with his uncle, and doing well, though Luis was worried about the company he was keeping. (This elicited "mmms" of approval, shading into concern.)

Nora, Darcy, and Elvie then reciprocated with their news. Each was funding children studying nursing at Manila universities. They planned for their children to migrate for professional jobs as nurses in Britain, Canada, or the United States. Theirs was an intergenerational strategy to give them security in their old age, and possibly to eventually relocate their families overseas. These three women described themselves as "the lucky ones." They had worked in Hong Kong for more than a decade. Remaining with the same employers, the children they had cared for had grown into teenagers. Each had negotiated a higher salary and taken on more complex tasks. Everyone reported fielding requests for funds to meet the rapidly rising costs of food and agricultural inputs at home. They were seeking part-time work (jokingly called "aerobics") and were looking for sideline businesses, as well as taking additional loans. They knew their earnings were the financial lifeline for their families and village. Everyone was pulling together. Those in Hong Kong were minimizing their own expenses in favor of remittances. Those at home were being, in Luis's words, "doubly thrifty."

Nora, Angelina, and Luis were all deciding to change their circumstances, but these moves led in different directions. After completing a series of face-to-face interviews with all three of them in Hong Kong in late 2007, I stayed in touch with voice calls, text messages, and the occasional letter in order to follow their lives.

Nora: Longtiming and Luck

Nora's fifteen years in Hong Kong made her a *longtimer*. Her luck was that she knew how to manage her relationship with her employers. She had become the indispensible "auntie" to the child she had helped to raise. Her employers envisioned an ongoing intra-familial relationship along a patron-client model. Nora's employer had created a business strategy based on the employer's own permanent residency in Australia. Her plan was to send Nora and her nursing-student daughter to run her Australian business, utilizing their superior English-language skills. Nora was not so sure her daughter, a professional, would want to be a lifelong client of her mother's boss. But the plan remained an option, depending on whether or not her daughter would be accepted into an Australian graduate nursing program.

Meanwhile, Nora was transforming her money-ubfu group into an Ifugao financial cooperative. The group was raising money with monthly deposits and then lending it to its membership at 5 percent per month. The membership fee was HK$20 (US$2.58), and the share capital was HK$500 (US$64) per month.[2] By January 2009 they had raised HK$500,000 (US$64,516) and had more than sixty members. Although the cooperative loaned money at a higher rate than the finance companies, they still undercut lenders in Ifugao by half, and the profits accrued to the group. The president and manager were Kiangan people, while Nora, representing Asipulo, was the treasurer. The cooperative loaned only to people known to them from Ifugao to make it easier to secure repayment. Since the cooperative was organized without NGO or government help, it had not yet registered with the Hong Kong Cooperatives Authority. The group was still experimenting with governance, deciding what proportion of the profits would be distributed to the members and what would be donated to charitable works in Ifugao, and determining how those decisions would be made. Nora was innovating within Ifugao traditions. While the membership of her group might be super-exploited in their work as domestic helpers, they were taking on the new identities of self-appropriating cooperative members and charitable patrons. The cooperative gave them a collective dignity in managing their own finances. If successful it would let them act collectively as a force in local Ifugao politics. Nora had thus become a big woman not just in Haliap but also among a wider group of Hong Kong–based Ifugao people and thus an expanded community at home. She is now an advisor and financial manager. With her employer, she does not describe her behavior as particularly "caring" or subservient. She argues back and states her case, but with sensitivity to her employer's pride. Nora does not consider herself to be imitating other micro-credit schemes. Instead, she considers herself to be an Ifugao innovator, working from within an adaptable local tradition of exchange that produces its own rules for governance. Nora has become an expert in managing the financial and social risks of the virtual village.

FRUSTRATIONS AND FAILURE

Luis and Angelina envied Nora; they had not found the same kind of luck. They were not the only domestic workers in their employers' household. Instead, they competed with several other helpers for their employers' generosity. Other than Luis's security shifts, they had not had pay rises or been given more responsibility or independence. Their workmates had been pressuring Angelina and Luis to seek loans in order to re-loan them again. Angelina had observed the housekeeper, Soledad, picking up some cash left on a night table by one of the employers' daughters and came forward when the employers investigated. Soledad was dismissed, and the other workers blamed Angelina for reporting her. Relations had soured, so their workplace had a heavy feeling. Their employer then decided to send Angelina to work in another house as full-time caregiver for his elderly mother.

Luis attended the Ifugao cooperative's 2009 New Year's Day picnic at Repulse Bay. The picnic was a kind of recruiting changa' (working bee) where the group asked him to become one of the officers who would be registered with Hong Kong authorities as the governing board of the formal cooperative. Luis had to refuse. His salary was already committed to repaying yet another finance company loan. He had decided to move on from Hong Kong. He explained to me, "It's already boring here. Always the same work. Instead, I want Angelina to go home and I will be the one to work." Luis drew on the ideals of nuclear family, gender, and progress that were familiar to him from Haliap and from his church to justify his next move.

In Luis's Iglesia worship service in Hong Kong, which I attended with him several times in 2005 and 2007, I had heard him sing hymns that emphasized how all lives were borrowed from God and must be invested wisely. When the pastor acknowledged the sacrifices that migrants in Hong Kong were making for their families, the congregation burst into tears and soft moans. The sermons emphasized the role of the male breadwinner. The church offered Luis an ideal of an ordered, just, and meritocratic society. He and Angelina not only were tithing but had also made an additional gift at the Iglesia thanksgiving. They still took Thursday as their day off. These commitments restricted their abilities to maintain their ties with the other Haliap migrants. But despite these sacrifices, Luis had not been made a deacon. Moving on was a step toward his old dream of being the sole overseas breadwinner and his new dream of reclaiming his status as a deacon.

Luis: Moving On to Canada

In October 2008 Luis had signed on with a Hong Kong–based recruiting agency that placed him in a job with a landscaping firm in Canada, outside Calgary, Alberta. The recruiting agency was licensed by the Hong Kong authorities and supplied Filipino workers, largely domestics, to Hong Kong and Canada. The agency had counterparts in the Canadian provinces of Alberta, British Columbia, and Ontario. Its Hong Kong staff was Filipino. Through this agency, Luis received a labor market order (LMO) under Canada's Temporary Foreign Worker (TFW) program. An LMO ties a worker to a specific job and can be converted into a two-year temporary working visa. Luis's LMO and the contract accompanying it described a forty-hour-a-week job, paid at C$15 (US$12.71) per hour.[3] From this salary, Luis would need to cover his own rent and other expenses. As a low-skilled worker under the TFW program, Luis should have had his accommodation arranged and airfare paid by his employer. From the contract he signed, Luis thus anticipated a salary of C$2,400 (US$2,033) per month, more than four times what he had been earning in Hong Kong. The agency gave him no information about taxes or the local cost of food, communications, utilities, housing, and transportation.

Luis paid HK$1,400 (US$180) for his medical exam and spent HK$1,000 (US$129) to apply for his temporary work visa that October. In late February 2009 he received a request for a letter of reference from his Hong Kong employer. Once the Canadian consulate in Hong Kong had that in hand, Luis was granted a two-year TFW visa. The speed with which his visa was approved is explained by his being in Hong Kong already; his Hong Kong employment meant his application was less likely to be fraudulent. The Canadian immigration system prefers applications from Filipinos who are already outside the Philippines, as their employment history and relevant work experience can more easily be verified.[4]

Beneath the apparently smooth visa approval process were irregularities. The Hong Kong recruiting agency charged Luis HK$30,000 (US$3,871) as a placement fee. The Citizenship and Immigration Canada labor market order itself specifies that this kind of fee is against the TFW program's rules. Luis thus queried the charge. His agent replied, "Why would I give you a job if you don't give me money? I have costs for processing these papers." Labor brokers for the TFW program are permitted to charge for preparing a resume and for settlement services, including communicating with Citizenship and Immigration Canada and completing work permit applications. But the amount Luis was being charged seemed excessive. He decided that he would lose the opportunity if he asked any further questions, so he paid HK$20,000 (US$2,580) in October and the balance in February. The agency told him to conceal the charge from the Canadian authorities: "When the Canadian Immigration will ask me if I pay anything, she tells me I will say no." Luis also paid his own air-fare. He was promised that his employer would reimburse him if he stayed in the job for six months. In the end, his Canadian employer did reimburse him for the HK$7,716 (US$995) ticket when he started work at the end of April. Luis found the conflicting information confusing. Though it said on the LMO paper that the government of Canada did not permit workers to be charged for recruiting, Luis saw there was nothing he could do to challenge the charge without putting his job offer at risk. The Canadian government did not seem to have any way to control what actually happened between Luis and the agent in Hong Kong and it was not the Hong Kong authority's concern.

Luis thus spent October 2008 to March 2009 in Hong Kong on a quarter of his monthly salary, working nights, waiting and dreaming. When he borrowed HK$20,000 to pay the first part of the placement fee, he agreed to repay HK$2,100 (US$271) per month for twelve months, starting in October 2008. (He would be paying 26 percent interest per annum whereas most Hong Kong banks charged approximately 15 percent for an unsecured loan and the interbank rate was well below 2 percent.) After re-loaning to the maximum HK$30,000, he paid the final HK$10,000 of the placement fee at the end of February. His total loan would cost him HK$3,200 (then roughly US$413) per month for twelve months, with his repayments running into February 2010. Even when he was working out his one-month notice with his Hong Kong employer in March 2009, he still had no information on the costs of his house and the number of people who would be sharing the property, the cost of utilities, or if he would have to pay transportation costs to work sites or spend money for equipment or a uniform.

Luis's plan was to repay his loan with money he would remit from Canada. He also planned to remit P15,000 (US$310) per month (approximately C$378 at the time, plus transaction costs) to Angelina once she had returned to the Philippines.[5] She was not a signatory to the loan. Luis felt that he absolutely had to repay this loan because dunning calls from the finance company could threaten Angelina's job and both their future employment references from Hong Kong. Luis explained, "It's my obligation, so it is me they are going to find" and "I will manage this thing; it will only take time, and with God's help." Luis saw dignity in honoring his debt, because he had agreed to the circumstances of it. If he were lucky and his accommodation and transportation costs were low, he planned to remit a bit more, about C$500 per month, to pay off the loan early. He was thus hoping to work overtime hours and find extra casual work in the underground economy that has arisen with the TFW program in

Calgary. Extra work is against the rules of the TFW program and could have led to Luis's being deported if he were to have been caught. Luis told me, "I'm not sure yet what is the good fortune there in Canada. I hope it will be fine. It's hard to save here in Hong Kong; we're spending too much. There are no fixed working hours. I work overtime, without pay. There's only one day off per week. Sometimes I'm working even until eight or nine at night." Luis had complained and been given a month off from his night duty but was now expected to go back to it. He found it lonely and thought it was making him sick: "It's really hard to work nights. It's boring and sometimes I get mailiw." But Luis was not worried about iliw in Canada. He would have Filipino companions and be busy with work. The job would exist for only two years, but as Luis said, it was "in my line," meaning suited to his skills and experience. The TFW program indicated there should be opportunities for training and advancement, and Luis's employer's website suggested that workers would receive on-the-job training that would qualify them for more responsible—and higher-paid—jobs within the industry. Luis saw working in Canada as being about work with dignity that would recognize his personal capacities and future plans. A dignified future was something Luis considered worth the risk.

Luis was seeking to become a client of more caring patrons: a better employer and a government that really cares for its people. He was thus looking forward to experiencing a place where the government provided health care, employment insurance, and other social benefits in return for taxes. The high rates of tax did not worry him, "as long as the people get some benefits, not like in Haliap." He hoped he and Angelina and Oscar might eventually become permanent there. He imagined a citizenship where, having state networks as exchange partners, people could reroute their earnings away from the redistributive claims of community. Luis thus thought living in a welfare state would give him economic stability.

Angelina: Going Home to the Philippines

Angelina's plan was to go home in mid-2009. She would live in Haliap with Oscar while he finished high school there. She and Luis had become concerned about Oscar. He was distracted from his schoolwork by his group of friends (*barkada*) and was squandering his academic promise. She explained, "It's really harder now that he is growing up; sometimes he is *makulit* [hardheaded]. He insists on what he wants. He has vices—he smokes." Once settled, Angelina planned to become a vegetable dealer, buying and selling while taking care of their rice fields and house. Their improved house, now empty, was another worry, "It's maybe no longer a home, just a house." Angelina had asked Tricia and Jesse to move out, anticipating their return in April 2008, when they had announced they would be going home "for good." But as Angelina explained, "We didn't manage to save anything, so we had to renew our contracts, again."

They had recently received a spate of messages and calls from Oscar. He had remained with Luis's brother's family in the lowlands but had been complaining that he had not been getting enough food. Luis sent his brother money to buy a separate gas stove so that Oscar could cook for himself. He and Angelina then asked that some of the P7,000 (US$145) allowance be given to Oscar to buy food. Oscar then complained that the money he was being given for his books, transportation, and other school expenses was not enough. Luis did not want to confront his brother again and blamed his brother's wife for being kuripot (stingy). As life had become more difficult in the Philippines, kin taking care of OCWs' children began to rely on their wards' allowances for their own expenses. Luis and Angelina understood, but they were worried about the impact on Oscar.

Though Angelina and Luis had been sending what had seemed like lots of money home, managing their investments seemed to be too much of a burden for their family. Dependency and resentments, rather than gratitude and obligation, were the result. Thus Luis and Angelina found they could never quite compensate for others' sacrifices with the cash they sent. Their various caretaking arrangements for the farm proved to be short-lived and unsustainable. Their kin expected to have a share in the apparent security Angelina and Luis enjoyed, not to be exploited. Angelina and Luis decided it would be better to have one of them at home. Equally, they resented staying abroad for so long in order to fulfill these kin requests. As Angelina said, "Even if it's small and small again, it adds up." As an example, she enumerated some of Luis's expenditures from his 2008 vacation. He had given P10,000 ($230) to his younger brother Samuel, who was now caring for his citrus plantation, to pay for the costs of a pig outstanding from his wedding in 2007.[6] It was shameful for their family to have had this lingering debt. Their citrus trees were still small, so they needed someone to come every few weeks to weed. Samuel was willing to help and to work with Angelina so that the farm would bear marketable fruit. Linda, Luis's sister who had been at the farm since arriving from Singapore, had been another disaster. Luis had given Linda P18,000 (US$413) to pay the recruiting fees for a job in Japan. But the job had turned out to be a scam, and the money was lost. Linda had also pulled out of plans to go to Dubai several years earlier, losing another deposit paid for by Luis. Angelina was despairing. They had made these gifts of money to compensate for the opportunities lost to Luis's siblings when they were managing his investments, but it seemed the recipients were careless and ungrateful.

All of this borrowing and donating can strain social relations just as much as it can strengthen them. Luis thought of borrowing from the Ifugao financial cooperative but decided against it. The job in Canada was such a risk that he wanted to preserve his Philippine social networks. It would be much worse to abandon a loan with Nora and the cooperative than to default with a Hong Kong finance company. Ifugao creditors like Nora would now seek restitution from Angelina and Luis's extended family in Haliap and beyond, forcing them to sell or mortgage land and thus diminishing his newly restored reputation. Luis wanted to avoid that at all costs. Angelina would need to renew and strengthen their Haliap ties to become a vegetable dealer and, finally, a Haliap-style housewife.

Risk and Dignity

The global regime regulating temporary migration requires workers like Luis to balance risk-taking with personal dignity, negotiating the two in a precarious space of interpersonal relations. This space lies outside the regulatory control of any one state. Luis applied for work in Canada without access to the Internet and lacking familiarity with impersonal bureaucracies.[7] He knew governing institutions as fundamentally large networks of personalistic relations. Though I mailed him materials outlining the rules and regulations that should govern the Temporary Foreign Worker program designed for workers, the personal approach remained his preferred strategy. Building good relations with his Hong Kong agent, he was disposed to go along with agency arrangements that contradicted published Canadian government regulations.

Luis texted me to ask for advice, and we spent much of early 2009 in close contact through text messages and phone calls. We found that the employer on his LMO was licensed and had an impressive website, including a Better Business Bureau approval, and a number of design awards. The site listed a number of jobs open for landscapers. These jobs paid C$15 (US$12.10) per hour, but employees had to provide their own transportation to work sites in the wider Calgary region. The labor broker (Canadian employment agency) who was filling the LMO for the employer was then also listed as licensed. The broker's website promised to assist arriving workers with settlement and to arrange their accommodation on behalf of the employer. Yet there was no insurance plan that would cover Luis if the contract he had signed misrepresented the actual working conditions he would encounter. The irregularities he had experienced in Hong Kong might have been of little concern, or they might have been ominous signs. Luis had no way to tell. Thus, waiting to travel, Luis felt at once extraordinarily hopeful and terribly vulnerable.

Alberta's TFW program has been praised as the best practice for temporary migration, but there have also been significant problems with it. The Alberta Federation of Labour reports that many TFWs are denied overtime, overcharged for cramped and substandard accommodation, overcharged for transportation to work, and forced to pay illegal placement fees.[8] Rather than working for employers directly, they are effectively being employed as subcontractors of their labor brokers. When workers have complained, they have been fired or threatened with being sent home. Some have been taken to the airport and forced to board a plane by their brokers. Workers' complaints about employment conditions have generally resulted in mediation, with only one successful prosecution leading to a fine for the labor broker investigated. The biggest constraint on workers' ability to file complaints is financial. During the complaints process, a worker cannot work for another employer without TFW program approval. Approval can be secured, but it is not immediate. It is illegal for a TFW to work for any employer not named on his or her temporary work visa. In order to hire a migrant, a prospective employer must have an approved LMO for the job being offered. With no financial support available during the approval period, the program has produced an underground workforce of temporary workers doing illegal work.

Luis's predeparture anxieties were commonsense ones. Landscaping was a seasonal industry. Would his employer be able to provide a full week's work for two years, even in the winters? The 2008 recession was deepening, and the Alberta newspapers reported that TFWs' hours were being cut. Could he find another job? Luis was inclined to think of these risks as new forms of more familiar problems. A dodgy agency, an inflexible employer, bullying, or threats are situations he hoped he could circumvent by relying on his relationships. He reminded me—and himself—that he had migrated to Kasibu, to Manila, and to Hong Kong under similarly risky circumstances. Over the phone, he told me again about his own history of migration in the Philippines, his ingenuity in negotiating working relationships, and his ability to break them—to walk away when not treated with respect. On his Hong Kong agency's behavior, he observed, "agencies are usually like that." He reminded himself that sometimes an employer does not know what the agency is actually doing. Thus he wanted to see what his employer was really like before he considered making a complaint. In this he saw himself as one of a group, although he had yet to meet the nine other men who would join him. "If I am already working, and if we will not be affected if we will complain, then we will complain soon. But if my employer won't support it; it will be very hard to complain, because at the end we will be the ones to suffer. We'll lose our jobs and we'll have no money." Luis planned to draw his coworkers into exchange relations and make his employer into a patron. In Filipino, he said "*bahala na,*" meaning "come what may, I can cope." In retelling his story, he was reshaping his feelings about himself, firming himself up to migrate again. He reevaluated his own history to recreate that endurable zone inside himself, the internal space from within which he could prepare himself to live with the potentially unendurable.

Building New Networks

Luis spent his first month in Canada living in his labor broker's house, waiting for his work to begin. The snow had not yet cleared, so the landscaping firm did not need him. He was not earning money. His broker used the placement fee to pay for his food and lodging until he started work. He was bored being stuck in the house, and he was worried. Once he started working, he learned, the landscaping firm would only have work for him until the snow came again, probably in November. This threw all of his financial plans into disarray, but he remained optimistic. His broker said she would help him to find another job, maybe a part-time one for the winter, and he could stay with her free of charge.

He talked about his financial problems with her, and she seemed upset to learn that his Hong Kong agency had charged him so much money as a placement fee. She then expressed astonishment and disgust at the high rate of interest applied to the loan. She said she had asked for C$2,500 (US$2,049), which would cover her settlement services, her costs for hosting him in her home, finding him a room in a shared apartment, and finding him a new job once the landscaping ended.[9] At the time, the definition of settlement services, as opposed to placement fees, under the TFW was subject to a legal challenge.[10] The Hong Kong recruiting agency had evidently kept a substantial extra amount (US$1,822) for themselves. Luis and his broker calculated that Luis would need at least C$1,000 (US$820) per month for his own expenses, so repaying Luis's Hong Kong debt with C$500 would likely use up nearly all of his additional money from his first six months of work.

According to Luis, his broker advised him not to repay his loan in Hong Kong. Luis said she had observed, "They won't chase you here, you know." Luis was not so sure about taking that risk, because he and Angelina would most likely need references from their Hong Kong employer in the future. His broker did dissuade Luis from sending the money reimbursing him for his air ticket back to Hong Kong and the Philippines, telling him he would need the money to set up his apartment, buy work clothes, buy food, pay for transportation, and use what was left as pocket money until he was paid by his employer.

Perhaps the worst thing Luis initially found in Calgary was that his mobile phone was locked and could not be used on Canadian networks. He bought a

SIM (subscriber identity module) card, but could only use it from a Canadian phone. Cut off from texting and calling unless he borrowed his labor broker's phone, he was desperate to maintain his Haliap and Hong Kong connections. He eventually bought a new cell phone and signed up for a C$50 (US$41) per month plan that gave him a rate of 25 Canadian cents per overseas text message—he had been paying about 1 Canadian cent (HK 10 cents) from Hong Kong. Constant contact, which had become crucial to Luis's ability to cope with migration and live in the virtual village, was now going to be incredibly expensive to maintain from Canada.

When finally Luis started work, he had another shock. He thought his employer would pay for transportation and some of the basic things inside his house. He had not anticipated that the money that had been deducted for income tax, a pension plan, and employment insurance would amount to so much. As required under the TFW, his employer was also paying his health insurance and worker's compensation payments. Luis began to understand that his relationship with his employer would be different from what he had become accustomed to in Hong Kong. His contract set his salary at C$18 (US$14.75) per hour, which was good. But he was given a shared room in a two-bedroom flat for C$635 (US$521) per month, deducted from his salary. This deduction covered heat and electricity too. After taxes, employment insurance and pension payments, health insurance, and rent, Luis had just over C$1,000 (US$820) each month. From that he had to pay for his food and his share of gasoline for the car his team had purchased, and then remit the HK$3,200 (US$413) he had contracted to Hong Kong to repay his loan. From what was left over, after his transaction costs, he then had to send an allowance to Angelina. He also needed to put some money aside for public transportation, tithing to his church, and savings for emergencies. So he was living on a very tight budget and controlling his food expenses in order to remit even part of the money he had promised Angelina. He rapidly lost the twelve kilograms he had gained when he moved from Haliap to Hong Kong. To help him cope with the stress, he started smoking again, having quit for his last two years in Hong Kong in order to save money.

Although Luis was working overtime each week, beyond the regular forty-four hours, his employer was banking what he considered to be his TFW workers' extra hours. Thus Luis's paycheck paid him for only thirty-five hours per week, and the rest of the hours would be paid out—at regular hourly rates rather than as overtime—on a series of checks to be issued after Luis's actual days of work had ended for the season. This would allow his employer to keep deducting rent for the apartment. It would also mean Luis was technically still employed, on his employers' LMO, meaning he would have to resign to find another job rather than being let go. Luis learned that if his employer didn't fire him, transferring his working visa between LMOs would be complicated, even if he did find another employer willing to hire him. He was looking at a long, dark winter, sitting in a ground-floor apartment in Calgary and waiting for spring.

Luis asked his labor broker for help. She initially promised she would demand that the Hong Kong agency return the extra money on a forthcoming trip to Asia. But the plan fell through. The labor broker's license was suspended for charging workers placement fees. She closed her business and then moved into a much smaller house. So no help would be forthcoming there. Luis then thought he could borrow an additional amount from Nora or her cooperative to pay off the Hong Kong loan all at once. He could then remit one payment to Angelina each month, repaying Nora through her Haliap connections and paying Angelina in a single transaction. This would have saved him about C$20 (US$16) per month in transaction fees. Unfortunately, he and Angelina then had a rupture in their relations with Nora.

Back at Home?

Angelina, back in Haliap since May 2009, found her return challenging. Over the phone and by text message, she told me she had been met with an unruly son, demanding relatives, and a seemingly endless stream of requests for loans and handouts. The Hong Kong earnings she had saved to start her buy-and-sell business were quickly drawn down by family medical emergencies, weddings, funerals, and daily living, while Luis, struggling to find his feet in Canada, could not send the money she had anticipated. In our calls Luis worried about Angelina; Angelina also worried about Luis.

Initially, Angelina explained she had been overjoyed to be home. The air was fresh, and the views were green and uninterrupted. Most importantly, she was finally in her own house, in her own place again. But, bit by bit, the things that were lacking began to attract her notice, she told me over the phone. For instance, there were some things in the house she thought had been fixed while she was in Hong Kong that were not what she had expected. The materials used in the bathroom were not of the quality she had expected. The living area (*sala*) was not completely finished; the walls were still bare concrete. And some of the items she had sent home in her last box had gone missing. She was almost apologetic when she explained to me that this had saddened her. She had intended them to be there on her return, but they had been distributed elsewhere. Just little things for the house: pillows, wall hangings, colorful bits of decor. When she had bought them in Hong Kong, she had found great pleasure in imagining how they would look in her kitchen and bedroom. Now what she saw was their absence. Tricia told her that the family had received them but was vague about who had taken which items and why. Angelina found herself looking for glimpses of the items when she visited her cousins.

Requests for money nonetheless came in as if she and Luis were both still working in Hong Kong. Angelina now depended almost entirely on Luis's remittances. Her kin expected her to share her continued good fortune with them, while Luis's siblings anticipated that they, too, would continue to access his earnings. When Angelina declined some of Luis's relatives' requests, they asked Trisha for his Canadian cell phone number so that they could outflank Angelina by texting and calling Luis directly. It was daunting to see just how much his family expected.

Angelina observed that their immediate relatives had been relying on these gifts to become big people themselves, sustaining their own dependents and redistributions. Moreover, they expected that the gifts she and Luis had given would be ongoing, not just some particular amount of money given once. When Angelina arrived in Haliap, she knew that Luis's father had already mismanaged the P50,000 (US$1,400) Luis gave him in 2007 to invest in motorized tricycles. That having failed, he had asked for another P70,000 (US$1,600), which she had been requested to give him on her arrival home from Hong Kong as part of Luis's loan, so that he could try his hand at running a piggery. Linda, too, having squandered the money for Japan and mismanaged the farm, expected more financial help would be forthcoming. No matter how much they had put in already, it never seemed that amount would be enough for the family. Angelina felt that she had come back from Hong Kong with much less money than she needed to enact her plans.

At the same time as the demands from their immediate families intensified, their kin networks were broadening. Over the phone, Angelina told me that almost immediately on her return, she had become reacquainted with a slew of long-lost third cousins who came to ask her for small loans. Angelina explained that she was finding it very difficult to say no to them. People who had supported her and Luis when they were struggling quite reasonably expected her to reciprocate and to be able to redirect this return flow of value from her to their own relatives. She was concerned that she would need to retain people's goodwill so that her new business, unlike her store, would prosper. To remain big, she must give, otherwise people would distance themselves from her and she would become small. Already, within a week of returning, she reported she had received some "negative comments" on her life. Her neighbors (she did not like to say which ones) had told her that people were saying she had not cared for her first son as she had for her second and that she and Luis had not contributed as they should to relatives' weddings. She was not sure which people her neighbors were referring to, just that there had been gossip.

In September 2009 Angelina admitted that she had become so focused on helping Oscar get organized to start the school year that she had not been able to see to the citrus plantation. Samuel, busy with his farm, his wife, and their two small children, had asked for an allowance larger than what she and Luis had budgeted. She had thus decided to wait a few more months, until Oscar was settled in school, to start her vegetable buy-and-sell business. In order to travel, she would need to ask Tricia and James to look in on Oscar and give him his meals. She had given Tricia the stove Oscar had been using at his uncle's house, but she believed it would be necessary to give them another big gift before she could ask them if Oscar could eat with them when she was away, tending to the citrus farm.

In a self-reflective moment, Angelina told me she was surprised to discover that she now felt much less close to her family and friends than she had when she had been away in Hong Kong. She was finding it difficult to share feeling—to make positive affective connections—with people who had made it quite clear to her that their own feelings about themselves depended on her sharing money with them first. Her fellow villagers tried to swallow their feelings of anger and shame when she declined their requests for money, but they then tended to avoid her for a while. Her extended family members, in contrast, did not take her polite refusals at face value or listen to her accounts of financial strain. Instead, they played up their own pitiable state, attempting to wear her down. Though she thought she had done so much for people at home while she was in Hong Kong, sometimes she could see their perspectives: it was still kurang; she had not done enough. But she did not always agree with this perspective.

By October 2009 Angelina had begun to accumulate a list of perceived slights, signs of ingratitude, and feelings of affective distance. Each item seemed trivial, she explained, but the overall pattern worried her nonetheless. Maybe it meant that Haliap would never quite feel like her home again, or maybe she was still adjusting to her return—and people were readjusting to the new version of her who had returned—and she should give it time. When I spoke about the situation with Luis over the phone, he told me he was concerned about Angelina's growing frustration, saying, "Maybe she will like to go back to Hong Kong again, once Oscar has completed his studies."

Becoming Balikbayan

From my mid-1990s fieldwork, I knew villagers would have identified Nora and Angelina as balikbayans, even on their occasional visits home, and most certainly on Angelina's return. It was not always so. *Balikbayan* combines the Tagalog for return, *balik,* with that for town or people, *bayan,* the term later extended to mean nation or fatherland.[11] *Balikbayan* initially recognized the profound changes in the self that occurred when migrants became permanent residents abroad, and was used to describe Filipino emigrants visiting the homeland from the United States from the 1960s onward. These balikbayans from America were typically snobbish and superior, disparaging the nation they had left behind. They brought with them distinctive boxes of gifts that offered locals a taste of the good life, displaying generosity while demonstrating local inadequacies. The surge in the number of contract workers leaving the country in the late 1970s and early 1980s brought a second, and much larger, group home with similar gifts and new attitudes. Initially, balikbayans were visitors who had permanent residence elsewhere, while OCWs came home on breaks within or between contracts. The contract workers also began to send home balikbayan boxes full of gifts, or bring them along on their intermittent visits. Eventually, when contract workers began to settle overseas after years of temporary work, the two categories—visitors and returnees—began to blend.

In 1989 the government had introduced special duty-free status for boxes of gifts (as long as the items were used goods) as a combined strategy to encourage return tourism from Filipino-American emigrants and to allow contract workers to send additional items of financial worth home to their households. This policy effectively included migrant workers within the visitor category of "balikbayan," reflecting how these identities were already being conflated in popular understandings when contract migrants settled permanently overseas. As my Haliap friend Saturnino had explained to me in 1997, "Because, here, we have no migrants in America, these OCWs, they are now our balikbayans here."

Since the mid-1990s, villagers have also described balikbayans as "our new kadangyans." They thus imagine migrant returnees replacing the old landed elite as patrons. Returnees' distinctive balikbayan style enables villagers to recognize returned contract workers and visiting emigrants alike. In the late 1990s the key elements of this style were fairer skin, a particular style of movement and of presenting the self (graceful for women, macho for men), distinctively imported clothes, high-quality footwear (like Merrell shoes), and, among women, makeup and jewelry. Female returnees cultivated straightened hair, polished nails, makeup, and imported clothes, much like the professional women working in the lowland Philippine cities. Among the returnees, those who had been farmers were thrilled to find that a few years in Hong Kong had seen their skin return to a paler shade. Villagers looking on explained that returned female migrants were "very Filipina now," embodying at once the stay-at-home wife and the self-made businesswoman, both of whom worked inside the house and thus maintained a paler complexion.

There is kind of a trick at work, one being supported by the government, in the bleeding and blending of categories here. Contract worker balikbayans are being named as such because they are not really expected by their fellow villagers, or perhaps themselves expecting, to return to Haliap for good. Instead, villagers think contract workers should seek to become true balikbayans—in other words, people who have become citizens of elsewhere, obtained security and "regained their profession," who are then visiting home again. Such a person is a true balikbayan because they have attained a similar or better class position abroad, relative to their predeparture status in the Philippines. When these successful permanents return, they do so as transformed persons, either removed from or able to cope effortlessly with the intensified demands of local exchange. Yet the same ability to cope with village demands is not true of returned contract workers.

The ways people evaluated balikbayan identity also marked new practices of excluding returnees from parts of the local economy. Tala, a returned contract worker whom I knew in 1995–1997, had invested her savings from domestic work in Singapore to become a local distributor of Tupperware in Haliap. Her in-laws, cousins, and neighbors took the containers from her on credit, then refused to pay their debts. After two humiliating months of trying to collect, Tala's business failed. Her neighbors explained that since Tala was "already rich from abroad," she did not need their money. Tupperware, for her, they claimed, was "just a sideline." Tala, however, told me that she had lost her savings in the venture. She was considering taking out a loan from a moneylender so that she could apply for another contract in Singapore, much as she disliked the idea of leaving her children again. Tala thought her other option, to run a small sari-sari store in her house, would be similarly doomed: "If you do not give credit, they will not buy anything, but if I give credit, they say 'never mind, she's OCW already,' and then it is only credits and never money. People are jealous here; they don't want to know how hard it is abroad." Tala's comments encapsulated the anxieties of many would-be returnees: if they were to be unable to balance what local people expected from them against personal success, they would fail as both balikbayan and Filipina. I was able to ask Angelina about her own return based on my knowledge of Tala's experiences several years before.

Angelina disliked how a balikbayan identity was being inscribed on her by her fellow villagers. She told me that she was feeling "dismayed . . . they say I am [a] balikbayan!" She explained, "I'm still the same person I was before Hong Kong." She also argued that she had not been staying somewhere where she could have become a permanent resident and taken another citizenship. Since she had never really left the Filipino bayan, how could she be returning to it? She explained, "We are not yet secured," meaning that their livelihood could not yet offer them the stability she and Luis were seeking. But Angelina's sojourn in Hong Kong seemed to have made her more, rather than less, vulnerable to the ways others evaluated her. Thus she waited to see how things would go for Luis in Canada. She was still texting and calling their Adyangan side friend Jojo to find out about the Canadian caregiver program and beginning to dream about "what if." What if Luis could have his contract renewed and Oscar had finished high school? Maybe he could go to college at the Iglesia university in Manila while she found work in Canada. Having yet to receive the full P15,000 (US$310) per month she and Luis had agreed he would send home, she remained hopeful that Luis could find a way to earn more. He was sending her what he could, usually about P7,000 or C$150 to C$160 per month.[12] In the interim, Angelina was doing what she could to subvert the expectations and prestige attached to balikbayan, starting by explaining Luis's situation in Canada to their kin.

Entangled Relations

Though the three of them were now living in different countries, at the end of 2009 Luis, Angelina, and Nora were nonetheless living village lives. Each was concerned, though in different ways, about village development, governance, and the local experience of the state.

Even on returning home, migrants like Angelina find they may not have arrived for good. Instead, the ways their kin and neighbors want to depend on them, along with their own dreams of progress, work against their previous resolve to remain in their home village. Going overseas again beckons with each new crisis or faltering relationship. I lost count of the times Angelina told me, on the phone, "It's still the same here in Haliap. Nothing has changed; it's still kurang." While Angelina was in Hong Kong, she had thought it was sad that Nora had spent so many years away, visiting her husband, children, relatives, and home only once or twice a year. Yet, after only six months back in Haliap, she was wondering aloud to me, over the phone, if she, too, might not be better off taking another overseas contract. Perhaps Nora had made the right choice.

Nora, in turn, told me that she had decided to remain abroad for much the same set of reasons: there were few opportunities for local investment and development in the barangay that would not depend on someone in the household earning a cash salary abroad to support them. She would rather be that earner abroad than the person struggling to cope with seeking approvals from and alliances with local regulations and development institutions: the projects, the land registry, the mayor's office, the government departments, and their agents.

Her husband struggled with these offices and their programs and regulations, unsuccessfully, on her behalf, each time they made an investment. She thought the sheer frustration involved in "putting up a business" was one of the reasons he would sometimes drink too much.

Luis, meanwhile, had fallen into many of the irregularities that persist beyond the Canadian state's current capacity to enforce TFW program rules in Canada. He experienced illegal recruiting charges, an unscrupulous broker, above-market rent, unpaid overtime, and a job that did not extend for the full two years of his visa. At the same time, his relations with Nora back in Hong Kong had also become strained. Just before Angelina's return, Nora had funded a land deal in Haliap in which her younger brother, Mark, Angelina's former fiancé, bought a field from Luis's eldest brother, Alfred. Custom dictated that the field should have been offered to Luis and Angelina first, but neither Alfred, nor Nora, nor Mark bothered to inform Luis of the transaction. As Luis explained: "We are IPs; we have protocols for this when it is a sale of ancestral land. If my brother likes to sell, he must inform me. If I cannot buy, then Mark must compensate me. They all know that. They just choose to ignore it. Even Nora; she knows I will not like it. If I will go home, I can make a problem for Mark, because the people will not respect what he has done." Luis thus wanted to advocate for a different kind of governance in Haliap to protect his customary interests in land.

As migrants, my three friends all carried their village with them. This village is virtual because it is at once a place being made through technically mediated intimacies and an ideal yet to be achieved, in the sense that its security, adequacy, and sufficiency are yet to come. By understanding themselves through the hopes and dreams they have pinned to migration as a solution to their financial concerns, villagers are in one way vulnerable, dependent on a fragile set of relations. At the same time, the shared sense the villagers have of their village and themselves as lacking progress actually makes their village relations robust. To transform themselves from failure and lack, migrants and those at home must remain intimately tied together by caring relations, even as their losses haunt them, and by their hopes for better futures. This means they remain intimately tied, too, to the things villagers expect government and development projects to deliver.

Nothing Changes?

What does not change very much for migrants while they are sojourning abroad is their experience of the national government in the village. It is, of course, a much more vicarious experience while they work overseas, but the government governs them at a remove through their exchanges with kin and investments in property and businesses at home. (We have seen this in the way that, by extending balikbayan box privileges to migrant workers, the government reinforced nascent popular notions that contract workers should or would eventually become emigrants.) Because it is their village exchanges and relations that define and sustain migrants during their overseas sojourns, migrants continue to see the state from a particular village vantage point and find themselves unable to move on from their entanglements with it. The government they experience as villagers is a rather incomprehensible patchwork of actors, discourses, and exchanges, incommensurable with the ideal they have of an omniscient and caring state that can meet their needs.

If we think about the state in the Philippines more broadly, statist accounts of people's experience of government abound. It is easy to describe the country's central administration (the bureaucracy and the legislature) and its landed elite as essentially one and the same. But it seems possible to recognize this kind of state—where the apparatus of rule has been captured by an elite—as problematic from all angles only if one has the vantage point of a virtuous, individuated national citizen who is not proximate to any stream of benefits from it. People in Haliap lack the institutionalized modern techniques to make something called the state appear as a distinct institution, governed by a central administration. Villagers find it very difficult to separate a state and its officers and institutions from "the people" and thus to treat government agencies and their officers as if the state they represent is actually a separate entity, existing beyond and above society. Instead of seeing the government as immune from the usual expectations for interpersonal reciprocity, they attempt to enter into patron-client relations with government officials and elected politicians. Their interests in doing so often coincide quite well with the interests of the governing elite in securing clients. But these relationships, though they may deliver flows of resources, do not create individuated modern subjects.

Development is certainly what villagers expect should bring their proper, longed-for caring state into being. In Haliap we should have seen village-level development initiatives, funded by the national government and international donors, working as techniques for making the state into a sphere people considered as separate from society. But as chapter 3 demonstrated, government offices, jobs, and salaries have not quite made Haliap people into the modern individuals who are the isolated, disciplined, receptive, industrious political subjects that this modern state needs to bring itself into being. Villagers' deficiency in this regard is the site of their lack. They alternately internalize their collective failure to separate state and society as "our poor Filipino values" and externalize it as "government corruption." And these two discourses about the state were the same ones my migrant respondents used to explain why their investments and plans at home were frustrated.

For example, Nora's first investment, a sari-sari store managed by her husband, failed, she said, because of poor values. People bought on credit, then refused to repay because they knew Nora was working in Hong Kong. Permits for other kinds of businesses they considered, like a long-distance transport vehicle, seemed to require Nora's husband to make donations to politicians' campaigns or pay expediting fees. The staff of local offices also knew that Nora was abroad and wanted their share of her earnings, exhibiting the same poor values. Angelina was worried that her buy-and-sell business would not be able to pay the bribes that she imagined might be required by people working with the Land Transportation Office in order for her to transport vegetables from farm to market. Encountering corruption in the regulation of transport links was a common Ifugao experience, particularly on journeys outside the province. Luis was angry that Haliap land had been approved for individual tenure and thought someone, somewhere in the Land Registration Authority, could have been bribed to give their approval, in another instance of government corruption. Since Luis's departure, a new series of projects had arrived, including building a new water system and providing more training in progressive farming. Angelina reported that all of these projects were having the familiar problems of nepotism and of officers diverting funds. Nora, Angelina, and Luis all blamed the government's flawed practices for Haliap's continued failure to achieve the progress required to let them come home for good.

That the development projects and programs at work in Haliap have not made people over into entirely modern individuals does not seem to be strictly an outcome of geography. It has, after all, been more than a century since colonization and forty years since development projects began in earnest in the village. Development failures cannot be explained solely by Haliap's position as a "far-flung barangay"; there are lots of places that are even more inaccessible and still lack phone coverage and electricity. There is not much evidence to suggest that the state is necessarily weaker or less fully articulated in Haliap only because Haliap lies on some particular social and internal margin of government influence. Haliap's out-migration sites on the agrarian frontier, though in the lowlands, are arguably even more remote in some ways from the caring state. Indeed, the National Commission on Indigenous Peoples, the Department of Agriculture, and the various donor projects have actually brought government offices and their officials into closer proximity to the village, but people have experienced their assessments and practices of evaluating identity as intrusive rather than supportive. Thus something other than sheer distance from the center of government in Manila must be at work.

The rituals, programs, projects, and discourses that have and have not been effective in making the state present in Haliap can tell us about the different and uneven set of practices and symbols that make up the state as a whole. Examining Haliap's encounters with government activities and institutions suggests that villagers often use state practices and symbols primarily to make and manipulate their own identities.[13] Haliap is thus a place where local culture has imposed contextual conditions that limit the ways the expected universal models of state practice can emerge. Thus, even though villagers would tell you they desire the state, they regularly reject, subvert, resist, evade, and ignore the very bureaucratic activities—the census, surveys, new community organizations, and so on—that bring it into being. They are, in James Scott's terms, past masters of the art of not being governed.[14] As their encapsulation by the postcolonial state has intensified, villagers have become experts at manipulating the various governing activities they encounter into competition, so there is a constant struggle to perform "stateness" in which no one set of networked institution prevails, but villagers can glean resources, protect their own interests, and ally themselves, on a shifting basis, with whichever set of governing rules seems most expedient.

Development projects intended to create the kinds of individual citizens on which effective governance depends seem to have been less than successful in the village for two reasons. First, Haliap people have largely been able to incorporate the local arms of the political and economic institutions of governing regimes, including Spanish, American, and those of the post-1946 Philippine Republic, into their indigenous exchange relations. Incorporating the state into village exchange has imbued governing institutions with particular meanings, reflecting local values, priorities, and collectivities. Villagers do not see the government and donor projects as the primary sources of a desirable modern individuality; the Protestant churches likely fulfill that role. Instead they see projects and offices, both political and physical, as sites of potential for other kinds of translations and exchanges, supporting relational personhood and exchange economies. Second, where they are effective, the individuating and modernizing aspects of the state must operate in concert with other kinds of governing power that similarly create modern individuals. Both state and other kinds of governing must use productive and disciplinary forms of power to individuate, creating discourses of responsibility and surveillance that are internalized by the people who recognize themselves as their subjects. Haliap people, however, are far more familiar with agents of government that act with sovereign power rather than the kind of disciplinary power that effectively makes them individuals.

Government agents have shelled them as a collective, stolen their lumber for violating the log ban without consideration of the claims of any individual owners, and claimed their commonly held land. Sovereign power has worked on the village as a collective, reaffirming a collective identity asserted against the national government. Villagers are much less familiar with governing that performs effective individuation through discipline and punishment. They have found that the census can easily be adjusted, votes can be created for ghost voters and also bought, government programs and projects can be modified to account for kin or sitio interests and identities, all through forms of exchange and patronage that are fairly transparent to villagers. And when they have made these adjustments and modifications or paid the bribes, nothing much has happened. Villagers have pretty much succeeded in their aims of continuing to have collectives of kin, faith, and propinquity and extended personhood recognized at the local level. While we should expect that governing institutions' intensified regulating of the boundaries of persons-as-individuals through development would produce the assemblage of a modern state in Haliap, there is little evidence for this. Villagers remain relational persons, still resisting being classified, enumerated, and distinguished as individuals by the projects and programs of governing they encounter. The village language of "stateness" that they have developed is all about exchange and reciprocity, networks and ties. As in other villages in the Philippines, people try to send their creditors, siblings, and spouses to perform their counterpart labor to access project benefits; might guess the state of their neighbor's contraceptive practices to support the success of health campaigns; and would go to the mayor's office in case of emergency, reluctant to recognize that the funds they are asking for will likely have been diverted from the development initiatives they await.

While villagers' accounts of the state they inhabit describe a government that is corrupt, inefficient, and irrelevant to much of Haliap's daily life, migrants overseas, on the other hand, continue to develop an ideal of a caring government that is the focus of much of the village's affective energy and full of compelling potentials.

The State of the Village

Looking at people's daily experience we find that the state villagers experience is both incoherent—a diffuse network of institutional arrangements and political practices with ambiguous boundaries—and attempting to become symbolically unified. This symbolic unity is being consolidated through the unsteady ways that people participate in a public imagery of the Philippine nation. But this national imaginary is one in which their very belonging has been continually debated. Both the political practices of incoherence and the production of symbols of unity generate a series of specific ways to distinguish state from society, bringing into being what historian Timothy Mitchell calls the "state effect."[15] By this he means the ways something called the state emerges from people's desires and becomes effective by existing in a set of mundane social processes through which people come to distinguish abstract categories of government, economy, religion, and society. This state effect causes people to set apart a distinct realm of social life as "the government," meaning an assemblage that structures, codes, generates information, produces expertise, makes plans, and forms intentions. As I've argued above, the state effect in Haliap is weak. Just where the government lies in Haliap is never clear. People play off the policies and programs of the elected barangay council against the interests of CECAP, national government-line agencies like the Department of Agriculture, the churches, various NGOs, and village elders as they see the need.

In Haliap this state effect emerges in ritual and symbol and in struggles over resources, as people claim belonging, recognition, and struggle for inclusion or to test their social size by exerting influence.[16] Contests over influence on village life then bring forth a local stateness that villagers then take as a metonym of the nation-state as a whole. Haliap's local stateness is uneven, the state appearing most clearly where and when particular practices and languages combine and coexist, supported by the patronage of big people. The kinds of institutions and political practices that shape local stateness are a defined territory, a knowable population, and the possibility of generating resources. But in Haliap, enacting the kind of practical governance that would produce territory, population, and resources (taxes) for government through these local institutions is where the national government is least successful, because it is these practices that threaten the existing networks sustaining big persons. While ancestral domain and the census have been attempting, in a faltering way, to bring practical governance into being over a defined territory and a knowable population for the last twenty years, villagers deem state efforts at resourcing to be the government's definitive failure.

Instead, resourcing has run in the opposite direction, with resources being removed from villagers' control. Generally the law has supported these extractions. Rather than being objective, national law and other nation-state practices have been captured and undermined by people's quite local efforts to secure political and economic survival through reciprocal exchange. Hence the law and government regulatory practices regularly intrude into reciprocal relations where people do not want them and tend to be absent or unavailable when people seek defense against predatory extractions. For example, the law could not be effectively invoked where villagers would want it—against the military seizing lumber or provincial officials grabbing land, for instance—but turns up where they do not. Such was the ban on extracting logs from the local forest—these logs being trees that village households have managed on land they have claimed for taxes whose sale would fund education—that was implemented by the military.

This daily experience of the state means that, beyond the barangay, people can rarely recognize state institutions, like POEA, as representing their village interests; rather, these institutions seem to actively work against them, so people find the institutions at best irrelevant, at worst corrupt and frightening. There is indeed much going on elsewhere in terms of governance in the Philippines, but these practices and activities are ones villagers find difficult to envision and make commensurate with their knowledge of how government works.

When the local state appears in people's everyday practices, it emerges through a symbolic language of authority. Officers representing national government institutions thus talk about the national law and make the government material and relevant in village life through signs and rituals. Signs include the placards on offices and projects and decals on vehicles. Some of these practices would be the endless project and community organization meetings and the working bees for counterpart labor on government-approved or -sponsored projects. Rituals would be found in the ways that development institutions and their categories and jargon are incorporated not only into events like the parade, but into the daily lives of villagers who attend offices and conform to surveys, aligning their own words with the stated goals of projects. One of the most visible rituals would be almost mandatory speeches feting development agency personnel at village festivals, usually offered by the very same big villagers who are most effectively undermining development efforts. For the state effect to work, all of these signs, practices, and rituals should inscribe a shared sense of state-level community and history—the nation of the Philippines—on local landscapes and cultures.

Clearly, Haliap's symbolic languages of authority instantiate a much more local and limited kind of state effect. What happens in the ethnic parade described at the opening of this book is the renewal of a kind of symbolic covenant. The parade offers a liminal space in which a story overseen by local state officials is intended to both condense and give shape to the world around it. This activity engages the mythical dimensions of the state, suggesting that if people perform the story properly in their real lives, the national government will then deliver development to them. But other symbolic exchanges call into question the state/society distinction established there. The Contemplacion incident was one such exchange, a reminder that the government's bureaucrats were not a state unto themselves but were beholden to the nation for their authority. A government that attempted to act as an autonomous entity, making decisions running counter to the affective forces in the society it claimed to govern, would be a fragile one. Beginning with the fall of the Marcos dictatorship, the Philippine history of both successful people-power revolutions and various unsuccessful attempts to launch them has shown how the public understands that government cannot be both autonomous and legitimate. Villagers enjoyed participating in the collective expressions that put the government back in its place, serving the people. That new laws resulted and that more resources were made available to support and recognize migrants were appropriate outcomes.

More problematic for villagers were the symbolic languages expressed around the government's local signs and rituals, such as the painted rocks on the road. These make the state present, but in ways that do not connect villagers to the resourcing practices they anticipate. Like Luis, villagers want rituals and symbols to deliver, to have a purpose, to be effective in creating durable, meaningful links to government. When it comes to inscribing a shared history onto the village by way of the parade, people are ambivalent. They find it a fun part of a festival day but also insulting—why do women have to be the primitives and professional women wear native uniform—and motivating—we do have Ifugao OCWs—in equal measure. People migrate to avoid allowing their engagements with a state that fails to deliver development to produce experiences of trauma and senselessness.[17] This is the state that villagers find they cannot move on from but must escape in order to negotiate with it more successfully.

THE STATE AS AN ARTICLE OF FAITH

We might anticipate that, unable to apprehend the Philippine state as whole, predictable, and meaningful, people would perform the rituals that align them to state goals in an affectively empty, automatic way. This is not the case. People participate in ways that both motivate and conceal their "divergent or contradictory affective commitments."[18] This means ritual performances of ethnic citizenship, like the parade, are not sufficient to recreate relational persons into individuated, modern subjects. Participants in the parade do not repress their awareness that those governing have no true political authority in order to allow their government to work. This awareness is actually very much at the forefront of their thoughts. Thus the parade does not produce faith in the state's ultimate "truth, justice, and functionality" by creating subjects who are oriented to care about their nation-state in particular ways.[19] Instead, participants engage with the story told by the parade through their own practices of mobility, experimenting with new roles and versions of themselves and their relations with others. One of the villagers' main purposes in migration is to test the idea that one could become a person who might develop this kind of faith in the state as a universal precept.

In Haliap, migration is an experiment in which migrants test the notion that one could come to believe, by living somewhere else, in a truthful, just, and functioning state. Only then might this universal be extended to the institutions and relations that govern home. Thus Nora in Hong Kong and Luis in Canada were exploring the possibilities of believing in government care elsewhere, before they could consider how they might bring about this caring state at home.

What Haliap people want from their state is care that would protect them from kurang, meaning insecurity and insufficiency. This term marks a set of interwoven ideas that layer on top of each other the exigencies of personalistic relations and ongoing obligations to reciprocate, unexpected natural disasters, and corrupt government expropriations. It is the failure of their mythologized state to care through development that motivates people to act on themselves and their sense of the world. Luis has turned to a religion that promises to offer him even more effective governance and symbolism, while Nora and her friends have decided to move forward with developing by themselves. Development here—what it should mean and who should enact it—is the site of a push-pull relationship that distinguishes people and government. People tend to attribute this failure to the statelike actors—the institutions with their projects, programs, NGOs, and their staff, the local officials—rather than attributing it to the alternative: a more profound failure among the people themselves, in their human capacities.

Haliap subjectivities are thus quite clearly oriented to the state. The state that they define themselves against and evade is one that originated in the violence of the colonial era; has been reshaped by the ongoing failure of development programs; and is then shifted further toward a neoliberal, facilitating model of governance by the export of contract migrants. Villagers, however, see becoming permanent elsewhere as the new way of becoming elite, achieving prosperity and becoming worthy of government attention or at least capable of negotiating with state officials on a more equal footing, and thus perhaps transforming the Philippine state itself toward delivering care. People attempt to achieve this change in status not simply by earning abroad but by becoming absorbed, as equal humans, by a better quality of state elsewhere. Migration, then, does not so much undermine villagers' ideal of the universal form of state but consolidate what they expect from it in terms of reciprocal care. Through migration, both in migrants' direct experience and the vicarious experience of the community, the ideal state becomes even more pivotal in how people imagine what security should be. Hence Luis and Angelina corresponded with Jojo to compare conditions in Hong Kong and Canada with things at home. Where would the government give them more support and a better deal? For them, migration is a way of negotiating with this more abstract ideal of the state by playing off its various aspects against each other across international borders.

Abroad, migrants like Luis find that the welfare state recedes before them. It is there but remains tantalizing, just out of reach. Migrants instead find openings for the kinds of personalism they are used to at home. Governments cannot truly govern people's interpersonal and affective connections by legislating and regulating, but their legislation and regulations can give some shape to the ways that these ties can be attenuated, minimized, and stretched by refusing to recognize them. To offer people the support they seek, the state must individuate, refusing to recognize certain kinds of relations of debt, of kinship, of sociality. Yet people can find and make gaps in which they can work around the ways that becoming an individual is required by state institutions, just as Luis had been negotiating with his employers in Calgary. What makes these experiments uneven and more confusing—for both the state and the migrants—is that the virtual village is not encapsulated within one state, but extends through several different ones: the Philippines, Hong Kong, and Canada. As much as they compare and contrast, as contract migrants move on, they learn that the problems of their weak postcolonial state are a set of entanglements that define them and that they cannot leave behind.

ANGELINA'S AND LUIS'S LIVES reveal how the new kinds of identities created by the global realm's new economic forms—here, temporary labor migration—shape dynamic cultures both at home and abroad. As Angelina struggled with being reidentified as balikbayan and Luis negotiated his new Temporary Foreign Worker status in Canada, their experience of virtual village life remade their intimate inner processes: intimacy, memory, feelings, and their senses of being selves in the world. The reverse has also been true. It is their village-shaped sense of self that in turn has scripted how they have interacted with family, neighbors, governments, agents, brokers, and employers, and thus shaped globalization—and the emergent global realm—itself, through interactions with different forms of the state.

Luis in Calgary

Initially, Luis felt that his life was going as well as might be expected with his work in Calgary. "I can accept my situation here," he explained to me. When I visited him in the summer of 2009, Luis was sharing a room in the two-bedroom, ground-floor condominium in southwest Calgary previously occupied by his employer's mother. Outside, in the parking lot that formed the forecourt of the apartment block, sat an old, dented sedan. Luis and his workmates had purchased the car secondhand to ferry their landscaping team around the Calgary area. Luis was not one of the drivers, but he helped pay for gas. His typical daily routine involved traveling to jobs, working for nine or ten hours, returning to the apartment and cooking with the group, then phoning Angelina, whom he had already texted early in the morning, using a discount phone card and the apartment's landline. The time difference between Haliap and Calgary meant Angelina received his morning text as she went to bed, and then they spoke on the phone mid-morning, her time. Once a week, or more often if he was able, he took the C-train (aboveground subway) to attend Iglesia services with his new Calgary congregation. He had met most of his nonwork Filipino friends through the church. Once a month he would travel on the C-train to Pacific Mall in the northeastern part of the city. There, at a business called I-Remit, he would send what money he could to Angelina's Lagawe bank account. Every month or so he would attend a Filipino social event, usually with members of his church, and eat Filipino food. In the few hours he had at the apartment outside his working time, he did laundry or went shopping in the stores in the sizable strip mall three blocks to the east. The complex was dominated by a massive Walmart, where Luis and I spent several hours shopping for work clothes during my stay at the nearby Big 8 motel. The vista to the south from Luis's apartment and the Walmart parking lot was an open prairie that rolled away toward the United States. Looking south, Luis lamented that his papers would not allow him to cross the Canada-U.S. border. But after all, this was not such a disappointment. "My purpose here is to earn," he told me. "Maybe later I can become a tourist."

Luis responded to the circumstance he found in Calgary by living up to the stereotypes of Filipinos as uncomplaining and hardworking. He concentrated on building good relations with his employer and with Ben, Albert, and Marlon, the three other Filipino TFWs on his landscaping team, who were also his roommates. In July 2009 he had not yet raised the question of working conditions with his boss, even though TFW conditions stipulate that workers should work no more than forty hours per week. Instead, he and his coworkers had been working to become the most efficient team in his boss's business. They could landscape in a day, he reported, what it took a Canadian team three days to do. They were thus a credit to their boss. But they were also vulnerable. The same labor broker had recruited all the members of Luis's team. Since their broker was now being investigated for breaking the rules of the TFW program, any applications she had made for them to transfer their labor market orders between employers were being scrutinized very closely by Citizenship and Immigration Canada.

At the end of July 2009, Luis was focused on the increasingly fragile relations within the landscaping team and apartment. Two of his coworkers, Ben and Albert, had arrived on visas attached to LMOs at another landscaping company but found it had gone into bankruptcy. They had then applied to transfer to Luis's employer and were waiting for approval. Technically, they should not have been working at all. Another of his team, Marlon, wanted to move out of the shared apartment, because the rent their employer was charging was far more than market rate. Other two-bedroom apartments in the same complex were being advertised for C$1,500 (US$1,389) per month.[1] Luis's employer was receiving C$2,540 (US$2,352). This amount included heat and light, but Luis did not know exactly what these services cost, as the bills went to the employer/owner directly. Luis's employer also should have been paying overtime for hours amounting to more than eight per day or forty-four per week at one and a half times his regular wage, with no day longer than twelve hours. With Luis's agreement, however, the employer could offer paid days off in lieu of overtime, and this is perhaps where banking Luis's hours fit in. All the workers were frustrated.

Luis's friend Marlon was responding to pressure from his family in the Philippines to send more money, having borrowed his placement fee from his sister-in-law, an OCW in Taiwan. Ben and Albert had borrowed money from their wives' families. Luis was the only one of the four on the team with a debt to a finance company. Though his repayments were eating up more than 40 percent of his monthly take-home pay, he observed that at least the finance company did not call him or pressure him to change circumstances that company representatives did not understand.

Luis counseled his team to wait to make any changes, saying that if one person left, the rest would suffer and the team dynamic would be ruined. Their employer could easily have terminated the contract of someone who did not have his papers in order, and might have done so, particularly if they stopped paying rent. Finally, in late August Luis's coworkers' papers were transferred to the landscaping firm. Their employer took all of them on a daylong trip into the Rocky Mountains to celebrate. Luis skipped the event. Instead, he traveled with me and two of his friends from the Iglesia to another site in the Rockies for a day out. Luis brought his camera phone and took many pictures; he enjoyed seeing mountain landscapes again, even if the Rockies were far bigger and more barren compared to the Cordillera.

The next week Luis led a delegation to speak with his boss. In response to Luis's telling his employer about his debts at home, family pressures, and the irregularities of their situation, his employer had lowered the rent from C$635 to C$335 (US$310) each per month and raised the number of hours in each fortnightly pay from seventy to eighty. So, Luis said at the end of August 2009, he now considered the money "okay." He thought he would now be able to send Angelina almost the full P15,000 rather than the P7,000 ($160) he previously had been sending. He even mused that he might be able to save a bit too. But all of this would quickly come undone.

Luis's next problem was to cope with his seasonal layoff. He planned to see if he could find a way to access his banked overtime in bulk and claim his employment insurance benefits rather than simply paying rent to his boss while unemployed. If Luis were a Canadian worker, he would have been able to demand the overtime he had worked at one and a half times the regular rates and claim employment insurance benefits for a seasonal layoff. Luis had heard that employment insurance applications from some TFWs had been successful when their employment had ended in a layoff. Again he needed the support of his employer to submit the necessary forms. If the employer had wanted to retain an efficient team and did not want any official attention drawn to the level of rent he had charged and the number of hours of overtime he had banked—both of which did not comply with TFW program standards and, in terms of overtime, Alberta's labor laws—he should have been reluctant to see his workers apply for benefits or to leave his employment. If it were discovered that Luis's employer had failed to comply with the TFW rules and the contractual conditions of employment for his TFW workers, the employer could have been refused future LMO applications. But the employer did not seem concerned about the possible outcomes of being investigated as a result of his workers' complaining, or at least he was not concerned enough to try to retain the team. In the end, Luis and the rest of the team moved out of the apartment and quit their jobs, eventually receiving their banked overtime after negotiating for several weeks. Their employer did not immediately provide them with the supporting documents they needed to claim employment insurance benefits.[2]

Luis was then unemployed for two weeks, working casually (and illegally) for cash for the employer of one of his friends from church. His labor broker helped him to rewrite his resume as a cook's helper, and he finally found a job for the winter in a Vietnamese restaurant. It was late October 2009. He texted me immediately, expressing huge relief because he would be able to continue to remit, if not the whole amount he had promised to Angelina, at least something. He would now be earning C$10 (US$9.25) per hour for a ten-hour day, six days per week. His working conditions once again contravened the TFW regulations, but Luis needed the extra hours to make up for the lower wage. The work itself proved monotonous and dull, and Luis did not want to tell me much about it, except that it was a low job and that he would be seeking better-paid work—and something better suited to his skills—in the spring. I interpreted his reluctance to talk about the work to mean that he did not yet have an LMO for the job and was thus working in contravention of his TFW visa conditions.

By February 2010 Luis had repaid his debt in Hong Kong and part of his travel expenses, also borrowed from friends there. His good news was that the restaurant owner might be able to nominate him for permanent residence as an employee with special skills under the Provincial Nominee Program. That would only happen if the employer found Luis to be a skilled, diligent, uncomplaining employee, plunging Luis into a now familiar situation of working long hours that were not always paid as overtime. Luis spent the spring and summer of 2010 applying for other jobs. He told me he had made four separate applications to Cargill Foods (the Canadian arm of the American agricultural commodities giant) for jobs in production but was never successful. His failure to secure a new job may have reflected the impact of the economic downturn but was most likely due to his original LMO being for unskilled work (landscaping was categorized as Class C and D in Canada's occupational tables in 2008).[3] Luis was now targeting the better-paying employers who would have approval to hire only those workers categorized as skilled under the TFW program, but he had not completed the skills training apparently on offer from his initial employer. At the same time as Luis was seeking work, the Alberta labor market had large numbers of skilled TFW workers who were ending their initial contracts and/or seeking better working conditions.

It seems Luis never did manage to find another job with an LMO. Perhaps his first employer blacklisted him as a troublesome employee or his skills set was no longer in demand. Instead, after he left the restaurant, my impression is that Luis continued to work in Calgary's informal economy, cleaning offices and doing odd jobs, for the rest of his two-year visa. He was never able to send Angelina the P15,000 per month he had promised her; instead, his remittances often dropped down to P3,000–4,000 per month. This was a matter of some shame for him, and other than saying he felt "ashamed" of his work and what had happened with his move to Alberta, he was very reluctant to talk about the job he was doing. In October 2010 his father became seriously ill, and Luis had to borrow money from friends in Calgary to meet the medical bills. This wiped out any savings he and Angelina had been able to accumulate.

Negotiating Difference and Distance

In negotiating his working conditions, Luis's personalistic strategies were both a result of the structure of the Canadian TFW program and a reflection of his experience of work in the Philippines and of his broader self-understandings and feelings about himself as a Haliap Adyangan and a Filipino. One reinforced the other.[4] Luis understood himself as more than an individual, finding his personhood in kin relations and village ties. Thus, when he arrived in Canada, he was accustomed to dealing with other similarly constituted persons rather than atomized individuals and abstract rules. If Luis could have found another, better-paying job for his second year in Canada, he knew there was a chance he would be able to save some of his Canadian earnings and have the capital he had always dreamed of to invest. This would have been possible if the temporary labor migration program had been what he had been led to expect. He also would have liked to stay on permanently, as he told me in July 2009. "If you have a stable job, you can have a nice life here. A house, a car, good schools, good health care," he observed. Luis would have had to convert his unskilled status to skilled to achieve permanent residency, but it did not seem to be possible for a Class C or D migrant working in a low-paying cook's helper position to become recognized as skilled. Luis never really understood the rules for switching visas, partly because he always seemed to hear stories of a friend of someone else who had just succeeded in breaking those rules.

Because of the inherent risks of his patronage relations failing, Luis knew he must simultaneously keep himself focused on ways to open up possibilities back in the Philippines. He involved himself with the Iglesia ni Cristo congregation, advising younger TFWs on workplace conflicts and mailiw. He hoped he could regain his deacon status, as church ties would help him face down the village expectations of balikbayans Angelina had met on her return home. Likewise, church ties could help him settle his family in Calgary. His plans for ongoing economic security at home, however, drew him back yet again to the ancestral domain process and the problems of indigenous identities, even as he struggled to cope with work in Calgary.

Luis wanted to see ancestral domain granted to Asipulo in order to enforce customary Ifugao law on the sale of rice fields. Yet, in late 2009 the land that had been certified "alienable and disposable" in Haliap—those areas under 18 degrees in slope—had been made available for private titling. The fields his brother had sold likely would have been assessed in this alienable and disposable area, but Luis wanted to see the paperwork in the land registry for himself. Haliap's commitment to the ancestral domain application had finally collapsed in the face of the interprovincial dispute between Ifugao and Nueva Viscaya over Barangay Camandag. In early 2010 Luis learned that his brother Alfred had subsequently sold a second field and moved his family to Manila, apparently permanently, with the proceeds. This field was also not offered to Luis but instead was sold to a woman from outside Barangay Haliap, who planned to have it farmed by local tenants.

Luis and Angelina decided their future plan would be to invest in more rice fields close by so that Angelina could manage investments that were both more secure in terms of production and markets and closer to home. Their frontier farm still had some potential, if only to sell on to another migrant, but Angelina had found that it was just too far away. She could not take care of it and take care of Oscar in Haliap at the same time, and Luis's younger brother Samuel had proven to be no help at all. Rice fields in Haliap would give Luis something to come back to, he reasoned. There would always be a demand for rice, and he could always hire someone to work the fields for him in Barangay Haliap. Thus, from Calgary, Luis began lobbying, through Angelina and his old friends, to try to undo the contract of sale on Alfred's rice field while being critical of the idea of individual, private landownership rather than Adyangan customary law. The virtue of the village as he now envisioned it was one of conserving Adyangan tradition, giving him access to secure sites of investment.

Luis's dreams were now of recreating Haliap as a more traditional indigenous village that would also be a hub of the Iglesia faithful.

On leaving Calgary, in March 2011, Luis was entertaining multiple sets of plans. What little money he had put together to take home he thought Angelina might use to reapply for work in Hong Kong. If they sold their plot in Nueva Viscaya and Angelina remitted her earnings from a good job there, they might have enough money to send Oscar to the Iglesia college in Manila. Or perhaps both Luis and Angelina might find work in Hong Kong again, marketing themselves as a housekeeping couple. To move on again, both Luis and Angelina will need references from their overseas employers. Thus Luis asked me to omit some details of their time in Hong Kong and, most especially, his recent employment in Calgary, details that would make it difficult to secure employment references from their previous employers. Luis is bitterly disappointed with what happened with his job in Canada and, understandably, wants to keep his options for the future open.

With Luis's having returned home, at least temporarily, and having maintained phone and text contact during his sojourn in Calgary, I can surmise some of the ways his approach to working in Canada led to his expectations being frustrated and his sense of personal failure. I am well aware that after the richness with which I can describe Luis's and Angelina's lives in Hong Kong, my subsequent account of Luis's life in Calgary feels flat. This is both because of the need to respect confidentiality and because Luis was struggling with feelings of betrayal and disappointment.

Our friendship in the early 1990s had painted for him a rather rose-tinted picture of middle-class Canadian encounters with the 1980s welfare state. By the time Luis got to Canada, that state had receded, somewhat unevenly, and was being shored up by the neoliberal temporary migration regime in which Luis became caught as an unskilled worker. As Luis's account of his experiences unfolded over the phone, I saw through his eyes a Canada that I no longer recognized as my own country. Some of Luis's resentments and sense of betrayal are directed toward the Canadian government and his specific employers, and some of this ill feeling is quite understandably currently shadowing our friendship. Having just migrated from Australia to the United Kingdom with a young family, and coming from Canada's eastern coast rather than its prairies, I found myself unable to provide him with meaningful help, advice, or contacts in his struggles in Calgary. Luis knows me as a village researcher, but he did not want me to use my research with him in Calgary to spark an exposé of the real-world conditions of TFW program workers, and he most especially did not want me to publish the names and details of his employers and labor broker.

Instead he wanted, somehow, to find himself in the decent, reasonably paying job he thought he had contracted for, a job that respected his human dignity. As much as the sense of a distance having opened up between us distressed me, my sense that Luis felt betrayed by Canada challenged me to explain how this has happened.

MAKING MIGRANT RIGHTS INSECURE

Perhaps the biggest risk that migration posed for Luis was to his own sense of himself in the world. This is the baggage he carries with him as a villager. Even before he left Hong Kong, I understood that his self-image was threatened by the idea that the outcomes of his migration would somehow be about his quality as a human being. Luis expected that this quality would be revealed to him through his success in building relations with others, so his self-concept as a migrant was founded on the premise that his broker and employer and broader Canadian society would recognize what he saw as his common human- ity. Luis thus dreamed of what he described as a "lenient" employer who would understand his sacrifices and follow the rules of the TFW program because they respected him as a fellow human being. The personalistic approach he brought with him to Canada was one that he already knew he could use to turn corruption and nepotism to his advantage, at least in the Philippines. This personalism also explained his frustrations in Hong Kong, attributing his lack of pay raises and days off to a failure of his relationship with his employer and his own personal qualities rather than to legal regimes or governments and the ways they do and do not regulate migration.

In both Hong Kong and Calgary, Luis conceived of employment relations as part of a gift economy. He understood that his work was a gift that could never be fully compensated by money—instead, work was a gift that left a residual claim for reciprocity with the recipient. Just as it did in his interac- tions with his siblings, Luis anticipated that a debt of gratitude for forgone earnings and opportunities would inevitably accrue with his future employer. Recognizing that this debt would build over time, he anticipated that he would enjoy better working conditions, a higher salary, and more respect the longer he stayed on in Canada, just like Nora had in Hong Kong. Because an employer, who would also be, by extension, Canada, would accumulate this debt to him and it could not be extinguished by payment alone, the initial patronage rela- tionship should have moved toward equality or parity of exchange. Luis thus arrived in Canada with an ideal of an employment situation that was likely far more complex and long lasting than the simple market-based relationship an employer might anticipate.[5]

The rules of the TFW program and the laws of Alberta require employers to remain immune from any extra requests workers like Luis might make. But noncompliance within what is a very lightly regulated program puts both the worker and the employer into a gray area. Here, workers might be in no position to complain, or they might be able to effectively leverage an irregular situation into better pay or working conditions. Outside the boundaries of the law, the outcome cannot be guaranteed. This gray area and the lack of guarantees were the space of both Luis's hopes and his insecurity while he worked in Calgary. Here, what Luis saw as an employer's responsibilities to his human dignity could have been secured only through interpersonal negotiations. Luis's claims on his employer could have been unwelcome or could have been considered to be the transaction cost of cheap, tractable labor—the travails and needs of the virtual village being laid at an employer's door.

COMMUNITY/IMMUNITY

To understand how global migration works, we need to acknowledge that Luis's expectations cannot be dismissed as the naïve approach of a premodern person encountering modern society. The relations Luis anticipates coincide reasonably well with the political traditions of citizenship and community in liberal democracies. Philosopher Roberto Esposito has suggested that the kind of reciprocity people like Luis anticipate is actually fundamental to how the Western liberal tradition understands community and thus shapes the role of the state. In Esposito's account the Western ideal of community is based on reciprocity. Community is built on the "giving of a gift that doesn't—indeed cannot—belong to oneself."[6] This gift of community demands an exchange in return, either in goods or in services. Villagers in Haliap recognize a similar idea of community: what they cannot keep only for themselves is their labor and its products. Traditionally, their rice fields may be individually owned but are cultivated by households and considered to be borrowed from future generations. When they are sold, their cultivators should compensate an extended kin group. Lives are likewise borrowed from God, as in the teachings of Luis's church. Esposito refers to this demand for ongoing reciprocity as the originary defect of community because reciprocal donations threaten individual identities.

Opposing and balancing community is the ideal of immunity—not to be and not to have in common. Conferred by the state, immunity exonerates individuals from ongoing obligations to reciprocate or from their previously contracted debts. The ideal state thus has a government that defends people against community attempts to expropriate their property. Such is Luis's imaginary of a caring state, where government services and benefits would buffer him from the predatory extractions of kin. In Luis's Haliap, people do not interact with one another and with the agents of the state with entirely bounded, individual identities. Rather, they experience a governing extending from a very uneven and conflicted assemblage, not all of which is regulated by what they recognize as the government. Just what the government is and is not remains a bit of a mystery. When the Philippine state confers immunity on people, it happens on a piecemeal and personalistic basis, more as corruption and nepotism than as smooth and equitable regulation. Thus soldiers can steal lumber, and the provincial officials can grab land, with immunity. Immunity can overturn and conflict with previous norms and laws, as in the case of ancestral domain.

Villagers see these contradictions, ruptures, and personal accommodations as at times being beneficial, but the politics they enact is one of pity and humanity rather than purposefully regulating an even social field to produce equality of treatment for all citizens. For Esposito, this fragmented and personalistic kind of state is grounded in a biopolitics where physically possessing land does not correspond to complete juridical ownership. In this biopolitics, familiar to villagers in Haliap and along the frontier, the possibility of violent death from the interference of others is almost always at hand. When Luis was mourning his murdered friend and destroyed the research notes on rice planting, he was expressing his resistance to this biopolitics. It gave others security and status at his expense while exposing him to risk and shame.

Compared to the weak state found on the Philippine frontier, the Canadian kind of state works somewhat differently. This does not mean it is more coherent in its operations, less contradictory, but simply that it operates along different lines of naming and governing. In states like Canada, Esposito sees that the concepts of liberty and private property guarantee individuals a kind of insurance against the interference of others. This state guarantee does not so much protect against violent death as permit "development of the life process of society as a whole."[7] The Canadian kind of state needs to provide flexible labor in order to afford its citizens the conditions in which to do business efficiently. The Canadian state form is grounded in a biopolitics that enables employers and brokers to contract noncitizen migrants with minimal regulation or interference. Its governing does not so much balance the rights and interests of the individual against those of sovereign power as emerge from a more distributed and complex set of relations between property and identities. The complexity of these relations produces a rationality that either integrates people as individuals into the society made by this state or excludes them, gathering them into special social spaces of non-belonging. Shaped by this kind of state, Canadian society is no longer governed by discipline and punishment, but by control. Thus the

Canadian government is not so much concerned with territorial integrity as with coding and controlling statistics, flows, and networks. This was Luis's lesson: migrants who are coded as unskilled cannot be transformed into skilled workers through any personal ties they might establish. Instead, they must either complete approved Canadian training or leave the country and reapply to become coded as skilled. The unskilled are thus used and excluded.

When a society of state control like Canada feels it is under attack, or threatened by global competition, it establishes new practices of biopolitical control that create generalized groups, gathering together individuals and making them indistinct. Such control practices are both social and spatial, producing what are called "zones of indistinction."[8] By creating special populations that are effectively excluded from national society, these zones are another form of Agamben's space of exception. This is the kind of space that has been created by expanding Canada's temporary migration programs to include temporary visas for low-skilled and unskilled workers in 2002. The exploitative outcomes of this change in migration policy are widely acknowledged in Canada. Alberta's complaints-activated system for protecting the rights of TFWs has been criticized for a reluctance to prosecute agencies and employers who contravene their legal and contractual obligations, and it has been noted that these contraventions seem to fall disproportionately on unskilled migrants.

Thus, as a TFW program worker, Luis was effectively denied access to the state institutions and public services that enabled Canadian citizens to remain immune from the demands of their fellows. Under the TFW program, Luis could remain in Canada for two years, but he should not have had any access to the Canada Pension Plan nor be able to rely on Employment Insurance benefits if he had become jobless, unlike the citizens and permanent residents that comprise the rest of Canadian society. Luis, as a TFW, was not eligible to receive assistance from immigrant settlement services supported by public funding. Taxes, pension contributions, and employment insurance premiums were nonetheless deducted from his salary. For most TFW program workers to change employers, it took, in practice, a minimum of two months' wait without income.[9] So Luis actually seems to have been comparatively fortunate in finding that he was able to fend for himself more informally.

Luis, however, had made his decision to come to Canada never having known the kind of immunity most Canadians take for granted. While he desired "a government that cares for its people," his virtual village perspective did not lead him to think of these people being cared for as bounded individuals. The Philippine state had never exonerated him from any communal demands on his property and labor. Though he had paid social security and health care contributions while he was working in Hong Kong, he expected that he would receive little tangible benefit from these payments when he returned to the Philippines for good. Instead, he believed his welfare and well-being would remain enmeshed within networks of virtual village interdependence. Luis thus understood himself as a node in an extended network. The terms of his visa, however, identified him as an individual worker, obscuring his preexisting—and foundational—debts and commitments to others.

IMMUNITY THROUGH BECOMING INDIVIDUAL

Persons attain immunity as individuals, not as villages, kin groups, or nations. In this, Esposito's theory and Luis's lived experience coincide. In Esposito's theory, persons are individuated—that is, they are shaped as modern individuals through the governing of an assemblage that creates subjects of civil and political rights.[10] People without full civil and political rights are less-than-complete—or in Luis's case, more-than-encompassable—persons. The assemblage marks out a space of the individual by cutting the preexisting networks of interdependence that sustain extended persons like Luis. Regulated regimes of migration, like the TFW program, individuate by abstracting persons from the relations of extended kinship and locality and placing them within tightly delimited employment contract and immigration categories. This is what has happened to Luis and his coworkers.

Regulating individuals this way does not discover and cultivate the worker as an autonomous actor. Instead, migration regimes try to produce the worker as an individual by cutting his or her previous ties and inscribing new identities onto the worker. This making of individuals is fundamental to the mode of governing through which the whole Canadian state assemblage of government becomes effective. Producing the individual justifies a sovereign state power that originates within the "artificial vacuum that is created around each person," making them "indivisible and united."[11] When the state extends immunity to individuals, it is providing them with a method to preserve their individual selves that works alongside the other ruptures of modernity: disenchantment and alienation. Yet this modern, sovereign assemblage, which protects life by reifying the individual, can govern effectively only if it is founded on the category of the exception: bare life or those people held beyond the state in zones of indistinction.

Excepted from their host society as Agamben's "bare life" or Haliap's "scratch," migrants without immunity make the immunity of Canadian citizens both possible and valued. Thus, by protecting individual life the state becomes sovereign. Its sovereignty exists, though, only if some exceptional lives are not protected. In daily life this means that Canadian citizens are afforded immunity from demands for reciprocity from people like Luis by institutions, such as taxes, social services, and development aid, and by identities, such as taxpayer, philanthropist, and donor. Globalization through migration and the unrecipro-cated gifts of cheap labor call into question the rules and norms sustaining this kind of becoming individual. The TFW program creates a bleed and a blend through which Canadian individuals—Luis's labor broker and subsequent employers—become both governors of others and gatekeepers, permitting and denying migrants rights. Geographer Geraldine Pratt argues that Canada's tem-porary migration programs allow "liberal, middle-class Canadians" to "adminis-ter" the space of exception inhabited by migrant domestic workers with "a clear conscience."[12]

Yet, migrations' blending together of persons of differing kinds, making individuals, is always in process, never complete. This process means modern individuals are never fully integrated into the totality of their state by the ratio-nalities of its governing.[13] Instead, even self-consciously modern people, like most Canadians, feel and understand themselves to be both constituted and dispossessed by their relations to others.[14] With their early-twenty-first-century turn toward neoliberal understandings of markets, governments, and persons, states like Canada have actually been attempting to divest people of their immu-nity, throwing them back onto their own relations and networks. Government policies seeking community care or denying benefits for persons previously supported by government programs have this effect. As immunity has become about more intensified forms of individuation, it has been made available on a more selective basis. This withdrawal of the caring state from Canadian society shapes migrants' lives through an affective politics.

Testing Global Empathy

Luis's path to Canada revealed how Canadian migration is governed by an assemblage of statelike institutions and actors. His Hong Kong recruiting agency, his Canadian labor broker, his employers—all are effectively able to grant or withhold his rights under the TFW program. There are sensible, struc-tural reasons for employment agencies, labor brokers, and employers to bend the rules. Employment agencies can earn more through offshore placement fees and charges to employers if they recruit new workers overseas. Employers can likewise keep wages low and training minimal with new batches of work-ers rather than offering second contracts to current employees. As an unskilled worker, Luis is not eligible to apply for "landed immigrant" status (permanent residency) through the Canadian Experience program, a program designed to offer highly skilled temporary workers a route to eventual citizenship. Instead he is positioned in a space where the market rationalities and his citizenship status combine to exclude him from permanency and push him toward contravening his visa with work in the informal economy.

Luis traveled to Canada with the goal of transcending the limits placed on him by regulatory regimes—apprehended only in his peripheral vision—with affective ties, intending to create empathy and mutual respect with his patrons/ employers and other Canadians. After all, he had been reasonably successful in building such connections with me and the other staff on our Canadian-funded project in Haliap. But his migrant predicaments remind his broker and employer of their own vulnerability to being dispossessed, shifting their focus to the questionable legality of their own actions and morality of their relationships with migrants. For Canadian employers, globalization of labor supply can be a face-to-face encounter with their own hypocrisy, so it was really no surprise that Luis found such moments of being recognized through affective links quickly repressed. By embodying the exception, Luis's presence and demands to have his past and ties to home accommodated was a challenge to Canadian accounts of liberal modernity. Canadians do not see that the way he expected to encounter reciprocity based on common humanity was, in itself, unfounded, but the obverse: his vision of humanity as shared is so compelling as to be difficult to confront. By expecting reciprocity, Luis's approach reveals the huge problems underpinning temporary labor migration as a way of coping with the global. Within societies like Canada, the fundamental conflicts are no longer physical battles for resources—those are now regulated by the state—but battles for self-understandings between aspects of the individuated and the extended or relational person. Being drawn into the affective intensity of the connections that constitute Luis's sense of himself reminds Canadians of their own uncomfortable sense of distance from kin and neighbors. It is as if migrants hold up a mirror in which host nationals see a distorted image of themselves, and hosts quickly realize that the distortions they see are not faults in the glass but the flaws they have had to ignore in order to hold on to their own self-identity.

Luis wants Canada to recognize him as an equal but more than individual person, confirming that his personhood is shaped as a node in a network of care and obligation. But while Canada governs migrants in ways intended to produce individuals, migration also produces public, collective practices that recognize a different kind of personhood as possible.

In January 2008 a Filipino immigrant to Canada, Arcelie Laoagan, was murdered as she traveled home from a night shift at a Calgary printing company. She was working two jobs while trying to qualify as an accountant. At the time of her death, she had applied to bring her family from the Philippines to Canada. After her death, Citizenship and Immigration Canada closed her family reunification application. Her sister, with the support of the Philippine Consulate in Alberta, has been trying to sponsor Laoagan's family to immigrate —"to ensure her dream of bringing her family to Canada comes true"—as a way of respecting the six years of sacrifices Laoagan made toward providing her family with a better life. They have had support from Laoagan's Canadian employer. When Laoagan's sister relocated from Toronto to Calgary, this company, West Canadian Graphics, gave her a job. They also started a trust fund with a gift of C$10,000 (US$8,196). Donations from the Calgary community have raised that amount to more than C$100,000 (US$81,967). Jane Mugford, vice president of the printing firm, explained, "Everything she'd [Arcelie] been doing here in Canada was to help her family back home so we sort of felt we wanted to do whatever we could to help take her place in that financial way." The funds collected have been sent to the family and used to pay the costs of reopening the application.[15]

Here, the Canadian employer became enmeshed in Filipino kinship, acting in ways that extended the personhood of a murdered employee. Filipinos would expect no less. Much of the money donated likely came from the more than twenty-five thousand Filipinos then living in Calgary. Rather than this outcome, most Canadians would have anticipated that state assistance, compensation, and life insurance should mean an employer would be immune from any claims to support from the family. In this case, workplace friendships and community support combined at the right moment to challenge Canadians' preconceived ideas. The case received media attention, focusing on its global context and the culture of mutual support in the growing Filipino community in Alberta. By asking the public to consider migrants' sacrifices as deserving a broader kind of compensation, this story recognized relational personhood as the basis for a global empathy. It also demonstrated that necropolitics and the discourse of martyrdom, so familiar to Filipinos at home, work globally too.

Luis could find no way of associating himself and his web of village obligations with the networks revealed by this singular case of martyrdom. Most Canadians he met likely saw him as just another unskilled, middle-aged manual laborer, one of many in Alberta seeking money, rather than any kind of potential martyr.

Shaping Coping Mechanisms

As Luis was finding his way in Canada, Angelina was finding her own sense of herself challenged at home. Their senses of self had been reshaped by their mobility, but theirs was never the kind of transformatory travel valued by middle-class metropolitan Filipinos. As I followed Luis's life in Calgary over the phone and by text messages in 2010, I was struck by the differences between Filipino experiences of travel. One of my true balikbayan friends, a dual citizen who spent most of childhood in the United States, explained on her Facebook profile: "I love traveling by myself because the farther I go, the closer I feel to the center of who I really am. It feels like the miles peel away the layers of your physical self (your roles, relationships, obligations, failings, false images, society's conventions) until you get to the core of who you are." Learning the core of who you are through solo adventure is not the project of contract workers like Angelina and Luis. Theirs has been a different kind of self-knowing, less a stripping away and more a wild oscillation between poles of being. Migration has made them bigger and smaller and revealed to them how their being has no core, but lies within their provider/advisor/investor roles and the intimate relationships they maintained with home while away, allowing them to find their true selves not within any center, but within their village dreams of possible futures.

These future dreams are the tools villagers rely on to shape the personal space from which they are able to cope, the endurable zone they inhabit. Recall how at the parade the returned migrant woman with the camera had fascinated my Haliap friends? Assuming that their account of her story accurately reflects their own dreams of the global, we can see how this woman is assembled, recorded, categorized, and measured by institutions governing migration. She has passed a medical exam, been issued a passport, had her qualifications assessed, described how her skills met those sought within a job description, acquired a visa or residency status, found an employer, met a partner, and had the Canadian state recognize her relationship. She is a citizen, a taxpayer, a tourist. She has earnings or savings to spend. The effect of her appearance, looking prosperous and detached, on my friends at the parade is immediate and visceral. Almost instantaneously, by projecting their affect they dreamed of how it would feel to inhabit her identities themselves, without comprehending the migration experience and its assemblage of personal ties and regulatory institutions. But there is nothing definitive in all of this. It tells us nothing much about this particular person—how she experiences herself, what contradictions she may juggle, her own dreams, or how she feels in the moment. We can only speculate from her appearance and from what we know of migration's governing institutions about some of the assortment of identities she carries. Her internal, self-reflective awareness is obscured. Instead of seeing this woman as a whole person, my friends at the parade became infatuated with a list of names and speculative musings on what they imagined to be her social identities.

Angelina found that returning home had placed her in this same role. She had become a screen onto which people projected what they expected from global possibilities, their own senses of themselves, and thus their sense of what Angelina ought to be to them. Becoming this screen gave Angelina a sense of affective rupture that made her anxious. She had spent her years in Hong Kong dreaming of how these people would see her and interact with her, the tenor of their imagined respect and affection sustaining her. But once at home, she quickly found that she had been made to feel small again one minute, big the next. This oscillating experience of being seen as a different sort of person seemed to be slowly moving Angelina toward a still-distant point of rupture, where her dreams became those of leaving Haliap to become a permanent, enabling her to cut more and more of her reciprocal exchange relations and to reorient herself to church networks or government services. Of course, Angelina's experience of return has been shadowed by unresolved land conflicts in the village and Luis's failure to remit the monies he had promised.

Their stories show how villagers who migrate are always more than migrants who are subjects produced simply by discourses governing migration. This approach posits the subject as made through a kind of doubling: "subject to others by control and dependence, and tied to his own identity by a conscience or self-knowledge."[16] This subject thus comes to know himself or herself in the terms set by his or her dependence and control by others. Applying such accounts of the subject to migrant Filipinos has suggested that those who migrate come to understand themselves primarily as technical objects of Philippine government programs and migration regimes. Yet, if we look at the ways Angelina and Luis reflect on their lives, their fundamental relationships and experiences, the institutions of migration seem to have dwindled away into memory as exercises in processing papers and waiting in apparently endless lines while visiting offices—just another everyday encounter with governance. These institutions, in themselves, have not produced particularly resonant inscriptions of identity. Angelina is more distressed and challenged by the discomfort she feels in being called "balikbayan" by her neighbors on her return to Haliap than she seems to have been by her predeparture orientation seminar at POEA that should have produced her as an overseas Filipino worker. "Balikbayan," while it has been inscribed into government regulations, emerged initially as a popular concept. So, while the idea that we can isolate a labor export apparatus within the assemblage and track the ways it is producing migrants for export seems elegant, it nonetheless tends to occlude how people who migrate may themselves conceive of their diverse personal histories, self-understandings, and affective attachments.

For Luis and Angelina, their new identities as migrants blended into ways of understanding and feeling about the mobile, extended self, about this self within the spatial and social forms taken on by village relations, and about this self within the activities of governing institutions. While Angelina and Luis have learned that migration can mean entrapment, encountering irreducible limits, and being coerced into compliance with regimes and rationalities they do not understand, they have also discovered new capacities and ways of enacting themselves as big persons. In the endurable zone they inhabit, their personhood remains one that is shaped by exchange. Their sense of self is deeply enmeshed within the expropriating features of community; their global does not allow them to escape or transfigure themselves. The claims of others at home do not diminish with distance but remain immediate and pressing, demanding to be honored. Finding themselves both within these claims and their new economic prowess explains their oscillating feelings of themselves as becoming big and small, amplified in the social, physical, and emotional distances across which they negotiate their relations with kin, friends, and employers. Thus they constantly waver between following strategies that would cut the networks that bind them to others and trying to help others expand their own personhood, building and folding new connections and exchanges into these very same networks. Remaining villagers, they have negotiated the limits of these intimate connections with money, yes, but also through faith, ghosts, and gifts.

Returns, Arrivals, Networks

Luis's Canadian migration story suggests both the radical potential for migration to force liberal democracies to confront questions of personhood, and how this potential comes up against a history of intransigent self-interests— all those things that don't change, come what may. His hopes of returning to Canada and Arcelie Laoagan's legacy in Calgary can offer a different kind of global imaginary comprised of a new set of relations between the ways people understand and feel about themselves in the world and the kinds of places where they live. In this global imaginary, migration builds a collective where the gift that makes community circulates among actors who are understood as networked, extended persons. The regulation of temporary contract migration here is the state's way of cutting global networks of care and deferring and rerouting people's human obligations to one another. Against this, people circulate in the gift of community, reenvisioning their responsibilities to others. Esposito describes this as a future "virtual community" that, much like Latour's cosmopolitical, will operate through an affirmative, inclusive biopolitics that values diversity.[17] But such utopian dreams remain remote. Instead, it seems to me that Luis's unskilled and temporary status meant he was unable to build the necessary intimacy to incorporate himself even into a permanently settled Filipino community or the broader Canadian community. His temporary status led him to redirect his energies, and earnings, back into the virtual village as his safety net.

To reveal that safety net, we need only to enter familiar Haliap surnames on Facebook. There, "friends" lists map most of my Hong Kong contacts, who are still there, as well as a new generation—their sons and daughters—who are not only domestic workers in Hong Kong but also doing factory and restaurant work in Singapore and caregiving in Israel. Almost all of them remain in temporary migration regimes, although a very few have found work with a path to permanent residency, either as spouses of skilled workers in Canada or as migrant nurses in the United States. Their social networking profiles celebrate marriages, births, baptisms, and anniversaries and mark deaths and departures across the virtual village space, the comments and images posted mapping the kind of extended personhood that characterizes villagers' sense of self.[18] As we might expect, the ties between cousins and neighbors persist across the generations: Marilyn's daughter in Singapore is friends with her cousin, Elvie's son, in Israel, and so on.

In this virtual village, however, there are radical and destabilizing potentials for further change. If these temporary migrants are repatriated, or must move on in ways that disconnect them, individuate them, the remittances and gifts that sustain Haliap and many similar places could fail. While government departments and development projects may still be representing Haliap as a village of progressive rice-producing farmers, village agriculture has long been extended into off-farm wage-earning activities that are now global in their scope. Thus, should migrants find their routes to successful returns denied, the village may be thrown into crisis. Overseas, migrant villagers cultivate a sense of self that challenges the fundamental precepts underpinning the liberal, democratic nation-states receiving them and thus the self-concept of their citizens. By remaining intimately entangled with the place they have come from, migrants carry with them everything they once were and desire to be in the future. On their return, they bring it all back. It is this burden that then impels them onward, seeking new citizenships and churches through which to extend their networks. Migrants become, in themselves, their own baggage.

CONCLUSION ◆ The Virtual Village

AS MIGRANTS KEEP HOLD of the intimate relationships between home and abroad, the ways they think and feel about themselves remain located in village relations. Having demonstrated this through the ethnographic detail of Haliap and of Angelina's and Luis's lives, I now turn to considering places and people more broadly. Though particular, these experiences can nonetheless tell us more about the lives of the 3.6 million Filipino temporary migrants working and living outside their nation and the places they have left behind. What I have described through their stories here is a pattern, a virtual village that reworks relationships between locality, meaning people's sense of placeness, and their sense of themselves in the world, meaning subjectivity, as mediated by the state and its absent presence. Personhood in this, the virtual village, remains relational rather than individuated, and people have a sense of themselves that is at once cosmopolitical and tied to locality yet simultaneously state-oriented, though they are unable to establish the kind of relationship with the state that they seek. In what follows, I unpack the more general attributes of the virtual village, returning to the ethnic parade and the questions it poses.

The Parade

The story the parade told mattered to people and motivated their actions, but it did so indirectly. Haliap people saw migration as an escape route to a place where they would no longer be underdeveloped and backward. They wanted an escape from development programs and projects in which they found no space for their own imagined futures. In the village they tended to prevaricate, elude, redirect, and move away, attempting to change themselves so that they might be recognized as different kinds of people. Because they thought of themselves as people with hopes, dreams, and possibilities that were different from the agricultural and tribal futures on offer in Haliap, they dragged their feet, ignored, derailed, and, most importantly, left. They departed imagining alternate futures and identities, evading, experimenting, and seeking adventure.

The parade condensed and performed a global imaginary that was thus clearly more than simply a localized image of a broader field.[1] The global described by the parade was one where perceived deficiencies in the village and its villagers were corrected. The parade inscribed new histories and identities onto villagers, ones appropriate to a Filipino national story of becoming a global nation through migration. But the parade's story was not what it seemed. Instead of portraying local realities, the parade performed its story of history as a kind of corrective to the village and its failure to progress. Rather than reflecting local realities, the parade attempted to reshape local attributes and desires by staging a competitive retelling of village history that linked progress to migration, and global to local. But beneath the veneer of compliance and celebration, participants' frustrations and disappointments simmered. Theirs was a resentful compliance. Like Sylvia, the performers knew that the village history and identities ascribed to them were dangerously different from their own self-understandings. To comply without really believing, the villagers imagined another space to inhabit that then took further shape through their migration.

To map this virtual space, we can begin with everyday connections. As we have seen, at the most basic level, migration means that village relations and identities come to depend on the electronic networks of the new communications technologies, including cell phones that enable villagers to send text messages and make voice calls. More profoundly, overseas migration actually enables the village to come into being in people's minds and thoughts much more effectively than ever before. This is the second sense in which the village is virtual. The village is never commensurate with the forms that government institutions imagine villages take; it has never been the ideal closed, corporate community described in some classic anthropological accounts and suggested by the parade's vignette of prehistory. Instead, what actually makes the village a place and distinguishes it as virtual is the way its villagers come to know it—and themselves—as lacking both progress and a suitable local history. While the village never quite fulfills its promise of place where it should—at home in Ifugao—it is instead constantly extending elsewhere. Beyond its apparent borders, village networks operate remarkably well to produce place, acting as a resilient safety net of mutual support for villagers, often where we might least expect it. Thus when villagers, wherever they are, express their feelings about their village's incompleteness, conflict, and lack (its insufficiency or failure to meet what villagers expect for their lives), they are actually never more at home. It is this shared feeling of connection through lack that shapes a shared sense of a village-based self that is at home in a global world. The flip side of seeing their village as lacking is villagers' vision of its potential and possibility. In this third sense of the virtual, the village becomes a space of perfectibility. This village, the site of future migrant returns home, is a locus of virtues. Migrants imagine they can return home to attain their new ideals for sufficiency, unity, and completeness that they find are denied them by the global world they encounter in sojourns abroad. Migrants thus reimagine the village as a sphere where they can transform their existing relations, either through the precepts of new religious confessions or reinvigorated tradition, in ways that transmute their village's lack of progress into a potential to bring into being a new kind of community.

The virtual village describes how migrants remain in the village while living abroad, both intensifying village social networks and expanding their senses of self. The virtual village inheres in the expansive space that their mobility creates within them, what Gilles Deleuze described as "an endurable zone in which to install ourselves, confront things, take hold, breathe—in short, think. . . . To live with what would otherwise be unendurable."[2] Inhabiting this zone allows villagers to sustain themselves during migration, but it demands in return that they stay focused on their ties at home. Thus, rather than being the frustrated, angry, despairing, and demanding villagers I came to know at their home in Haliap, migrants abroad become self-effacing, hardworking, compassionate carers-for-others who focus on religious and community events. Villagers like Luis thus take on the national attributes of Filipino migrants overseas despite, and perhaps because of, their previous emotive, drunken, cranky, public eruptions of frustration and anger. It is the fraught, everyday relations of village politics and social life—rather than the institutional apparatus of labor export and the inefficient, fragmented, and corrupt mechanisms of national government—through which migrants find they are most profoundly changed by their mobility. From the vantage point of this virtual village zone, a new pattern of place, subjectivity, and state becomes visible.

Place: Virtual

Despite the changes I have documented, Haliap has not suddenly become a porous place. Village boundaries have not been opened up by the impetus of external cultural influences, communications technologies, and financial investments that comprise globalization. Instead, the village was never a traditional closed community; its boundaries were porous to begin with. In a place like Haliap, acquiring knowledge, land, and capital elsewhere has almost always been the prerequisite for people to produce security and thus a sense of home. Migrants like Luis, Angelina, and Nora are never really at home in the nation per se. Instead, they know that home is where one's claims on others, through reciprocal exchange or property rights, will be recognized, and these others can be held accountable. Village relations persist as the key locus of security, and this is why Nora's nascent Hong Kong financial cooperative lends only to people from home. It is also why when Luis was in Calgary, he decided he should invest in village land. Their stories show that migrants move in search of a very local kind of recognition. While it seems contradictory that their village's administrative boundaries and indigenous identity are actually more likely to be secured with their migration than without it, this contradiction actually marks the conflicted relations that virtual villages have with national governments, further revealing the contradictory position of place in a global world.

This book started from the premise that globalization might actually be solidifying places rather than dissolving them. I argued that we needed to distinguish between the qualities of social relations that make placeness and the physical forms of settlements themselves in order to really understand place. Anthropologist Arjun Appadurai has done this work of distinguishing placeness and settlement form in elaborating his concept of locality. Locality is a quality of social relations produced by successful place making. Appadurai describes it as "a variable quality constituted by a sense of social immediacy, technologies of interaction, and the relativity of contexts, with the maintenance of its materiality or place-ness requiring ongoing work."[3] Those projects of place-making that exhibit locality are what Appadurai calls "neighborhoods." Haliap has this quality; its neighborhood emerges both from people's familiar face-to-face ways of interacting and from relations brokered by communications technologies.

Observing that locality is a feature of communities that have an established presence not only in the real world but also in the spaces of media and communications technologies—in other words, cyberspace—Appadurai reminds us that locality is not only a property of a traditional village. It is also a property of any community that has the potential to maintain and reproduce its sense of place. Locality can also emerge from an Internet chat room, a social networking site, or a diasporic religious congregation. It has been tempting, however, to understand traditional—indigenous, peripheral, or small-scale—places like Haliap as being obliged to exhibit vigorous forms of locality while apprehending new global spaces, such as migrant detention centers, refugee camps, airports, and shopping malls, as precluding almost any emergence of locality at all. Appadurai's conception of locality challenges any idea that globalization universally threatens placeness. He argues instead that locality can now emerge without meeting the requirement that a place should have a contiguous geography. What Haliap demonstrates for this argument is that a supposedly traditional place, rather than falling apart, can exhibit a more vigorous locality even as its geography loses its contiguous character. It is not that some places become less local while others become more so; instead, it is their placeness itself that is being redefined by migration.

Villagers, however, are no more satisfied with their long-distance locality than they were with their local neighborhood before they migrated. For them, locality continues to be what it has always been: a problematic, an achievement created against a background of flux, disorder, and competing ties that villagers worry will overwhelm them. While their concerns about unity, sufficiency, adequacy, and security may be expressed as complaints about the quality of their place, they are actually signs of a robust affective engagement with their village and their fellow villagers. They maintain this kind of engagement even when they have been sojourning abroad for several years, like Nora, Dalen, and Elvie. In Hong Kong these Haliap migrants meet up as a village, defining themselves on the basis of a new kind of expanded territoriality while self-consciously recreating shared histories. They make space for cultural diversity and change rather than fashioning cultural homogeneity, even though they only coalesce, face-to-face, each week in Central. In these gatherings Haliap's locality is produced by the reflexive practice of collective lives extending back and forth to the Philippines.

Appadurai would argue that it is Hong Kong itself—through these migrant gatherings in Central—that exhibits a distinctive new form of locality produced by globalization, what he calls "translocality." This is a locality made by engagements with complex and abstract power relations lying elsewhere, beyond the neighborhood. In a translocality, locals mix with circulating populations. Its emergent sense of place is constituted through this flux and diversity. Appadurai thus uses translocality to describe spatially extended communities where the boundaries of social networks no longer correspond with the familiar kinds of administrative borders that states might expect to contain such networks: citizenship, religious confessions, beneficiary identities, and civil society groups. For him, translocality marks a new awareness that, around the world, people's everyday experiences are increasingly mediated by global flows of goods, information, and power relations. Yet in Haliap this spatially extended form of locality does not really represent something new.

We have seen how Haliap's social relations, culture, topographies, built environments, and ritual have always been shaped by colonialisms and their aftereffects. From one angle, what the ethnic parade offers us is really just an inventory of the various ways people inhabit identities, economies, and polities produced through and against power emanating from these centers elsewhere. Thus, instead of translocality emerging as a novel sense of global placeness, as Appadurai predicts, it actually describes the long-standing shape taken by Haliap as a remote, marginal, or frontier village. With globalization such villages become more likely than ever to be places that move—neighborhoods whose borders are porous and boundaries flexible, inhabited by people who are actively seeking to extend into and incorporate new terrains and networks of relations. This movement does not become possible because they are no longer proper places, but because they are. In Haliap's struggles with property, gender, and development, we see how the village appears as a village only by constantly revising performances of locality against an ideal it will never achieve. This kind of negative awareness—the idea that village locality is threatened, insufficient, shaky—actually produces a very resilient, adaptable, and mobile sense of place.

LINKING PLACE AND SUBJECTIVITY

Insisting that locality, the distinctive aspect that gives a sense of placeness to sites of settlement, is fundamentally about how people connect with one another, Appadurai offers a useful starting point from which to think about territory and personhood. The biographies of Luis, Angelina, and their friends show that villagers carry a distinctive sense of their place in the world with them, grounding their self-understandings wherever they go. Though time and distance do not extinguish this subjective self-awareness, it can be profoundly stretched and transformed. This relationship between locality and subjectivity is territoriality. By this I mean in the sense of territoriality (or territory) developed by Gilles Deleuze and Félix Guattari rather than the more familiar kind of political/administrative box that is inscribed on a map. Deleuze's concept of territoriality describes people's place-based self-understandings. Where the ritual of the ethnic parade produces locality by modifying the ways people think and feel about themselves in the world, Deleuze and Guattari would describe the parade as de- and reterritorializing selves. I have shown how Haliap selves have been de- and reterritorialized multiple times, often without people ever leaving the village, through processes like ancestral domain, the introduction of new crops, the activities of development projects, and so forth. Territoriality names the way locality and subjectivity, the way people think and feel about themselves in the world, are configured in a particular pattern before that pattern shifts yet again.

If we then think of territoriality as a dynamic relation between locality and a sense of self, rather than a fixing of identity within static networks of power, we are some way toward a more nuanced, less flat account of the person. This account should acknowledge how the multiplicity of identities that people inhabit, and their capacities for change motivated by dynamic reflection and self-awareness, are fundamental to the ways they think and feel about themselves in the world.

Subjectivity: Shifting

Revisiting the parade, we can see how identities are inscribed on people by naming. Naming is the mode through which the parade governs, even if all the names that people bear are not written on placards. In the parade, naming works through its performative effects.[4] That is, the placards naming people as Stone Age primitives, as anticolonial resistance fighters, as progressive farmers, or as overseas contract workers identify people by citing previous performances and histories. The identities people take on in this process are real yet intangible. Though they are abstract ideas, they do have effects in the material world. Identities are attached to individuated bodies by institutions—censuses, categories of colonial governing, research forms, development programs, and bureaucracies—and work to form the social groups, organize the economies, and constitute the religions that these institutions govern. Though created effortlessly in mind and thought, these identities are inherently unstable. They invariably produce frictions with people's other identities and thus generate ambivalent feelings in their performers. Villagers' lives are thus shaped by experiences of spanning these contradictions, being simultaneously identified as both ——— and ———; for example, both progressive farmers and Stone Age tribals, both proud anticolonial warriors and compliant global migrants. Such colliding and contradicting identities make the virtual village a space where people's own self-reflective awareness emerges as something more than simply an effect of discourses from any set of bounded institutions' discourses. Instead, they inhabit a much more fluid field of feelings and self-understanding.

This space of villagers' self-awareness is subjectivity. Subjectivity describes the complex set of emotions and sensations that constitute the way a person thinks and feels about himself in the world. The term encompasses the internal life of the person, his thoughts, the ways he is disposed to act and feel, and his embodied and affective awareness; it is shaped by his physiology, memory, and imagination, not merely by discourses of governing. The idea of subjectivity as mobile and multivalent challenges Western and modern conceptions of the subject's self-awareness. Feminists and those working in non-Western contexts have sought to develop a theory of an enculturated, social person that both incorporates and exceeds an account of the self-regulating individual of biopolitics who comes to know himself as singular and fixed through encounters with particular kinds of governing discourse. When explaining people's everyday lives this biopolitical account of the subject feels flat, because it tends to, as Uli Linke argues, "dismiss the emotive agency of persons as merely an outcome of their formation as subjects of discourse."[5]

Here, subjectivities are about affect, the energy that motivates people to connect with others and with concepts in order to transform themselves and the world. Affect is the precursor for and substrate of emotions. Villagers reveal this when they talk about showing and sharing feeling. They are more interested in using affect to connect with and disconnect from others and less interested in labeling the intricacies of specific emotions. For them, affect either shows you something nice that draws you toward other people, or shares with you a not nice feeling that pushes you away. In this push and pull, people feel in themselves big, meaning expanding in connection, recognized as a fellow human, and small, meaning distanced, isolated, and objectified. Where I would tend to use English emotion words like *humiliation, anxiety, elation,* and *envy,* Luis and Angelina and their friends would talk about their "feeling" (in the body) as being "heavy" (for negative affects) and "light" (positive affects).

My respondents' subjectivities are continually reshaped through their multiple, shifting, and contradictory experiences of their connecting selves, these selves being always in process and never simply reducible to any single identity. Their subjectivity emerges through reversals and self-reflection; it is labile and multivalent, having different timbres or modes over the course of their biographies, or even within a single conversation. Luis, for example, shifted from an account of himself as abject and exploited to angry and defiant when he repudiated development projects. Yet, when he arrived in Canada, he described himself as "accepting," although he was yet again confronting circumstances where his job was not what he had been led to anticipate.

Though subjectivity is unique to each person, people's subjectivities take on collective valences when their self-understandings are shared across affective interpersonal ties. Affect thus moves not just from public connections and meanings into intimate sensibilities but also the other way around. A collective valence of subjectivity is the ground for people's affective agency, as shown by the Contemplacion furor.

In Contemplacion collective agency extended beyond people's capacity to act in ways delimited by the identities inscribed on them by the institutions that attempted to govern the nation. Because people's affective experiences of connection shape their personhood, their sensual inner spaces of self-reflection often work against their social identities.[6] People's intersubjective connections with others and the ways others recognize them call into question the ways the identities they bear limit, define, and exclude them from the nation. The affective origins of people's agency in querying their identities explain why that agency lies at least partly outside institutional practice and discourses. In chapter 2 we saw how villagers began to dream of the possibilities that might come from aligning themselves with a femininity they had been continually told they lacked in response to a public crisis. Motivated by the same event— the execution of a migrant worker—elite film stars performed public service and augmented their family's popularity by taking up the cause of exploited working-class migrants, simultaneously shifting their own class identities downward and those of migrants upward. Contemplacion did this political work, not fundamentally through logic, but through the outpouring of affect, which then shaped the accompanying rationalities that questioned state practices of recognizing citizenship. The ethnic parade is intended to work as a similar affective exercise.

In both of these events, the parade and Contemplacion, bodily affects and valences of subjectivity become the media through which the collectivities of nation and village, or bayan, emerge.[7] But this collectivity is not what the government intends it to be. An affective account of subjectivity explains the origins of this political agency within the parade. In the parade the intended outcomes are subverted. Those performers who are making faces and poking fun at their uniforms are transforming the story through the affective connections they make with one another and the audience, if not yet in an entirely conscious or self-reflective way. Luis, who marched as a progressive farmer in the parade, went on to question the idea of progress in agriculture and the efficacy of the government itself. People's agency here does not emerge from a single set of discourses regulating migrants. Instead, their agency comes from subjectivities as they form and shift in movement through and with affective recognition or refusal of the multiple and contradictory ways they were being identified by a whole assemblage—multiple, conflicting institutions, discourses, and practices. We see such agency emerge in interpersonal frictions, such as Angelina's refusal of being considered "balikbayan," Luis's claims to human equality with his employer, conflicts over customary tenure, and the meaning of *housewife*.

When subjectivity shifts, it is through such moments of becoming recognized, and these moments are affective and immediate. They occur in everyday interactions and through material objects or embodied ritual that connect "the singular to the cultural, the personal to the social, and the self to the other."[8] The frailty and changeability of recognition is why the health worker's census activities and the rest of their program fail. People recognize that they themselves and their fellow villagers could occupy the role of the government staff or the developers just as easily as they could fill the role of the targets for development interventions. Villagers thus dispute the ways they have been relegated to the status of project beneficiaries. They are not particularly interested in the rationale behind the NGOs' practices of identifying some people in one role and some in another. They take being looked down on to heart. They want to prove those who would make them feel small or low to be wrong. As with the migrants' photographs, they do this by cutting others down to size. Thus my account has revealed how in describing themselves as feeling big and small, my respondents mark the ways people are comprised of multiple, simultaneous, and often conflicting identities, with everyone having a mobile and shifting awareness of how they think others see them and how they feel about themselves.

Personhood here is thus something people experience as a fragmented trajectory rather than as a unitary whole. In this trajectory, experiences of becoming, of bleeding and blending one identity into another, give form to people's self-understandings most powerfully. People find that their ability to adapt and combine and to shift the meanings of identities enables them to inhabit contradictions and gaps. Thus they always hold a little bit of themselves back even as they perform. In the parade the performers may reorder their outward practice into the moral categories of social evolution, but they do not find their sense of themselves totally absorbed by the roles that they take on. Instead, the parade is, at one level, one of those everyday experiences of governing that is fun but of limited relevance to their daily lives. At another level the parade does help to shape people's dreams by moving them against its story. It leads them to experiment with alternative ways to interpret themselves and gives them impetus to seek different approaches to make sense of global possibilities. These kinds of experiments in becoming appear in the blending and bleeding of identities into one another in migrants' solo portraits, the village ideal of housewife (chapter 2), the health workers' drag show (chapter 3), and in Tricia's photomontage (chapter 5). These material objects and performances are the tools people use to shape the imaginative, vicarious experiences of migration—their virtual, global realm—negotiating relationships with their real-world kin and neighbors and employers. In doing so, they come to know themselves through their own global dreams.

All of this means that personhood in Haliap is not delimited by identities attached to people through institutional discourses alone. Instead, Haliap personhood emerges from that intangible and interior but nonetheless real space where subjectivity expands the ideal of the self beyond the bounds established by identities. Personhood is constituted in the affective experience of an "I" that bleeds and blends into other identities, other groups, and other persons. This affective flow is, of course, continually truncated by people's real-world, intersubjective encounters; they are made (to feel) small when their attempts to connect to and to make claims on others are repudiated, limited, or ignored. Instead of a clearly delimited and individual subject, Haliap personhood takes on an extended, relational shape in contexts where the truth of the self emerges through relationships with others—people seek to feel big. With an emphasis on interpersonal recognition and social belonging, this mode of personhood is open and expansive, producing a social self that is relatively undifferentiated and nonautonomous. This mode of personhood is not at all unique to Haliap. The anthropologist Marilyn Strathern is famous for distinguishing this as dividual rather than individuated personhood in Melanesia. Much closer to

Haliap, in the Philippines, Renato and Michele Rosaldo found this relational kind of personhood revealed by traditional Ilongot mourning practices.[9]

To see this personhood at work, we can ask just who were the nameless people calling Angelina a balikbayan? She could not tell me; she had only heard it secondhand. Or was that secondhand comment perhaps itself a way for her neighbor to call her a balikbayan at a remove? Villagers' stories of their lives continually referred to deciding on a new course of action based on the reported impressions and preferences of "we" and "they," but people were often unable to specify the groups these collective identities bounded for them. People thus experienced themselves as mattering through others' eyes. They needed continual reassurance that others gave their needs priority and saw their relations to those others—and flowing through them—as primary. When Luis and Angelina faced dilemmas abroad, they would sometimes ask me for advice. When I would suggest they should not give, or should deny requests from their friends, they were amazed at not just my perceived stinginess but at my insensitivity to the ways persons were constituted. From my own Western perspective, they seemed to be caught up in something I ought to have recognized as close to narcissism, becoming obsessed with the images that others may or may not have of oneself. Yet, as an approach to understanding and feeling about themselves in the world, locating the self through others' imagined gaze was clearly constitutive of the sense of self that sustained my respondents abroad. In their village context this approach was no psychological defect, but a shared mode of subjectivity.

Of course, villagers did not always experience themselves as persons in this relational mode. They could also choose to think of themselves as individuals. This more individuated mode of personhood tended to emerge in contexts where people could seek a sense of self in the pleasures of being recognized as an individual: consumption and romance. Individuated personhood tended to be marked by distinctive subjective valences for a self that was more atomized and clearly bounded—the hard-hearted, hardheaded, stingy self. This is the kind of self some villagers read into Luis's photographic portraits. To resist being tempted to see themselves too much this way, Nora had villagers in Hong Kong playing Scrabble (chapter 6), gambling with women to whom they were already indebted, rather than shopping or seeking extramarital romance.

Village personhood emerges from an interplay between these two modes: the monologue delivered by the lone self of the photograph and the kind of dialogical self that finds its truth in the response of the other. It shifts between an individuated narcissism and a relational collectivism. While such an interplay of selves may describe personhood for most people, village history gives it particular moments and tendencies of expression. Personhood is thus never set but is a matter of how selves can be performed within a given context and thus of knowing what to do when being oneself. These modes of personhood can be distinguished by particular sets of feelings and fears, emotions and dreams, giving shape to what feels like a truthful way of presenting who one is, and it is this shared mode of subjectivity that, collectively, produces distinctive territoriality.

What distinguishes a virtual village, then, is not just its long-distance form of locality but also this oscillation of personhood. This territoriality, the kind of personhood and locality relationship I have described, is further shaped by villagers' engagements with the state and, now entwined within those engagements, religion.

STATE-SEEKING SUBJECTIVITIES

My data suggest approaching the state through a subjectivist lens. This is a viewpoint from which we can trace how the state emerges from, inhabits, and reproduces itself through people's actions and thoughts, not least their thoughts about themselves and their desired futures.

We can see the state emerge from the ways virtual villagers demonstrate their adequacy by testing their development capacities themselves. People cope with their disappointments in government and development through the blend and bleed of performances, finding the truth of themselves within their dreams of becoming someone else, somewhere better. Against a model that seems to posit a more or less immobile subject, encapsulated within a single state, virtual villagers actively seek somewhere better across several states. If there is an ideal state form, they expect to find it elsewhere. Thus, symbolically, they march on past the congressman, seeking good governance abroad, or into the networks and programs of statelike institutions, such as the European Central Cordillera Agricultural Program or the Iglesia church, that claim to have a worldwide reach. Villagers sustain and define themselves by dreams of becoming something different, as a permanent (resident or citizen) of elsewhere. Thus, at just those points where villagers claim the state to be most absent from their lives, the state is actually being made present through their dreams, complaints, desires, and mobility.

The state appears in villagers' lives as an ideal that has been lost and which then haunts migrants, one among the other hauntings that migrants experience. This is because people's practices of movement and becoming always entail some form of loss, and this loss, when not recognized and mourned, then comes back as a ghost. For instance, Luis's mother was "disturbing" his sister, people said, because the family had not held the proper burial rites for the Adyangan pagan tradition and thus did not "feed" the community. While he was in Hong Kong, Luis also had his emotional equanimity disturbed by the apparent impossibility of attaining the future self he had portrayed in his photographic portraits. Unable to acknowledge this and mourn it as a loss, he seeks greener pastures and new networks of relations to bring this self into being. Whether it is Luis's mother's ghost or his anxieties about photographic images, the connections Luis may have allowed to attenuate keep calling him back to the village so that he can reaffirm his affiliations by giving. Luis is likewise reluctant to accept the impossibility of encountering the kind of caring state he desires to engage. Thus he is, in effect, haunted by his ideal version of the state, seeking it in new places but unable to locate it in his everyday relationships, and perhaps even actively subverting its emergence by relying, quite sensibly, on the already familiar forms of exchange he has established.

In the virtual village, then, we can see that the local experience of stateness is, paradoxically, about the global. Where government projects and projects of governing throw up resistances, slippages, innovative practices, and unexpected outcomes, gaps and disjuncture result. These frictions occur not because the global is out there, impinging on people's ability to make decisions about their daily lives, but because it dwells within the desires of villagers themselves. Their global realm takes its shape through their collective, affective investment in the idea of a frictionless space of mobility and possibility. This is a realm of dreams, where affective connections are given shape and the vistas of unlimited futures open up their imaginative possibilities. Thus the Philippine global nation and its state, even in apparently remote Ifugao, both emerge from the complex ways affect is being mobilized across space. Such exchanges of feeling are now an integral part of the ways that states reproduce themselves through flows of people and value.[10]

All of this means that virtual village subjectivities are state-oriented. Villagers' self-understandings and feelings are shaped by a collective desire for the state to instantiate itself as a functional, transparent, resourcing government. One of the key features of this way of seeing the state is a culture of complaint among people who do not have the kind of state they want. Across the village, people devote time and energy to dreaming about and debating what they would have—infrastructure, projects, markets, jobs—if they had the right kind of government. Local inscriptions of the state, such as ancestral domain, labor recruiting, and development projects, are projects in which they find it very difficult to locate the forms of caring (and exchange) they desire. People find that the state they experience is, disappointingly, not undivided and instrumental, but an assemblage that governs the world through projects, processes, institutions, and programs, making social groups and attaching social identities to individuals only by producing friction and contradictions. People want these identities to be accurate, and fair, but they are not. The assemblage of governing institutions acts as a channel for their affect, trying to direct people's sense of self-awareness toward identifications with objects and outcomes, thus encouraging people to define themselves as nationalist, family-oriented, and so forth. However, such connections are never produced in an entirely coherent way, nor do they emerge without contradictions. People want this assemblage of statelike actors to manage these contradictions, balancing things, like families and migration, that justify each other. And such balancing easily comes undone.

Virtual villagers then respond to the perceived failings of the state by seeking networks and personal recognition within religion. Luis, for instance, shifts between approaching development as a kind of secular religion and seeking religion as development through his engagements with a church that has a particular mode of governing its members. Although villagers can quite clearly find much more within religious beliefs and communities, recognition and networks seem to have a fundamental appeal. This kind of reversal, and migrants' awareness that faith and church are playing both supporting and conflicting roles in sustaining locality and its particular territoriality, produce the last characteristic of the virtual village as a form of territoriality: a cosmopolitical subjectivity tied to locality.

Engaging States: A Virtual Cosmopolitics

When Luis found that progress-as-religion did not work, he returned to seek progress with or through religion. Many more migrants like Luis intensify their engagements with churches while working abroad. Luis's particular church is interesting because it operates as a kind of para-state, even in the Philippines, enforcing government rules on illegal stays and working visas in its governance of the congregation. Thus, though his church is not the government per se, it functions as part of an assemblage that is engaged in the governance of the village and its migrants. Within the village, his Iglesia faith can offer him a way of cutting the network of local reciprocity attached to paganism to accumulate wealth and perhaps competing forms of prestige. From this angle, Luis's experience of the positive connections of his church may well be less about his own becoming individual and more about situating a relational self within a new and more global kind of collective.

In Haliap, while development is officially secular, in that people expect it to enable them to meet their obligations without redefining them, it moves with a broader Christian faith and against animism. Development, however, is supposed to be secular and thus cannot itself transform how people are obliged to sustain customary exchanges prescribed by local culture: kinship and animism. Instead it is religion that seems to offer villagers their own, better programs of personal development. These faiths work by redefining people as individuals and delimiting a much smaller range of obligations to others, redirecting the faithful away from animist exchange toward God and a new family of coreligious, addressed as brothers and sisters. Thus, while religion should be familiar to modern people as a separable sphere of action, meaning affiliation to formal churches rather than paganism, this is not really a distinction that holds in the village. Instead, villagers expect churches to be part of the process of governing.

This is as we might expect. As Louis Dumont has famously suggested, the modern state more generally seems to work as a kind of transformed church based on individualism.[11] Certainly the Christian idea of the world as existing in a state of lack has been picked up by development—and government—in the Philippines, to offer people a kind of secular faith in progress.[12] But as Luis shows, this faith is tested by failures. When Roberto Esposito argues that states can maintain immunity only by continually individuating their subjects, he indicates that this individuating should happen through administrative means within a modern, secular state. But his account seems to depend on a distinctively post-Christian understanding of social evolution. Rather than a European genealogy, where religion has ceded the ground of individuation to a secular administration, Haliap's history sees this sequence reversed. If immunity becomes possible only where the modern individual has already been produced by religious conversion, what happens where religious conversion is never quite complete? Haliap's spiritual and material exchanges—how to get pigs and chickens to sacrifice, or how to find the money to tithe and make cash offerings—depend on relational personhood and networks with others rather than on individuated earnings or merit. So people are more or less right when they observe that you need to become a Christian to be progressive, but you cannot turn your back on tradition without risking your defining kinship and exchange networks. This is Nora's cosmopolitical argument: honoring traditional beliefs in spirits of place and the beliefs of village-mates—being "open"—is the only way the village and those it comprises will be able to move on.

Such a cosmopolitics has its consequences. Drawn into Luis's exchange networks by default, Luis's employers, like that of Arcelie Laoagan, may have been asked to take on a new role as patron within his networks. They could have found that rather than addressing concerns over working hours or overtime pay directly, Luis attempted to compel them to contribute value to his networks by sponsoring festive occasions, donating pigs, and finding jobs for his kin. Whether such requests would have been successful likely depended on the employer's sense of himself as generous, his curiosity about Filipino culture, his reliance on his Temporary Foreign Worker team, and his own perceived vulnerability to complaints from his TFW employees about the irregularities in their working conditions. Only this last sense of an employer's self as exposed, vulnerable to state sanctions for his treatment of migrant employees, is effectively open to the regulation of state institutions. Luis found that in Alberta the TFW only appeared to have been structured to make the employer responsible to the regulatory framework of the program. In practice it proved quite difficult to draw the Canadian state's regulatory presence into the migrant's employment relationship after the work had commenced, at least without making the migrant even more vulnerable to other TFW regulations. Cosmopolitics here thus also lies in the employer's superior knowledge of the everyday Canadian state—in knowing which TFW regulations are being effectively implemented and which are not. This is the kind of local knowledge of the receiving state that Luis could only acquire on the ground in Calgary.

Living in this space, with relational personhood, a cosmopolitics tied to locality, and a state-oriented subjectivity that cannot find the state it seeks, all driven by affect, means that people have a particular way of thinking and feeling about themselves in the world. This is why when they become migrants they are particularly concerned with establishing caring, personalistic relations; with opening up new networks and incorporating others into them; and with practicing expansive, global forms of faith. Migrants become people who can neither go back home nor cut the ties that bind them, because home and these ties increasingly constitute their sense of self. Coping with a global world only by continually drawing others into their personal networks through giving and mutual obligation, they seem self-effacing and hardworking. These are migrants' strategies to seek human recognition. When the ways they can be recognized are limited by the regimes through which receiving states regulate migration, virtual villagers then pursue faith and spirituality as ways of building new networks with others. All of this suggests that we can expect a continuation in current trends in the expansion of transnational churches and faith movements and an increase in faith-based advocacy for migrant rights and local development in sending areas. But we may also see, as a result, more potentially damaging practices emerging from institutions that may deploy faith to redirect migrants' remittances to particular ends or to intervene in resource politics in migrant-sending villages, thus increasing rural insecurity and instability.

VIRTUAL VILLAGES / GLOBAL POLITICS

If we have understood globalization as breaking open the boundaries of place, we should expect the spatial patterns produced by the globalized world—repeated moves away from family and friends for education and work—to have fragmented and distributed the social networks of traditional, small-scale societies.[13] And certainly an affect of becoming alienated is one that many people in the industrialized West associate with the changes wrought by globalization. Yet my account here shows that this affect is not necessarily a universal one, at least not in a migrant-sending village like Haliap. In the global encounters between these migrants and their employers and hosts, patterns of intimacy, of self-understanding, of investment and support, as well as the inherent power imbalances and regulatory structures governing temporary migration regimes tend to suppress friendships from forming. Nonetheless, the various kinds of work that migrants perform, and the ways they perform it, undoubtedly draw on the ways they attempt to negotiate new affective ties of care, humanity, belonging, and faith. Thus those people whose experience of social connection is fragmented—that "we" who think life has been disrupted by global mobility—are actually depending on the multitude who still live virtual village lives to sustain them. And while popular accounts may describe villages as self-sufficient, for many people who are living lives bounded by village as administrative containers, as opposed to the expansive and dynamic network I have described here, the village has rarely been able to offer them a secure livelihood. These migrants and their villages need work to find the security they seek. They have grasped at global migration in hopes of expanding their exchange networks by participating in making the global, seeking respect and dignity. Their mobility produces a new kind of global affective politics. This politics is not a zero-sum game where care is drawn out of villages and delivered to metropolitan consumers at a loss. Instead, this politics challenges the ways we understand our relations to the world, because the virtual villages are living alongside and within host societies, carried along by migrants to their sites of sojourn.

ON AFFECT ◆ A Methodological Note

IN WRITING THIS BOOK, I wanted to produce an intimate account of the changes and continuities produced by globalization—and global migration—in the Philippines. I have tried to show how migrants carry with them histories and subjectivities that have been transformed through their encounters with states and host societies as well as changes in their home villages. I see the book as providing a useful platform for follow-on work.

As a contemporary village ethnography gone global, this book opens up into key questions explored by anthropology's subdisciplines. The text not only points readers toward debates on migration and affect, but it can also direct readers to compare ethnographies of development in Southeast Asia, examine the political anthropology on the margins of the state, study informal economies, explore accounts of subjectivity, investigate contemporary indigenous identities, and develop accounts of the uptake of new media and communications technologies. I have tried to work from my specific village case study toward general claims in order to demonstrate how far these claims can extend and where they fail. I anticipate that my readers will be reading ethnographies like this one not only to learn about the wider world but also with the aim of making their own research projects more interesting and entirely different pieces of scholarly work.

Part of this book is about care and migration. But it provides only a partial answer to some of the bigger questions about Filipino migration: if care is a universal disposition or a technical proficiency, why is it that Filipino migrants are able to market themselves as the quintessential caring people, almost as a brand name? The answer, this book suggests, comes from the ways Filipinos conceptualize care as based on an ethic of shared labor and mutual affective exposure, much as Luis (and Esposito) considers work. This book thus foreshadows how the explanation for Filipino care lies in the affective experience of mutual exposure and the elaborations of exchange in caring work as these coincide with Filipino relational personhood and the obligations of kin and village exchange that constitute it. I am currently working on this follow-on project with a group of Filipino migrant friends in London.

Methodologically, the question posed by my approach here is how I can claim to understand affect when much of this book has been written as secondary description rather than reporting directly what my respondents have said and the context for their statements. While I flag this in my introduction, here I want to draw together the reasons behind this approach.

If I had offered the reader more interactive dialogue, reported in the actual language spoken by respondents, and described its context in greater detail, I would nonetheless have failed to reveal affect in any transparent way. The book is written against the suggestion that affect and emotions are related to each other in a universally applicable formula that would make reporting simply an act of translating emotion rather than my own authorial representation. My use of the secondhand and descriptive is intended to mark that and to provide the sense of dynamic ebb and flow, offering the staid ground against which outbursts stand out. To make producing a written text even more complicated, Adyangan Ifugao does not have a rich vocabulary for emotional expression that can be easily translated into equivalents in English. People don't say the equivalent of "I'm angry . . . (sad, happy, etc.)" or "so-and-so was showing enthusiasm or was diffident." They talk about showing a feeling that is (in English) "nice" or "good" or "not nice" and "not good," and they do this after the fact, interpreting facial expressions and gestures. So to explain any exchange, one would need to interview both sides to find out what people intended to convey and then what they thought about what was shown and shared—good or bad and what particular English feelings they attributed to it—and then how they themselves identified those feelings in their interlocutors. Even after years of fieldwork, I have had only a few opportunities to do this where people were then comfortable with my sharing the results with an academic audience.

My methods and tools in this project have been those of classic long-term participant observation, trying to understand the world through what happens in a singular neighborhood. I visited the various sites of Haliap in 1992–1993, 1995, 1996–1997, 1999, 2002, 2004, 2005–2007, and 2009 and have stayed in intermittent contact with some of my respondents by letter, text, phone, and, now, Facebook, in the interim. My key strategy has been attending to—and returning to—those moments of fieldwork that are particularly challenging or problematic and that carry an emotional baggage for me as ethnographer. I have been working mainly with people who have sought to sustain our long-standing research friendships, which go back almost two decades now. I am writing about themes I can discuss more generally on the basis of these years of intermittent participant observation in the village, drawing on a large body of data: notebooks of observations, my field diaries, transcripts of interviews, tapes of events, text messages, and commentaries on all these kinds of data recorded in analytic notebooks, notes from recent phone conversations, and my own memory. All of this fieldwork has generated a great deal of data, but it has not necessarily been in the form of taped exchanges and accurate verbatim records of conversations between two or more people that offer tidy quotes.

To provide focus and detail, I have elected to focus on Luis's and Angelina's lives because I know them well, and I believe the depth that can be achieved in such a longitudinal approach is revealing. It has not always been possible to stay in touch on such a long-term basis with other villagers who migrated, nor would they be comfortable having me report on their personal histories in such a revealing way. Luis and Angelina had the benefit of having a strong marital relationship set within a very large extended family, with whom I also have good relations. Though I may be able to report on affective outbursts for other villagers, I would not always be able to offer as much of a sense of the respondent's character or personal history for the reader.

Underpinning these choices about representation are some practical and ethical considerations. In Haliap, conversational exchanges happen in Adyangan Ifugao, Filipino English, Ilokano, and sometimes Tagalog, often with rapid code switching. It is much easier to retrieve the kind of verbatim exchanges a reader might like to see from intimate observations of dyadic interactions rather than group discussions. But villagers enjoy groups and often pass the time in busy shop fronts and other noisy locations with distracting conditions that rarely produce a high-quality recording. All of this is compounded by the way that, in Adyangan daily speech, sentences are often unfinished and subjects and agents go unidentified. This kind of grammar is typical in Malay languages, where "they" and "them" become potent disciplinary tools because the specific actors remain undefined. In those sections of my recordings where voices are not drowned out by chickens crowing, trucks passing, or children playing, multiple dialects and the imprecision of daily speech mean that verbatim transcripts would become heavy with *sics,* multiple translations, and authorial brackets identifying missing subjects and agents.

Apart from making things messy for the reader, *sics* are a big problem for respondents who speak Filipino rather than American English. My respondents are quite understandably deeply sensitive about how their English skills, educational attainment, and ethnicity are represented. Thus the conventions for presenting transcripts in translation, with their nonstandard use of English words in scare quotes and *sics,* could be interpreted as belittling them, a situation I want to avoid. Those Filipino English terms that I initially italicized are words that virtually all of my respondents used in everyday English. Though my respondents' use of these terms may be unfamiliar to non-Filipino readers, their meaning is often fairly clear in context. To define and then contextualize each of these words in a longer quotation would take up a great deal of space. Since only key terms advance my arguments here, I've tried to be selective.

Because what people are usually most provoked by is being spoken to (in terms of tone) as if they are small or having their shortcomings pointed out in public, I would need to implicate myself in any approach that detailed affect in conversational exchange. And as my respondents do, in everyday conversations I convey the affective part of my meaning by speaking in incomplete sentences, using slang, changing my tone, changing my volume, stuttering, repeating things, shifting topics, and communicating my meaning with sighs, grunts, and various other non-word noises. I titter, snort, mumble, and clear my throat. Sometimes, when I am really feeling strongly about a topic, I tear up and my nose runs, so I sniff. That's me. But there is a different kind of relationship here between my text and my respondents. I am reluctant to publish something my respondents would read as making them sound uneducated or describing them as lacking in the emotional self-control that marks people as functional Filipino adults. Thus I have tried to be sensitive in selecting excerpts and to make these choices with my respondents' permission. I offer some examples of affective outbursts in my interactions with Luis, with his permission. Other examples I could offer I have been asked to keep confidential.

Villagers' reluctance to acknowledge and discuss affective outbursts comes from local cultural norms. Haliap villagers, like most Filipinos, tend to repress (they say "swallow") a lot of negative affect and publicly perform positive affect as part of the emotional grammar that generates norms for proper conduct. In the village, huge outbursts of affect are comparatively rare and may be dangerous, often involving alcohol, shame, and grief. These moments are not the time for an ethnographer to get in there with a tape recorder or notebook, but they do resonate. Such outbursts end up being rehashed with participants, observers, and others much later on. Often they are retold in the conditional, at a kind of secondhand remove, as a series of stories on how one should and should not behave and when. So there is a kind of reconstruction in this text where I have left as secondhand accounts materials shaped by my own interpretations as much as village gossip to mark them as such. I could offer the reader vignettes that put together partially quoted sentences in which an ellipsis would mark not three sentences but three months or even three years. That seems to me a problematic strategy, providing a reader with a false sense of immediacy rather than clearly marking how my learning has emerged from the ethnographic work of recording, remembering, connecting, reminding, and reinterpreting in an ongoing dialogue with my respondents.

NOTES

INTRODUCTION

1. Republic of the Philippines, National Statistics Office, 2000 Census, www .census.gov/ph/census2000. Indigenes may comprise 20 percent or more of the Filipino population, according to an unofficial count from the Philippine National Commission on Indigenous Peoples when compared with the last complete survey (1995) by the Republic of the Philippines, National Statistics Office. ("The Indigenous People of the Philippines," *Indigenous Peoples/Ethnic Minorities and Poverty Reduction—Philippines,* Asian Development Bank [2002], 7, http://www.adb.org/documents/reports/ indigenous_peoples/phi/chapter_3.pdf.)

2. Republic of the Philippines, National Statistics Office, 2000 Census.

3. Tsing 2000, 330; Tyner 2008.

4. Kelly 2000, 1.

5. Kelly 2000; Tyner 2004, 2008.

6. Rafael 1997; Tyner 2004.

7. International Organization for Migration 2005; Tyner and Donaldson 1999; Tyner 2008.

8. Philippine Overseas Employment Agency, www.poea.gov.ph/stats/Skills/ Skill_Country_Sex (accessed 12 February 2011). Sea-based workers, of which there are approximately 330,424 (2009), remain almost entirely male.

9. Francisco 2006.

10. Bello 2005.

11. Mendola 2006.

12. International Labour Organization 2010; International Organization for Migration 2010, 171; "Stock Estimate of Overseas Filipinos as of December 2008," Commission on Filipinos Overseas, Philippine Overseas Employment Agency, www .poea.gov.ph/stats/stats/stock_est_2008.pdf (accessed 15 April 2011).

13. Ribas 2008.

14. Appadurai 1996, 48.

15. Friedman 1994.

16. Urry 2000, 2007.

17. Li 2007; Tsing 2005; Wilson 2004.

18. W. Watson 1958.

19. Gamburd 2000; Gardner 1995; J. Watson 1975.

20. Levitt 2001.

21. Mercer et al. 2008.

22. Constable 1997; Lan 2006; Parreñas 2001.

23. Guevarra 2010; Rodriguez 2010; Tyner 2004, 2008.

24. Parreñas 2005b; Pingol 2001.

25. Aguilar 1999, 2002; Pertierra 1988, 1992, 1994, 2001; Pertierra et al. 1992.

26. Abu-Lughod 1991.

27. Guevarra 2010; Rodriguez 2010; Tyner 2004, 2008.

28. Constable 1997; Parreñas 2001.

29. Collier and Ong 2005; Deleuze and Guattari 1987, 165.

30. Linke 2006, 210.

31. "United Nations' World Population Prospects: The 2008 Revision, Highlights," http://www.un.org/esa/population/publications/wpp2008/wpp2008_highlights.pdf (accessed 15 April 2011).

1 ◆ FINDING THE VILLAGE

1. Republic of the Philippines, National Statistics Office, 2000 Census.

2.Ibid.

3. W. Scott 1974, 1976.

4. Radio DZNV, broadcasting from Solano, Nueva Viscaya, 2 December 1996.

5. For an account of the evolutionary ladder, see Rydell 1984.

6. W. Scott 1994, 4–6.

7. The Summer Institute of Linguists classifies Ayangan Ifugao as a dialect of Batad Ifugao. See Ethnologue: Languages of the World, www.ethnologue.com (accessed 15 February 2011).

8. The 2000 census records the name as *Ayungan,* but this does not fit the orthography for Ifugao. Republic of the Philippines, National Statistics Office, 2000 Census.

9. The 2000 census reports 760 persons living in 133 households in Panubtuban, thus the village as a whole has 310 households. Republic of the Philippines, National Statistics Office, 2000 Census.

10. Kerkvliet 1990, discusses Philippine client patronage.

11. Pertierra 2002, 88.

12. For Filipino syncretism, see Cannell 1999, 101–102; Cannell 2006b; and Pertierra 1988, 109.

13. Lynch 1986.

14. Hirtz 2003; P. Perez 2000.

15. See Republic Act 8371 (for details, see Prill-Brett 2000; Hirtz 2003; P. Perez 2000, 18), and see also National Commission on Indigenous Peoples for a full text of the act.

16. Keesing 1962.

17. Renato Rosaldo (1980) and Michelle Rosaldo (1980) studied the Ilongot people in the 1970s.

18. W. Scott 1974.

19. Keesing 1962; W. Scott 1974.

20. Keesing 1962, 289, 296.

21. For an account of Tuwali practices, from which my munfahi respondents suggested Adyangan ritual has borrowed, see Barton 1946.

22. C. J. Bates, Report to Captain W. E. Thompson, 28 July 1904. Typescript document, Beyer Collection of Filipiniana, Yale University (microfilm), New Haven, Connecticut, cited in Jenista 1987, 42.

23. Li 2000, 6, after Trouillot 1991.

24. Jenista 1987; Paulet 1995.

25. W. Scott 1974, 1994.

26. Republic of the Philippines 1990. *Ifugao Socioeconomic Profile*. National Statistics Office, Lagawe, Ifugao.

27. Ifugao people were also reported in the neighboring areas of Region 1 (Ilocos coast; 1,027), Region 2 (Cagayan valley; 61,752), and Region 3 (Central Luzon; 1,033). National Commission on Indigenous Peoples, http://www.ncip.gov.ph/resources/ethno_region.php, accessed 25 August 2009).

2 • BECOMING A GLOBAL KIND OF WOMAN

1. The 2000 census for Ifugao shows 1.04 males for each female for the 15–19 age cohort, 1.08 for the 20–24 cohort, and 1.16 for the 25–29 cohort. Republic of the Philippines, National Statistics Office, 2000 Census.

2. Malumbres 1919, 311, and typescript letters held in the Dominican archives in Manila, provided to the author in the original Spanish, with assistance in translation courtesy of Fr. Wilfred Vermuelen. The quote is taken from a letter from Fr. Bonifacio Corujedo to Fr. Provincial, dated 5 September 1898, held in the Dominican archives (DOC.NR.646).

3. Lim Pe 1978, 237.

4. Aguilar 1998, 219.

5. Barton 1930.

6. The 2000 census reports a 2:1 ratio of Ifugao women to men in tertiary education. Republic of the Philippines, National Statistics Office, 2000 Census.

7. Eviota 1992; Israel-Sobritchea 1990.

8. Tyner 2004, 2008.

9. Aguilar 1999.

10. Margold 1995.

11. Ileto 1997; Rafael 1988.

12. Rafael 1997.

13. Shenon 1995; Rafael 1997; Hilsdon 2000; Cheah 2006; Latif 1995.

14. *Singapore Law Reports* quoted in Anon. 1995a.

15. Anon. 1995c.

16. Shenon 1995.

17. Rafael 1997.

18. Fernandez 1995.

19. Cheah 2006, 235, 234; Magay 1995.

20. Fernandez 1995.

21. L. Perez 1995.

22. Magay 1995.

23. Anon. 1995b.

24. Magay 1995, 3.

25. Quoted in Cheah 2006, 237.

26. A mestiza is a Filipino woman of mixed ancestry, traditionally Spanish and/or Chinese, but also now American, Japanese, or European.

27. Ramos 1995.

28. Anon. 1995d; Fernandez 1995.

29. Fernandez 1995.

30. Agamben 1998; see Das and Poole 2004, 13.

31. Cohen 2005, 82.

32. Rafael 1997.

33. See POEA, OFW Statistics, www.poea.gov.ph/stats/statistics.html, Deployment per Skill per Sex, 1992–2009 (accessed 19 September 2011).

34. In 2005 another Filipina working in Singapore, Guen Aguilar, was convicted of murdering her neighbor from the Philippines, Jane Parangan La Puebla. There was no widespread protest of Aguilar's innocence. See "Filipina Maid Guilty of Grisly Slaying," *Asian Pacific Post,* 30 May 2006, www.asianpacificpost.com/portal2/ff8080810b870c2d010b8766fb8701a2_grisly_slaying.do.html (accessed 2 June 2009).

3 ◆ FAILING TO PROGRESS

1. Data from the CECAP Haliap Area Team, 1996.

2. Republic of the Philippines 1990.

3. Republic of the Philippines, National Statistics Office, 2000 Census.

4. Lauby and Stark 1988; Trager 1988.

5. Eggan 1960, 39, 49.

6. Eder (1994) reports similar findings.

7. Strathern 1996.

8. Andrew Bacdayan, Professor of Economics, Northwestern State University, Louisiana, in a speech to the second International Igorot Consultation, Arlington, Virginia, 5 July 1997.

9. Herzfeld 1992, 28.

10. Dulnuan 1996, A3.

11. Lewis 1992.

12. Pertierra et al. 2002, 8.

13. $US 1 = P26.31 at 24 January 1997, the time of the fieldwork reported here.

14. Pertierra (1994) reported that some areas of the Ilocos had 13 percent of their adult working population overseas. In his study sites, 62 percent of households reported migrant workers, and 70 percent of migrants were women.

15. Palmer-Beltran (1991, cited in Lan 2003 n18) reports on a survey of 3,099 prospective overseas workers conducted in 1990–1991. Of these, 61 percent of respondents were ages 21–30; 28 percent were 31–40; 43 percent were high school graduates; 36 percent had a college degree or some college education, and 11 percent had completed a vocational course. More than 80 percent of the respondents reported they were single, 18 percent were married.

4 ◆ NEW TERRITORIES

1. US$1 = P51.15 as of 25 September 2001, the date of Angelina's departure from Haliap.

2. POEA, OFW Statistics, www.poea.gov.ph/stats/statistics.html, Deployment per Country per Sex, 2004 (accessed 29 September 2009).

3. $US1 = $HK7.77 as of 22 July 2005, the time of the fieldwork reported.

4. For accounts, see Guevarra 2010; Rodriguez 2010; and Tyner 2008.

5. Law 2001.

6. Constable (1997) discusses the history and role of a maid in Hong Kong.

7. Aguilar 1998, 74; 1999.

8. Callon and Law (2004, 10) and Pertierra et al. (2002) offer insights into the impact of cell phones.

9. Francisco 2006.

10. Szanton-Blanc 1996; Rafael 1997.

11. Sotelo-Fuertes 2003.

12. These costs were calculated in 2004 on the basis of prices in SM (Shoemart), a nationwide department store, using prices obtained from goods in the branch in Baguio City.

13. Pertierra 1992.

14. US$1 = P40.40 in late 1999; see Guinid 1999.

15. "Black Man" refers to the statue of a British colonial official, Sir Frank Jackson.

16. In July 2005, HK$1 = P7.40 and US$1 = P56.25. See Chin 1997, cited in Momsen 1999, 9; Tung 2000.

17. Personal communication, mayor of Asipulo, December 2005.

18. US$1 = HK$7.78 = P49.90 in November 2006.

19. Thrift 2004, 57.

20. Yeates 2004, 371.

21. Lynch and McLaughlin 1995, 256–57, cited in Yeates 2004, 371.

22. Ehrenreich and Hochschild 2003; Hochschild 2000; Hochschild quoted in an interview with Sutherland 2005.

23. Geladé 1993, 244.

24. Parreñas 2001, 2005a, 2005b; see also Ehrenreich and Hochschild 2003; Hochschild 2000; Sørensen 2005; Yeates 2004, 2005. Subsequent detail from Parreñas 2005a, 333–34.

25. Jamieson 1998.

26. Berlant 2000, 1.

5 • HAUNTED BY IMAGES

1. Appadurai 2003, 23.

2. Ibid., 22.

3. Tagg 1988, 63, as quoted in Pinney 1997, 11.

4. Lozada 2006, 95; Cannell 1999.

5. Barthes 1981; Bloustein 2003, 2; Lury 1998, 3; Sontag 1977, 9.

6. Lury 1998, 3.

7. Das and Poole 2004, 14.

8. Strathern 1988, 161.

9. US$1 = P53.34 at 10 December, 2005.

10. Harper 2001.

11. Latour 2004.

12. Latour 2004, after Stengers 1997; Hannerz 2005, 95; Hannerz 1990, 239.

13. Beck 2005, 5; 2002, 17, 37, 2, 35–36.

14. Aguilar 1999; Pigg 1996; Tyner 2008.

15. Venn 2002, 73.

16. Personal communication from Rosario Cañete, Asian Migrant Center, Hong Kong, October 2007.

17. For forms of cosmopolitanism, see Werbner 1999; and Beck 2005, 7; Rabinow 1996, 56; Clifford 1992, 108; Hall 2001, as cited in Nava 2002, 89; Werbner 2006, 7; Beck 2005, 3.

18. Latour 2004, 455.

19. Ibid.

20. Englund and Leach 2000.

21. Esposito 2006, 28.

22. Englund and Leach 2000, 226.

23. Mitchell 2000, xxvi, xi; Englund and Leach 2000, 239; Mitchell 2000, xii.

24. Englund and Leach 2000, 228.

25. Cannell 2006a.

6 ◆ MOVING ON

1. Constable 1999.

2. US$1 = P43.95 and HK$1 = P5.67 as of 18 October 2007, the time of the fieldwork reported.

3. US$1 = C$1.18 = HK$7.75 as of 15 October 2008.

4. Personal communication, Canadian Embassy, Manila, December 1999.

5. As of 28 April 2009, when Luis arrived in Canada, US$1 = C$1.22 = HK$7.75 = P48.43.

6. US$1 = P43.63 in May 2008, when Luis visited Haliap.

7. Luis is much less sophisticated than the typical Filipino temporary worker. Filipino migration to Canada has been dominated by tertiary-educated and middle-class Filipinos (see Parreñas 2005a; Pratt 2005).

8. Alberta Federation of Labour 2007.

9. US$1 = C$1.22 on Luis's arrival in Canada.

10. Alberta Federation of Labour 2007.

11. Szanton-Blanc 1996, 178; Rafael 1997.

12. C$1 = P44.07 in July 2009, when I visited Luis in Calgary.

13. Das and Poole 2004, 1.

14. J. Scott 2009.

15. Mitchell 1999, 86.

16. Blom Hansen and Stepputat 2005, 9.

17. Žižek 1989, 43–44, as discussed in Linke 2006, 217.

18. Linke 2006, 217, drawing on Žižek 1989, 211–12.

19. Žižek 1989, 37–38, as discussed in Linke 2006, 218.

7 ◆ COME WHAT MAY

1. US$1 = C$1.08 during my August 2009 conversations with Luis.

2. Government of Alberta, Employment and Immigration, http://employment .alberta.ca/documents/WIA/WIA-IM_tfw_employee.pdf, details conditions current at the time of my research (accessed 15 September 2009), and Human Resources and Skills Development Canada (hereafter HRSDC), Temporary Foreign Worker Program, http://www.hrsdc.gc.ca/eng/workplaceskills/foreign_workers/questions-answers/ removalextlmo.shtml, details conditions current at the time of my research (accessed 15 September 2009).

3. For details on the Temporary Foreign Worker program current at the time of the research, see HRSDC.

4. Stiell and England (1997, 211) argue that this also holds true for Canada's Live-In Caregiver Program.

5. Luis did not want me to approach his Canadian employers to ask for interviews, because he was concerned that his participation in my research, though outside his working hours and largely mediated by phone calls and text messages, could jeopardize his employment contract.

6. Campbell 2006, 4; see also Esposito and Campbell 2006.

7. Arendt 1961, 150, as quoted by Esposito 2006, 44.

8. Fischer 2007, 439.

9. Alberta Federation of Labour 2007, 13.

10. Campbell 2006, 12.

11. Esposito 2006, 34–35.

12. Pratt (2005, 1065), discussing Canada's Live-In Caregiver Program.

13. Esposito 2006, 44.

14. Butler 2004, 24.

15. Canadian Broadcasting Corporation report archived at "Arcelie Laoagan: One Year Later," Canadian Broadcasting Corporation, 17 January 2009, http://www.cbc.ca/calgary/features/arcelielaoagan (accessed 3 February 2009).

16. Foucault 1982, 212.

17. Campbell 2006.

18. McKay 2010.

CONCLUSION

1. Miller 2002, 260.

2. Deleuze 1990/1995, 111 and 113, as cited in Fischer 2007, 423.

3. Appadurai 1995, 204.

4. Butler 1997.

5. Linke 2006, 207.

6. Ibid., 214.

7. Biehl et al. 2007, 29.

8. Berlant 2002, 2.

9. Strathern 1988; R. Rosaldo 1980, 1983, 1989; M. Rosaldo 1980; also Scheper-Hughes 2007, 180.

10. Thrift 2004, 58.

11. Dumont 1985, 93–122; Cannell 2006a, 21.

12. Cannell 2006a, 5.

13. Dunbar 2010.

BIBLIOGRAPHY

Abu-Lughod, Lila. 1991. "Writing against Culture." In *Recapturing Anthropology: Working in the Present,* edited by Richard Gabriel Fox, 137–62. Santa Fe, N.M.: School of American Research Press.

Agamben, Giorgio. 1998. *Homo Sacer: Sovereign Power and Bare Life.* Translated by Daniel Heller-Roazen. Stanford, Calif.: Stanford University Press.

Aguilar, Filomeno V., Jr. 1998. *Clash of Spirits: The History of Power and Sugar Planter Hegemony on a Visayan Island.* Honolulu: University of Hawai'i Press.

———. 1999. "Ritual Passage and the Reconstruction of Selfhood in International Labour Migration." *Sojourn* 14: 98–139.

———. 2002. "Beyond Stereotypes: Human Subjectivity in the Structuring of Global Migration." In *Filipinos in Global Migration: At Home in the World?* edited by Filomeno V. Aguilar Jr., 1–36. Manila: Philippine Migration Research Network.

Alberta Federation of Labour. 2007. "Temporary Foreign Workers: Alberta's Disposable Workforce." Six-Month Report of the AFL's Temporary Foreign Worker Advocate, 21 November. Calgary: Alberta Federation of Labour.

Anon. 1995a. "Beyond the Rage," *Asiaweek,* 7 April, 18.

———. 1995b. "The Fallout from Flor," *Asiaweek,* 7 April, 30.

———. 1995c. "Ministry Rebuts New Charges about Maid," *Straits Times Weekly Edition,* 25 March, 7.

———. 1995d. "Savage Blows," *Asiaweek,* 14 April, 33.

Appadurai, Arjun. 1995. "The Production of Locality." In *Counterworks: Managing the Diversity of Knowledge,* edited by Richard Fardon, 204–25. New York: Routledge.

———. 1996. *Modernity at Large: Cultural Dimensions of Globalization.* Minneapolis: University of Minnesota Press.

———. 2003. "Archive and Aspiration." In *Art and Theory on Archiving and Retrieving Data,* edited by Joke Brouwer and Arjen Mulder, 14–25. Rotterdam: V2 Publishing/NAI Publishers.

Arendt, Hannah. 1961. *Between Past and Future: Eight Exercises in Political Thought.* New York: Viking.

Barthes, Frederic. 1981. *Camera Lucida: Reflections on Photography.* Translated by Richard Howard. London: Vintage.

Barton, Roy Franklin. 1930. *The Halfway Sun: Life among the Head-Hunters in the Philippines.* New York: Brewer and Warren.

———. 1946. *The Religion of the Ifugaos.* American Anthropological Association Memoir 65, 1–219.

Beck, Ulrich. 2002. "The Cosmopolitan Society and its Enemies." *Theory, Culture, and Society* 19(1–2): 17–44.

———. 2005. "Neither Order nor Peace: A Response to Bruno Latour." *Common Knowledge* 11(1): 1–7.

Bello, Walden. 2005. "Letter from the Philippines." *Nation,* October 31.

Berlant, Lauren. 2000. "Intimacy: A Special Issue." In *Intimacy,* edited by Lauren Berlant, 1–8. Chicago: University of Chicago Press.

———. 2002. "Critical Inquiry, Affirmative Culture." *Critical Inquiry* 30(2): 1–5.

Biehl, João, Byron Good, and Arthur Kleinman, eds. 2007. *Subjectivity: Ethnographic Investigations.* Berkeley: University of California Press.

Blom Hanson, Thomas, and Finn Stepputat. 2005. "Introduction: States of Imagination." In *States of Imagination: Ethnographic Explorations of the Post-Colonial State,* edited by Thomas Blom Hanson and Finn Stepputat, 1–38. Durham, N.C.: Duke University Press.

Bloustein, Gerry. 2003. "Envisioning Ethnography: Exploring the Meanings of the Visual in Research." *Social Analysis* 47(3): 1–7.

Butler, Judith. 1997. *Excitable Speech: A Politics of the Performative.* New York: Routledge.

———. 2004. *Precarious Life: The Powers of Mourning and Violence.* London: Verso.

Callon, Michel, and John Law. 2004. "Absence-Presence, Circulation, and Encountering in Complex Space." *Environment and Planning D: Society and Space* 22: 3–11.

Campbell, Timothy. 2006. "*Bios,* Immunity, Life: The Thought of Roberto Esposito." *Diacritics* 36(2): 2–22.

Cannell, Fennella. 1999. *Power and Intimacy in the Christian Philippines.* Cambridge: Cambridge University Press.

———. 2006a. "Introduction." In *The Anthropology of Christianity,* edited by Fennella Cannell, 1–50. Durham, N.C.: Duke University Press.

———. 2006b. "Reading as Gift and Writing as Theft." In *The Anthropology of Christianity,* edited by Fennella Cannell, 134–62. Durham, N.C.: Duke University Press.

Cheah, Peng. 2006. *Inhuman Conditions: On Cosmopolitanism and Human Rights.* Cambridge, Mass.: Harvard University Press.

Chin, Christine. 1997. "Walls of Silence and Late Twentieth Century Representations of the Foreign Female Domestic Workers: The Case of Filipina and Indonesian Female Servants in Malaysia." *International Migration Review* 31(2): 353–85.

Clifford, James. 1992. "Travelling Cultures." In *Cultural Studies,* edited by Lawrence Grossberg, Cary Nelson, and Paula Treichler, 96–116. London: Routledge.

Cohen, Lawrence. 2005. "Operability, Bioavailability, and Exception." In *Global Assemblages: Technology, Politics, and Ethics as Anthropological Problems,* edited by Aihwa Ong and Stephen Collier, 79–90. Malden, Mass.: Blackwell.

Collier, Stephen, and Aihwa Ong. 2005. "Global Assemblages, Anthropological Problems." In *Global Assemblages: Technology, Politics and Ethics as Anthropological Problems,* edited by Aihwa Ong and Stephen Collier, 7–21. Malden, Mass.: Blackwell.

Constable, Nicole. 1997. *Maid to Order in Hong Kong: Stories of Filipina Workers.* Ithaca, N.Y.: Cornell University Press.

———. 1999. "At Home but Not at Home: Filipina Narratives of Ambivalent Returns." *Cultural Anthropology* 14(2): 203–28.

Das, Veena, and Deborah Poole. 2004. "State and Its Margins: Comparative Ethnographies." In *Anthropology in the Margins of the State,* edited by Veena Das and Deborah Poole, 3–33. Santa Fe, N.M.: School of American Research Press.

Deleuze, Gilles. 1990/1995. *Negotiations.* New York: Columbia University Press.

Deleuze, Gilles, and Félix Guattari. 1987. *A Thousand Plateaus: Capitalism and Schizophrenia.* Translated by Brian Massumi. Minneapolis: University of Minnesota Press.

Dulnuan, M. 1996. "Rape Cases Increasing." *Philippine Daily Inquirer,* 19 September, A3.

Dumont, Louis. 1985. "A Modified View of Our Origins: The Christian Beginnings of Modern Individualism." In *The Category of the Person: Anthropology, Philosophy, History,* edited by Michael Carrithers, Steven Collins, and Steven Lukes, 92–122. Cambridge: Cambridge University Press.

Dunbar, Robin. 2010. *How Many Friends Does One Person Need? Dunbar's Number and Other Evolutionary Quirks.* London: Faber.

Eder, James. 1994. "State-Sponsored 'Participatory Development' and Tribal Filipino Ethnic Identity." *Social Analysis* 35: 28–38.

Eggan, Fred. 1960. "The Sagada Igorots of Northern Luzon." In *Social Structures in Southeast Asia,* edited by George Peter Murdock, 24–50. Chicago: Quadrangle Books.

Englund, Harri, and James Leach. 2000. "Ethnography and the Meta-narratives of Modernity." *Current Anthropology* 41(2): 225–48.

Ehrenreich, Barbara, and Arlie Russell Hochschild, eds. 2003. *Global Women: Nannies, Maids, and Sex Workers in the New Economy.* New York: Metropolitan Books.

Esposito, Roberto. 2006. "The Immunization Paradigm." (Excerpted from *Bios: Biopolitica e Filosofia.* Turin: Einauidi, 2004.) Translated by Timothy Campbell. *Diacritics* 36(2): 23–48.

Esposito, Roberto, and Timothy Campbell. 2006. Interview. Translated by Anna Paparcone. *Diacritics* 36(2): 49–56.

Eviota, Elizabeth Uy. 1992. *The Political Economy of Gender: Women and the Sexual Division of Labour in the Philippines.* London: Zed Books.

Fernandez, Warren. 1995. "Making Sense of Filipino's Fury over the Contemplacion Affair." *Straits Times Weekly Edition,* 22 April, 14.

Fischer, Michael. 2007. "Epilogue—To Live with What Would Otherwise Be Unendurable: Return(s) to Subjectivities." Biehl et al. 423–46.

Foucault, Michel. 1982. "The Subject and Power." In *Michel Foucault: Beyond Structuralism and Hermeneutics,* edited by Hubert Dreyfus and Paul Rabinow, 208–26. Brighton, U.K.: Harvester.

Francisco, R. 2006. "Philippine Malls Thrive as Diaspora Dollars Roll In." *Philippine Daily Inquirer,* 24 May.

Friedman, Jonathan. 1994. *Cultural Identity and Global Process.* London: Sage.

Gamburd, Michele Ruth. 2000. *The Kitchen Spoon's Handle.* Ithaca, N.Y.: Cornell University Press.

Gardner, Katy. 1995. *Global Migrants, Local Lives: Travel and Transformation in Rural Bangladesh.* Oxford: Clarendon Press.

Geladé, G. 1993. *Ilokano-English Dictionary.* Quezon City, Philippines: CICM Missionaries Inc.

Guevarra, Anna Romina. 2010. *Marketing Dreams, Manufacturing Heroes: The Transnational Labor Brokering of Filipino Workers.* New Brunswick, N.J.: Rutgers University Press.

Guinid, Angie. 1999. "Ifugao Mayors Visit Hong Kong," 13–15 November 1999. http://www.ifugaos.org/newsarticles/HKreport.htm (accessed 20 February 2003).

Hall, Stuart. 2001. *The Multicultural Question.* Milton Keynes, U.K.: Pavis Papers.

Hannerz, Ulf. 1990. "Cosmopolitans and Locals in World Culture." *Theory, Culture, and Society* 7(2–3): 237–51.

———. 2005. "Speaking to Larger Issues: The World, if It Is Not in Pieces." In *Clifford Geertz by His Colleagues,* edited by Richard A. Schweder and Byron Good, 89–97. Chicago: University of Chicago Press.

Harper, Ann C. 2001. "The *Iglesia ni Cristo* and Evangelical Christianity." *Journal of Asian Mission* 3(1): 101–19.

Hilsdon, Anne-Marie. 2000. "The Contemplacion Fiasco: The Hanging of a Filipino Domestic Worker in Singapore." In *Human Rights and Gender Politics: Asia-Pacific Perspectives,* edited by Anne-Marie Hilsdon, Martha Macintyre, Vera Mackie, and Maila Stivens, 172–91. London: Routledge.

Hirtz, Frank. 2003. "It Takes Modern Means to Be Traditional: On Recognizing Indigenous Cultural Communities in the Philippines." *Development and Change* 34(5): 887–914.

Herzfeld, Michael. 1992. *The Social Production of Indifference: Exploring the Symbolic Roots of Western Bureaucracy.* Oxford: Berg.

Hochschild, Arlie Russell. 2000. "Global Care Chains and Emotional Surplus Value." In *On the Edge: Living with Global Capitalism,* edited by Will Hutton and Anthony Giddens, 130–46. London: Jonathan Cape.

Ileto, Reynaldo. 1997. *Pasyon and Revolution: Popular Movements in the Philippines 1840–1910.* Honolulu: University of Hawai'i Press.

International Labour Organization. 2010. *International Labour Migration: A Rights-Based Approach.* Geneva: International Labour Organization.

International Organization for Migration. 2005. *World Migration Report 2005: The Costs and Benefits of World Migration.* Geneva: International Organization for Migration.

———. 2010. *World Migration 2010: The Future of Migration—Building Capacities for Change.* Geneva: International Organization for Migration.

Israel-Sobritchea, Carolyn. 1990. "The Ideology of Female Domesticity." *Review of Women's Studies* 1(1): 26–41.

Jamieson, Lynn. 1998. *Intimacy: Personal Relationships in Modern Societies.* Cambridge: Polity Press.

Jenista, Frank. 1987. *The White Apos: American Governors on the Cordillera Central.* Quezon City, Philippines: New Day.

Keesing, Felix M. 1962. *The Ethnohistory of Northern Luzon.* Stanford, Calif.: Stanford University Press.

Kelly, Philip. 2000. *Landscapes of Globalization: Human Geographies of Economic Change in the Philippines.* London: Routledge.

Kerkvliet, Benjamin T. 1990. *Everyday Politics in the Philippines: Class and Status Relations in a Central Luzon Village.* Berkeley: University of California Press.

Lan, Pe-Chia. 2003. "Maid or Madam? Filipina Migrant Workers and the Continuity of Domestic Labor." *Gender and Society* 17(2): 187–208.

———. 2006. *Global Cinderellas: Migrant Domestics and Newly Rich Employers in Taiwan.* Durham, N.C.: Duke University Press.

Latif, Asad. 1995. "The World We Live In: Contemplating Contemplacion." *Singapore Business* 19(7): 96.

Latour, Bruno. 2004. "Whose Cosmos, Which Cosmopolitics? Comments on the Peace Terms of Ulrich Beck." *Common Knowledge* 10(3): 450–62.

Lauby, Jennfier, and Oded Stark. 1988. "Individual Migration as a Family Strategy: Young Women in the Philippines." *Population Studies* 42: 473–86.

Law, Lisa. 2001. "Home Cooking: Filipino Women and Geographies of the Senses in Hong Kong." *Ecumene* 8(3): 264–83.

Levitt, Peggy. 2001. *The Transnational Villagers.* Berkeley: University of California Press.

Lewis, Martin. 1992. *Wagering the Land: Ritual, Capital, and Environmental Degradation in the Cordillera of Northern Luzon, 1900–1985.* Berkeley: University of California Press.

Li, Tania Murray. 2000. "Articulating Indigenous Identity in Indonesia: Resource Politics and the Tribal Slot." *Comparative Studies in Society and History* 42(1): 149–79.

———. 2007. *The Will to Improve: Governmentality, Development and the Practice of Politics.* Durham, N.C.: Duke University Press.

Lim Pe, Josefina. 1978. "Spanish Contacts with the Ifugaos, 1736–1898." *Philippiniana Sacra* 13(38): 193–249.

Linke, Uli. 2006. "Contact Zones: Rethinking the Sensual Life of the State." *Anthropological Theory* 6: 205–25.

Lozada, Eriberto P., Jr. 2006. "Framing Globalization: Wedding Pictures, Funeral Photography, and Family Snapshots in Rural China." *Visual Anthropology* 19: 87–103.

Lury, Celia. 1998. *Prosthetic Culture: Photography, Memory, Identity.* London: Routledge.

Lynch, Kathleen, and Eithne McLaughlin. 1995. "Caring Labour and Love Labour." In *Irish Society: Sociological Perspectives,* edited by P. Clancy, S. Drudy, K. Lynch, and L. O'Dowd, 250–92. Dublin: Institute of Public Administration.

Lynch, Owen. 1986. "Philippine Law and Upland Tenure." In *Man, Agriculture and the Tropical Forest: Change and Development in the Philippine Uplands,* edited by Sam Fujisaka, Percy Sajise, and Roberto del Castillo, 269–92. Bangkok: Winrock Institute for Agricultural Development.

Magay, M. 1995. "Flor Contemplacion: Requiem for a People." *Sunday Inquirer Magazine,* 28 May, 3–5, and 20.

Malumbres, Julian, Fr. 1919. *Historia de Nueva Viscaya y Provincia Montañosa.* Manila: Tipog. Litog. del Colegio de Sto. Tomas.

Margold, Jane. 1995. "Narratives of Masculinity and Transnational Migration: Filipino Workers in the Middle East." In *Bewitching Women, Pious Men: Gender and Body Politics in Southeast Asia,* edited by Aihwa Ong and Michael Peletz, 274–98. Berkeley: University of California Press.

McKay, Deirdre. 2010. "On the Face of Facebook: Historical Images and Personhood in Filipino Social Networking." *History and Anthropology* 21(4): 483–502.

Mendola, Maripia. 2006. "Rural Out-Migration and Economic Development at Origin: What Do We Know?" Sussex Migration Working Paper No. 40. Brighton, U.K.: University of Sussex Centre for Migration Research.

Mercer, Claire, Ben Page, and Martin Evans. 2008. *Development and the African Diaspora: Place and Politics of Home.* London: Zed Books.

Miller, Daniel. 2002. "Coca-Cola: A Black, Sweet Drink from Trinidad." In *The Material Culture Reader,* edited by Victor Buchli, 245–63. Oxford: Berg.

Mitchell, Timothy. 1999. "Society, Economy and the State Effect." In *State/Culture: State-Formation after the Cultural Turn,* edited by George Steinmetz, 76–97. Ithaca, N.Y.: Cornell University Press.

———. 2000. "Introduction." In *Questions of Modernity,* edited by Timothy Mitchell, xi–xxvii. Minneapolis: University of Minnesota Press.

Momsen, Janet. 1999. "Maids on the Move." In *Gender, Migration and Domestic Service,* edited by Janet Momsen, 1–21. London: Routledge.

Nava, Mica. 2002. "Cosmopolitan Modernity: Everyday Imaginaries and the Register of Difference." *Theory, Culture and Society* 19(1–2): 81–99.

Palmer-Beltran, Ruby. 1991. "Filipino Women Domestic Helpers Overseas: Profile and Implications for Policy." *Asian Migrant* 4(2): 46–52.

Parreñas, Rhacel Salazar. 2001. *Servants of Globalization: Women, Migration, and Domestic Work.* Stanford, Calif.: Stanford University Press.

———. 2005a. "Long-Distance Intimacy: Class, Gender and Intergenerational Relations between Mothers and Children in Filipino Transnational Families." *Global Networks* 5(4): 317–36.

———. 2005b. *Children of Global Migration: Transnational Families and Gendered Woes.* Stanford, Calif.: Stanford University Press.

Paulet, Ann. 1995. "The Only Good Indian Is a Dead Indian: The Use of United States Indian Policy as a Guide for the Conquest and Occupation of the Philippines, 1898–1905." Unpublished PhD dissertation, Rutgers University.

Perez, Leticia. 1995. "Della Maga's Murderer 'was Left-handed.'" *Straits Times Weekly Edition,* 29 April, 5.

Perez, Padmapani. 2000. "Contested Domains: Philippine National Law, Indigenous Peoples, and the Environment." Unpublished MA thesis, University of Kent.

Pertierra, Raul. 1988. *Religion, Politics and Rationality in a Philippine Community.* Honolulu: University of Hawai'i Press.

———. 1992. "Trust and the Temporal Structure of Expectations in a Philippine Village." *Australian Journal of Anthropology* 3(3): 201–17.

———. 1994. "Lured Abroad: The Case of Ilocano Overseas Workers." *Sojourn* 9(1): 54–80.

———. 2001. "Multiple Identities, Overseas Labour, and a Disaporal Consciousness in a Local Community." In *Going Global: Asian Societies on the Cusp of Change,* edited by Armando Malay Jr., 74–91. Manila: Asian Centre, University of the Philippines, Diliman.

———. 2002. *The Work of Culture.* Manila: De La Salle University Press.

Pertierra, Raul, ed., with Minda Cabilao, Marna Escobar, and Alicia Pingol. 1992. *Remittances and Returnees: The Cultural Economy of Migration in Ilocos.* Quezon City, Philippines: New Day.

Pertierra, Raul, Eduardo F. Ugarte, Alicia Pingol, Joel Hernandez, and Nikos Dacanay. 2002. *Txt-ing Selves: Cellphones and Philippine Modernity.* Manila: De La Salle University Press.

Pigg, Stacey. 1996. "The Credible and the Incredulous: The Question of Villagers' Beliefs in Nepal." *Cultural Anthropology* 11(2): 160–201.

Pingol, Alicia. 2001. *Remaking Masculinities: Identity, Power, and Gender Dynamics in Families with Migrant Wives and Househusbands.* Quezon City, Philippines: University of the Philippines–University Center for Women's Studies.

Pinney, Christopher. 1997. *Camera Indica: The Social Life of Indian Photographs.* London: Reaktion.

Pratt, Geraldine. 2005. "Abandoned Women and Spaces of the Exception." *Antipode* 37(5): 1052–78.

Prill-Brett, June. 2000. "Concepts of Ancestral Domain in the Cordillera Region from Indigenous Perspectives." In *Perspectives on Resource Management in the*

Cordillera Region, Research Report I, Ancestral Domain and Natural Resources Management in Sagada, Mt. Province, Northern Philippines (NRMP 2), 2–21. Baguio City: Cordillera Studies Center, University of the Philippines–Baguio.

Rabinow, Paul. 1996. *Essays on the Anthropology of Reason.* Princeton, N.J.: Princeton University Press.

Rafael, Vicente. 1988. *Contracting Colonialism: Translation and Christian Conversion in Tagalog Society under Early Spanish Rule.* Ithaca, N.Y.: Cornell University Press.

———. 1997 "'Your Grief Is Our Gossip': Overseas Filipinos and Other Spectral Presences." *Public Culture* 9(2): 267–91.

Ramos, G. 1995. "The Other Flor Contemplacion." *Today,* 31 May, C22.

Republic of the Philippines. 1990. *Ifugao Socioeconomic Profile.* Lagawe, Ifugao: National Statistics Office.

Ribas, Natalia, Victoria Simmons, and Mar García Domínguez. 2008. *Gender, Remittances and Development: The Case of Filipino Migration to Italy.* Santo Domingo, Dominican Republic: United Nations International Research and Training Institute for the Advancement of Women (INSTRAW).

Rodriguez, Robyn Magalit. 2010. *Migrants for Export: How the Philippine State Brokers Labour to the World.* Minneapolis: University of Minnesota Press.

Rosaldo, Michelle Zimbalist. 1980. *Knowledge and Passion: Ilongot Notions of Self and Social Life.* Cambridge: Cambridge University Press.

Rosaldo, Renato. 1980. *Ilongot Headhunting, 1883–1974: A Study in History and Society.* Stanford, Calif.: Stanford University Press.

———. 1983. "Grief and a Headhunter's Rage: On the Cultural Construction of Emotions." In *Text, Play and Story,* edited by Steven Plathner and Edward Bruner, 78–195. Washington, D.C.: American Ethnological Society.

———. 1989. *Culture and Truth: The Remaking of Social Analysis.* Boston: Beacon Press.

Rydell, Robert W. 1984. *All the World's a Fair: Visions of Empire at American International Expositions, 1876–1916.* Chicago: University of Chicago Press.

Scheper-Hughes, Nancy. 2007. "Violence and the Politics of Remorse: Lessons from South Africa." Biehl, 179–233.

Scott, James C. 2009. *The Art of Not Being Governed.* New Haven, Conn.: Yale University Press.

Scott, William Henry. 1974. *The Discovery of the Igorots: Spanish Contacts with the Pagans of Northern Luzon.* Manila: New Day.

———. 1976. *On the Cordillera: A Look at the Peoples and Cultures of the Mountain Province.* Manila: MCS Enterprises.

———. 1994. *Barangay: Sixteenth-Century Philippine Culture and Society.* Quezon City, Philippines: Ateneo de Manila University Press.

Shenon, Philip. 1995. "Manila Minister Dismissed in Furor over Singapore Hanging." *New York Times,* 15 April, A7.

Sontag, Susan. 1977. *On Photography.* New York: Dell.

Sørensen, Nina. 2005. "Transnational Family Life across the Atlantic: The Experience of Columbian and Dominican Migrants in Europe." Paper presented at the International Conference on Migration and Domestic Work in Global Perspective, Wassenar, the Netherlands, 26–29 May.

Sotelo-Fuertes, Y. 2003. "AC's 2nd Homecoming Was Her Last." Inquirer News Service, available at http://www.inq7.net/nat/2003/apr/24/nat_13–1.htm (accessed 24 April, 2004).

Stengers, Isabelle. 1997. *Pour En Finir avec le Tolerance.* Paris: La Decouverte.

Stiell, Bernadette, and Kim England. 1997. "'They Think You're As Stupid As Your English Is': Constructing Foreign Domestic Workers in Toronto." *Environment and Planning A* 29(2): 195–215.

Strathern, Marilyn. 1988. *The Gender of the Gift: Problems with Women and Problems with Society in Melanesia.* Berkeley: University of California Press.

———. 1996. "Cutting the Network." *Journal of the Royal Anthropological Institute* 2: 517–35.

Sutherland, J. 2005. "The Ideas Interview: Arlie Russell Hochschild." *Guardian,* 12 December.

Szanton-Blanc, Cristina. 1996. "*Balikbayan:* A Filipino Extension of the National Imaginary and of State Boundaries." *Philippine Sociological Review* 44(1–4): 178–93.

Tagg, John. 1988. *The Burden of Representation: Essays on Photographies and Histories.* Basingstoke, U.K.: Macmillan.

Thrift, Nigel. 2004. "Intensities of Feeling: Towards a Spatial Politics of Affect." *Geografiska Annaler Series B* 86(1): 57–78.

Trager, Lillian. 1988. *The City Connection: Migration and Family Interdependence in the Philippines.* Ann Arbor: University of Michigan Press.

Trouillot, Michel-Rolph. 1991. "Anthropology and the Savage Slot: The Poetics and Politics of Otherness." In *Recapturing Anthropology: Working in the Present,* edited by Richard Gabriel Fox, 17–44. Santa Fe, N.M.: School of American Research Press.

Tsing, Anna Lowenhaupt. 2000. "The Global Situation." *Cultural Anthropology* 15(3): 327–60.

———. 2005. *Friction: An Ethnography of Global Connection.* Princeton, N.J.: Princeton University Press.

Tung, Charlene. 2000. "The Cost of Caring: The Social Reproductive Labor of Filipina Live-In Home Health Caregivers." *Frontiers* 21(1–2): 61–82.

Tyner, James. 2004. *Made in the Philippines: Gendered Discourses and the Making of Migrants.* London: RoutledgeCurzon.

———. 2008. *The Philippines: Mobilities, Identities, Globalization.* New York: Routledge.

Tyner, James, and Daniel Donaldson. 1999. "The Geography of Philippine International Labour Migration Fields." *Asia Pacific Viewpoint* 40(3): 217–34.

Urry, John. 2000. "Mobile Sociology." *British Journal of Sociology* 51(1): 185–203.

——. 2007. *Mobility.* London: Polity Press.

Venn, Couze. 2002. "Altered States: Post-Enlightenment Cosmopolitanism and Transmodern Socialities." *Theory, Culture, and Society* 19(1–2): 65–80.

Watson, James L. 1975. *Emigration and the Chinese Lineage.* Berkeley: University of California Press.

Watson, William. 1958. *Tribal Cohesion in a Money Economy: A Study of the Mambwe People of Northern Rhodesia.* Manchester: Manchester University Press.

Werbner, Pnina. 1999. "Global Pathways: Working Class Cosmopolitans and the Creation of Transnational Ethnic Worlds." *Social Anthropology* 7(1): 17–35.

——. 2006. "Cosmopolitans, Anthropologists, and Labour Migrants: Deconstructing Transnational Cultural Promiscuity." Paper presented at the ASA 2006 Conference, Keele University, 10–13 April.

Wilson, Ara. 2004. *The Intimate Economies of Bangkok: Tomboys, Tycoons, and Avon Ladies in the Global City.* Berkeley: University of California Press.

Yeates, Nicola. 2004. "Global Care Chains: Critical Reflection and Lines of Enquiry." *International Feminist Journal of Politics* 6(3): 369–91.

——. 2005. "Global Care Chains: A Critical Introduction." Global Migration Perspectives No. 44, Global Commission on International Migration, Geneva.

Žižek, Slavoj. 1989. *The Sublime Object of Ideology.* London: Verso.

INDEX

Page numbers in italics indicate illustrations.

murder story and, 43–45; market
price of rice, 70; native varieties
of rice, 94; origin of rice terraces,
33–34; shifting cultivation and,
28–29, 31; shortage of land for, 32;
water shortages and, 66, 67
rituals: cosmopolitanism and, 147–49;
debate over, 140–41; *fogwa* ritual,
136, 137, 147
Rodriguez, Robyn, 10
Rosaldo, Renato, and Michele Rosaldo,
208

"Saudi" (Arabian Gulf region), 90
Scott, James, 172
"scratch" concept, 58–59, 190
security, livelihood, 47
sex-related work, 5
sharecropping, 25, 75
sharing, 74, 119
shopping, 98, 100, 208; for *balikbayan*
boxes, 103; shopping malls, 201
SIM (subscriber identity module) cards,
101, 162
Singapore, 3, 91, 117, 197; Contemplacion murder case in, 54–58;
deportation from, 152; Haliap
OCWs in, 90; temporary ban on
OFWs in, 62
Skype, 101
social networking sites, 8, 18, 201
Social Security System (SSS), 118
Spanish colonialism, 2, 19, 63; barangay
unit and, 21–22; Christianity as
marker of civilization and, 37; history of, 30–32; patriarchal nuclear
family introduced by, 45; resistance
to, 34, 44–45
Spanish-American War, 34
state, the, 17, 168, 170–72, 179; as
article of faith, 176–78; Canada
compared with Philippines, 188;
ideal of caring government, 173;
spaces of exception and, 59, 189;
"state effect," 174; subjectivist
viewpoint and, 209–11; symbolic
languages of authority, 175–76; villagers' experience of, 173–76; virtual

cosmopolitics and, 211–13. *See also*
government institutions; nation-
state; politics/politicians
Strathern, Marilyn, 207
subjectivities, 10, 17, 128, 215; placeness and, 9, 198, 203; in search
of caring state, 209–11; shifting,
203–209
suicide, 99
swidden cultivation, 29, 31, 66; development projects and, 84; home gardens
in contrast to, 86; women and, 46

Tagalog language, 20, 22, 37, 95, 217;
in Hong Kong, 99, 147; hymns
sung in, 83; *maybahay lang* (simple
homemaker), 50; *pakikisama* (being
solicitous, yielding), 62; *puhunan*
(planting stock or capital), 68
Taiwan, 90, 181
taxes: in Canada, 155, 157, 162; *cedula*
(head tax), 31; failure of practical
governance and, 174; land claims
and, 66–67; in Philippines, 2, 15, 22
teachers, 49, 50
technologies: communications, 7, 16,
199, 200, 215; information technology, 5; limits of, 128; Spanish colonialism and, 31
Temporary Foreign Worker (TFW)
program, 155, 156–57, 159–60,
186; employer-paid benefits, 162;
enforcement of rules of, 169, 181–
82; immunity denied to migrants,
189; individuation and, 190, 191;
settlement services under, 161; virtual village and, 179; working conditions, 180, 183, 184, 185, 212–13
territoriality, 40, 203, 209, 211
text messaging, 90, 101, 107, 110, 152,
159; "migrant archive" and, 128;
participant-observer methodology
and, 216
third world, 17, 112
Thompson, Captain W. E., 34
tourism, 2, 180
translocality, 202
tribe concept, 35–38, 39

TRACKING GLOBALIZATION

Recycling Indian Clothing:
Global Contexts of Reuse and Value
Lucy Norris

Music and Globalization:
Critical Encounters
Edited by Bob W. White

Global Filipinos:
Migrants' Lives in the Virtual Village
Deirdre McKay

DEIRDRE McKAY is Senior Lecturer at Keele University.